China's Foreign Relations Survival of Autocracies

C000182774

The Chinese government has frequently been criticized for propping up anti-democratic governments. This book investigates the rise of China as an emerging authoritarian power. By comparing China's bilateral relations to three Asian developing countries – Burma, Cambodia and Mongolia – it examines how China targets specific groups of actors in autocracies versus non-autocracies. It illustrates how the Chinese non-interference policy translates into support for incumbent leaders in autocratic countries and how the Chinese government has thereby profited from exploiting secretive decision-making in autocracies to realize its own external interests such as achieving access to natural resources. In a statistical analysis of the patterns of Chinese external cooperation and their impact on the survival of autocratic leaders, the book finds some evidence that China is more likely to target autocracies with economic cooperation. However, only some forms of bilateral interaction are found to increase the prospect of survival for autocratic leaders.

This important contribution to the understanding of both external factors of authoritarian endurance and China's foreign relations, a field of study still lacking systematic investigation, will be of great interest to students and researchers in Development Studies, Asian Studies, International Relations, and International Political Economy.

Julia Bader is an Assistant Professor for International Relations at the University of Amsterdam, the Netherlands and an Associate Fellow of the German Development Institute (DIE). Her work focuses on the political economy of authoritarian regimes, foreign aid and democracy promotion.

Routledge Explorations in Development Studies

This Development Studies series features innovative and original research at the regional and global scale.

It promotes interdisciplinary scholarly works drawing on a wide spectrum of subject areas, in particular politics, health, economics, rural and urban studies, sociology, environment, anthropology, and conflict studies.

Topics of particular interest are globalization, emerging powers, children and youth, cities, education, media and communication, technology development, and climate change.

In terms of theory and method, rather than basing itself on any orthodoxy, the series draws broadly on the tool kit of the social sciences in general, emphasizing comparison, the analysis of the structure and processes, and the application of qualitative and quantitative methods.

The Domestic Politics of Foreign Aid
Erik Lundsgaarde

Social Protection in Developing Countries
Reforming Systems
Katja Bender, Markus Kaltenborn and Christian Pfleiderer

Formal Peace and Informal War
Security and Development in Congo
Zoë Marriage

Technology Development Assistance for Agriculture
Putting Research into Use in Low Income Countries
Norman Clark, Andy Frost, Ian Maudlin and Andrew Ward

Statelessness and Citizenship
Camps and the Creation of Political Space
Victoria Redclift

China's Foreign Relations and the Survival of Autocracies
Julia Bader

China's Foreign Relations and the Survival of Autocracies

Julia Bader

Routledge
Taylor & Francis Group

LONDON AND NEW YORK

First published 2015
by Routledge
2 Park Square, Milton Park, Abingdon, Oxfordshire OX14 4RN

and by Routledge
711 Third Avenue, New York, NY 10017

First issued in paperback 2016

Routledge is an imprint of the Taylor & Francis Group, an informa business

© 2015 Julia Bader

The right of Julia Bader to be identified as author of this work has been
asserted by her in accordance with sections 77 and 78 of the Copyright,
Designs and Patents Act 1988.

All rights reserved. No part of this book may be reprinted or reproduced or
utilised in any form or by any electronic, mechanical, or other means, now
known or hereafter invented, including photocopying and recording, or in any
information storage or retrieval system, without permission in writing from
the publishers.

Trademark notice: Product or corporate names may be trademarks or
registered trademarks, and are used only for identification and explanation
without intent to infringe.

British Library Cataloguing-in-Publication Data
A catalogue record for this book is available from the British Library

Library of Congress Cataloging-in-Publication Data
Bader, Julia, 1981-
China's foreign relations and the survival of autocracies / Julia Bader.
pages cm
ISBN 978-0-415-66095-2 (hardback) – ISBN 978-0-203-07382-7 (e-book)
1. China–Foreign relations–21st century. 2. Authoritarianism–Asia.
3. China–Foreign relations–Cambodia. 4. Cambodia–Foreign relations–China.
5. China–Foreign relations–Burma. 6. Burma–Foreign relations–China.
7. China–Foreign relations–Mongolia. 8. Mongolia–Foreign relations–China.
I. Title.
DS779.47.B34 2015
327.51–dc23
2014019808

Typeset in Times New Roman
by FiSH Books Ltd, Enfield

ISBN 13: 978-1-138-69302-9 (pbk)
ISBN 13: 978-0-415-66095-2 (hbk)

Contents

Figures

Tables

Acronyms

ASEAN	Association of Southeast Asian Nations
CCP	Chinese Communist Party
CDC	Council of the Development of Cambodia
CPP	Cambodian People's Party
CRDB	Cambodian Rehabilitation and Development Board
DAC	Development Assistance Committee
DP	Democratic Party
FDI	Foreign direct investment
FUNCINPEC	Front Uni National pour un Cambodge Indépendant, Neutre, Pacifique et Coopératif
GDP	Gross Domestic Product
IR	International Relations
MPRP	Mongolian People's Revolutionary Party
NLD	National League for Democracy
ODA	Official development assistance
OECD	Organisation for Economic Cooperation and Development
PLA	People's Liberation Army
PRC	People's Republic of China
RCAF	Royal Cambodian Armed Forces
SCO	Shanghai Cooperation Organization
SLORC	State Law and Order Restoration Council
SOE	State-owned enterprise
SPDC	State Peace and Development Council
UN	United Nations
UNTAC	United Nations Transitional Authority in Cambodia

Acknowledgements

From the very first idea to its publication, this book project has been accompanying me for several years. I am indebted to a number of people who have generously supported me in writing this book. To begin with, it would never have materialized without Jörg Faust, who hired me for a project at the German Development Institute/Deutsches Institut für Entwicklungspolitik (DIE). With his faith in my abilities and his encouragement to start a PhD project on China, he planted the seeds of this book and pushed me to engage with this topic. This book builds on my PhD project.

Also, my PhD supervisors, Aurel Croissant and Stefanie Walter from Heidelberg University, have been extremely helpful in developing my research. However, throughout most of my work on this project, DIE was my institutional home. It offered a very convenient working atmosphere and many opportunities to travel to Asia to participate in conferences and summer schools. I gratefully acknowledge the financial support of Germany's Federal Ministry of Economic Cooperation and Development.

Nonetheless, this institutional infrastructure and funding would have been much less fruitful without the inspiring interaction with and support from DIE's staff. I would therefore like to thank my friends and former colleagues at DIE for their continuous encouragement and generous support. The discussions on the theoretical framework with the members of the DIE project team, Jörn Grävingholt, Antje Kästner and Oliver Schlumberger, were always inspiring. I would also like to thank Sebastian Ziaja, Melody Garcia and China expert Doris Fischer, and I am especially grateful for Julia Leininger and Jörg Faust's valuable feedback on parts of the manuscript in various versions, their mentoring, and help along the way. Christine Hackenesch has been a careful and critical reader and an extremely valuable partner for discussion at the later stage of this book project, and I am especially indebted to her.

Furthermore, I would like to extend my sincere gratitude to the numerous conversation partners in China, Mongolia, Cambodia, Vietnam, Singapore, Berlin and Bonn who took the time and exchanged their views with me. Even though they remain anonymous in this book, the conversations and encounters with these individuals offered invaluable opportunities to me to learn and get useful insights and perspectives. Thanks are also due to Milan Svolik who, even before its publication, kindly shared his dataset with me (though it has not been used in the final version of this book) and to the student assistants at DIE, Kathrin Becker, Viviane Raub, Stefanie Hirsch as well as my friend Jule Krüger, who have helped me with collecting and coding some of the data.

It is impossible to list all those who have asked crucial questions or given critical remarks on the project, for instance, during various conference presentations or the review process. These challenging commentators have greatly contributed to the project by stimulating my own reflection and pushing me to improve the clarity and rigour.

There is no doubt that I would not have succeeded in completing this project without the affectionate support of my family and friends. I thank all my family members, my parents, my friends and Clemens for their patience, faith and encouragement. This kept me going.

Part I

Supporting dictators

If so, why and how?

1 What we know and why we know so little

As the third wave of worldwide democratization ebbed away in the 2000s, a growing interest in the causes for autocratic survival emerged. After a decade dominated by a focus on democratization and transitology, the 'turning tides' in freedom (Puddington 2007) and the 'rollback of democracy' (Diamond 2008) was declared. Even those who view the current situation more optimistically, as one in which liberal democracy is not in retreat and competition between political regime type as merely frozen, come to the conclusion that the number of autocracies is unlikely to decrease soon (Merkel 2010). Indeed, the global financial crisis has been another backlash for democracy. In many developing countries, the breakdown of the global financial system was interpreted as more than just a failure of the liberal economic order. As several Western democratic governments under political and economic pressure appeared unable to prevent social disruption, democracy as a political model was critically questioned too.

Against this background, one parallel trend, the emergence of China as an autocratic major power, is undeniable (Gat 2007). Since the beginning of the new millennium, China has become increasingly active in other parts of the world. Specifically, since the global financial crisis set in, China has bolstered its profile as a foreign investor, alternative donor, and trade partner (Kobayashi 2008; Lum *et al.* 2008; Brautigam 2009; Wolf Jr *et al.* 2013). Moreover, in the context of retreating liberal values, China's experience is increasingly viewed as an alternative to the Western development path and value system (Kurlantzick 2008; Halper 2010; Kopinski *et al.* 2011).

This rise of China has created much suspicion and criticism among Western countries. For example, observers have called China a 'rogue donor' (Naim 2007), because of its policy of providing development assistance without strings attached; that is, without political conditionality. By doing so, it has been argued that China is undermining the efforts of traditional Western donors to promote good governance and democracy. In countries like Sudan or Angola, China's 'oil diplomacy' was accused of feeding a civil war or, at least, of disregarding transparency and human rights (Taylor 2006; Halper 2010). At the same time, observers have identified the potential to stifle free expression abroad in China's attempts to expand its international media cooperation (Farah and Mosher 2010).

Whether or not democracy is really on the retreat, given their simultaneity, some have tried to establish a link between the trends of stagnation of democratization and China's rise as a powerful non-democratic player (Puddington 2007; Kagan 2008). While the Chinese government itself has only reluctantly acknowledged China's weight as an economic, military and normative power, it remains keen to portray itself as a developing country with no ambition to interfere in the domestic politics of others (State Council 2011a, 2011b). This has by no means resolved the debate about the intentions, the empirical nature and the implications of China's rise. In particular, it remains controversial whether the Chinese government patronizes autocratic regimes, and whether such alleged support has helped autocratic leaders to bolster their power and makes the world more authoritarian.

Empirically, it is not evident that China is indeed a cause of authoritarian persistence. Firstly, while China has reportedly supported autocracies (Kleine-Ahlbrandt and Small 2008), China might not be the only source of external assistance: other authoritarian powers such as Russia or Iran, but also many Western countries have questionable relations to autocratic regimes. For example, recent research revealed that the US is no less inclined to sell arms to authoritarian states than China (De Soysa and Midford 2012). Others have criticized the activities of Western corporations and banks in autocracies for being just as condemnable and questionable as the Chinese (Brautigam 2009). Moreover, there is evidence that natural resource exports from Africa correlate with human rights violations no matter whether they are sold to China or the US (Meyersson *et al.* 2008).

Secondly, the effect of China does not necessarily need to be negative for democratization (Hackenesch 2014). As modernization theory claims, the social and cultural changes associated with economic development enhance democratization in the long run (Lipset 1960; Inglehart and Welzel 2009). Hence, assuming that China has a developmental effect on some developing economies – through the provision of aid and infrastructure investments, or by driving up prices of natural resource exports – one would expect China's rise to have a positive effect on democratization in these countries ultimately. Empirically, China's doing-business approach in Central Asia, for example, appears to have positive effects on governance aspects that are usually associated with democratization (Melnykovska *et al.* 2012). Thus, the theoretical and empirical effects of China's rise on other autocracies are unclear and we do not know whether they differ from that of other actors.

This book attempts to improve our understanding of China's role as an external factor in authoritarianism. Does China profit from the persistence of other autocratic regimes? Do China's leaders strategically cooperate with other autocrats? And, to what extent is linkage to China a cause of longevity of other autocrats?

The answer to these questions is of relevance not only for those who are interested in the theoretical causes – and lack thereof – of democratization, but also to practitioners in the field of development assistance, and particularly to policymakers in international relations. As will be elaborated in more detail, the effects of external influences on democratization and authoritarianism are underresearched. The impact of non-democratic external influences, and especially of China, remain particularly opaque. At the same time, policymakers in the field of development cooperation and foreign relations disagree about the role of China and the debate about this becomes increasingly heated. While there is little to no systematic analysis of the impact of China's rise, this phenomenon shapes our contemporary world to a great extent and will continue to do so in the future.

This book connects the growing scholarly interest in the survival of autocracies with the debate on the external factors of political stability and with the discussion of the particular role of China in international relations. It provides a theoretical perspective on the potential causes of the persistence of modern autocratic regimes that explicates the role of external autocratic powers. This forms the base of the subsequent empirical investigation of China's external relations. Given the still weak understanding of China's foreign relations, and given the early stages of the debate on external autocratic support, the book's contribution consists as much in providing insights into the recent Chinese engagement in the developing world as in systematically assessing the particular role of China as an external factor in the survival of other autocracies.

As will be discussed in more detail below, there is a recent, lively debate about the role of autocratic major powers, such as Russia, Iran, Venezuela and China, in sustaining authoritarianism abroad. However, in extant literature, there is no consensus on how to conceptually capture the phenomenon of such external 'autocracy support', 'autocracy promotion' or 'black knight' support (Tolstrup 2009; Burnell 2010; Vanderhill 2013). For one, a variety of mechanisms and instruments of external autocracy promotion has been proposed. Another important line of contention relates to the degree to which external support or promotion involve a deliberate intention of the external actor and whether or not the concepts also comprise unintentional actions that have the consequence of strengthening autocratic features. Autocracy promotion, according to some experts, contains the deliberate intention to induce or strengthen autocratic structures elsewhere (Vanderhill 2013). Some also make the distinction between situations where autocratic features are already present, and hence can be supported by the outside actor, versus contexts in which they are absent or weak, where authoritarianism only can be promoted.

This book does not seek to solve this conceptual debate, but takes on a rather flexible position which is defined by and varies with the diverse subquestions raised. More specifically, the theoretical argument provided in this book covers both the *motivations and mechanisms* of autocracy support, while the empirical focus of this book lies on *the mechanisms and the impact* of external factors, and pays less attention to intentions. Empirically, the main interest lies on the interactions between existing authoritarian regimes, i.e. what some would call autocracy support. However, the investigation seeks both to shed light on China's external behaviour and to assess its impact on other countries. Therefore, it looks not only at China's interaction with, and effect on autocracies, but strives for a comparison with China's external relations to and effects on non-autocratic countries.

The book thus contributes to the autocracy promotion debate by proposing and testing a theoretical framework that takes the motivation of authoritarian powers as the starting point, by providing empirical insights into the interaction between elites in and outside of China, and by assessing the empirical relevance of linkages to China for autocratic survival elsewhere. At the same time, while the book delivers insights into the patterns of China's foreign relations it neither provides an anatomy of China's approaches to, or instruments of, autocracy promotion in the narrow sense of the debate, nor any proof that such intention exists. So, the reader should neither expect a book on the 'Chinese way' of autocracy promotion (as opposed to the Russian or Iranian), nor an analysis of Chinese rhetoric, motivations or intentions. Whereas the book suggests that a preference for authoritarianism abroad is theoretically plausible, it does not claim to explain how such preferences relate to other plausible foreign policy interests or that they necessarily obtain priority over other objectives; it also does not claim to prove that such preferences empirically exist. Finally, as mentioned above, the empirical focus of the book lies on China's role in autocratic survival. Therefore, the questions of whether or how China effects democratic institutions, whether it makes countries less democratic, or even induces transition from democratic to autocratic rule are not investigated here.

Why should we expect China to patronize other autocratic fellows? The starting point of the investigation is a theoretical reasoning, broadly based on selectorate theory (Bueno de Mesquita *et al.* 2003). This actor-centred political economy argument identifies the different distributional patterns that can be observed in autocratic and democratic regimes as an incentive for major powers to cultivate autocracies elsewhere (Bader *et al.* 2010). The main argument is that the highly discretionary redistribution of resources in autocratic systems makes these systems prone to exploitation from outside. Accordingly, it should be easier for external players – be they autocratic or democratic major powers – to realize their external interests in autocratic than in democratic countries. However, for autocratic major powers such as Russia or China, the interest in autocratic persistence is topped up by the fear of democratic diffusion and the spillover of rebellions to overcome autocratic rule, as could be observed most recently in North Africa and the Middle East. The possibility to exploit autocratic regimes and the fear of democratic dominos – which in a globalized world extends beyond the country's immediate neighbourhood – both deliver a motivation for why the Chinese leadership is expected to prefer cooperation with autocracies over democracies.

But the actor-centred political economy approach also provides insights into how such external preferences and interaction affect autocratic longevity elsewhere. For actors in such countries, interaction with external players can form a crucially important source of power. Accordingly, international cooperation affects the distribution of power in a country and so impacts on the survival of specific leaders (Smith 2009). As external actors can decide to interact only selectively with a specific partner, they have some influence on the distribution of power in a given country. Such influence is, however, conditioned on the pre-existing institutional constraints in a country that define the degree to which external interaction priviliges specific political actors over others.

The book investigates the empirical validity of this argument by combining in-depth case study research with a quantitative regression analysis. First, it investigates a core assumption of the theoretical argument; namely, that Chinese decision-makers find it easier to realize their interests in autocratic than in democratic countries. Because it is also of interest to investigate whether this is achieved by exploiting the distributional logic in authoritarian regimes, this investigation is pursued by the means of three comparative in-depth case studies. The three compared countries – Burma, Cambodia and Mongolia – capture the spectrum between outright autocracy and democracy. (For practical reasons, I refer to Burma rather than Myanmar throughout the book. During most of the period of investigation, Burma was considered to be authoritarian.) With respect to their compliance with Chinese interests, the comparison finds that the Chinese government is very successful in realizing its interests in the more autocratic small-coalition countries Burma and Cambodia, whereas it faces greater difficulties pursuing its objectives in the more democratic or large-coalition country Mongolia. Moreover, the investigation also finds empirical evidence that the Chinese government adapts to the distribution patterns in small- and large-coalition systems in order to increase the responsiveness to its interests. Specifically, there are indications that the Chinese government is more inclined to target members of the political and economic elite in Burma's and Cambodia's autocratic small-coalition regimes, whereas it seems to be more concerned with considering the interests of the broader population in the Mongolian large-coalition democracy. Interestingly, it appears that the Chinese approach has also adapted to the recent changes in Burma's domestic political situation.

Second, the book quantitatively examines what determines China's recent international economic cooperation projects and whether these are specifically targeted at autocrats. Finally, I assess whether different forms of interaction and cooperation between China and other autocrats increase the autocratic survival of the latter. Analysing the allocation of Chinese economic cooperation projects, the book finds that autocratic small-coalition countries are, indeed, targeted by China's foreign engagement. When investigating the impact of interaction and cooperation with China on the survival of leaders elsewhere, the effect is, however, found to be much more limited than expected: for several interaction channels, such as high-level diplomatic relations, economic cooperation and arms sales from China, no effect on autocratic leadership elsewhere can be shown. However, export dependence on China seems to increase a leader's survival in power in autocracies, but not so in democracies, suggesting that autocratic leaders are better able to capitalize from external interactions. Thus, while China's rise is found to have a stabilizing effect on autocratic rule elsewhere, the channels through which such external support enforces authoritarianism are very specific.

The book's findings have several implications. First, the fact that the degree of compliance seems to vary with coalition size supports the suspicion that powerful incentives exist for external actors to prop-up other autocrats. Without arguing that this translates into a preference for political stagnation, we can expect that for China, these incentives will only increase in the future. This is because with China's increasing outward orientation and spiralling investments in other autocratic regimes, the country's material stakes in the stability of existing authoriarian regimes are dramatically changing. Second, the findings underline the ambiguity of China's rise and its impact on leader survival, and on international relations more generally. On the one hand, China's rise becomes increasingly sensible elsewhere in the world. On the other hand, the fact that most forms of linkages were not found to have any observable impact implies that the impact and influence that China supposedly has on others tends to be overestimated, and is sometimes even misreported. Most importantly, economic power seems to be more influential than other forms of political linkages.

The external factors of political regimes

In general, it is fair to say that we know relatively little about the external determinants of regime type. The majority of democratization literature attributes the question of whether, or to what degree, a country is ruled in a democratic or an autocratic manner to internal factors, such as the level of economic development (Lipset 1960; Moore 1960; Inglehart and Welzel 2009) cultural factors and the heterogeneity of a country's population (Lerner 1958; Almond and Verba 1963; Pye 1985; Fukuyama 1995; Putnam *et al.* 1993; Huntington 1996), or domestic agents and institutions (Rustow 1970; Dahl 1971; Sartori 1976; Lijphart 1984). Regarding authoritarian rule more specifically, there is some consensus on the idea that authoritarian rule is established and maintained by a combination of two complementary strategies, repression and co-optation (Tullock 1987; Wintrobe 1990). In addition, authoritarian rule is sometimes legitimized, ideologically or religiously. Taking this as the starting point, there are a number of different scholarly traditions with varying foci on aspects of authoritarian rule. Aspects such as specific types of authoritarianism (Geddes 1999), the role of institutions (Gandhi and Przeworski 2006, 2007; Magaloni 2008), and their ability to co-opt internal and external oppositional forces (Svolik 2012; Conrad 2011) as well as their implications for authoritarian stability have been investigated, to name a few.

Only a small number of approaches have tried to build an external perspective into these considerations. One of the very early approaches linking external and internal factors of regime type during the Cold War are world-system (Wallerstein 1974) and dependency theory (Cardoso and Faletto 1979). These theories implicitly argued for the importance of external factors in shaping a state's regime type. Both approaches perceived a division between more and less developed countries where the more developed 'core countries' exploit the dependent underdeveloped 'periphery'. Dependency theorists argue that since authoritarian leaders are supposedly more receptive to the interests of international economic centres, this system of exploitation is maintained by stifling democratic rule in peripheral countries (Teorell 2010: 77f).

As Teorell (2010) summarizes, the empirical evidence for dependency theory is mixed: early studies did not find strong support for it, but in an era of increased globalization, trade and portfolio investments appeared to hinder democratization. His own quantitative investigation, in which he contrasted the effect of trade volumes against other international factors of democratization (such as diffusion or the influence of regional organizations, as discussed in the following), found that largely trade-dependent countries were, indeed, less likely to democratize. Interestingly, however, according to Teorell's research, this outcome is not affected by the nature of a trade-dependent country's trading partners. Thus, it does not matter whether a country's trade is dependent on democratic core countries such as the US, France or the United Kingdom, or on autocratic cores such as China or Russia (Teorell 2010).

After the Cold War, the debate on the external effects of regime type and regime stability was predominantly shaped by the democratization discourse. With only a few exceptions, this debate neglected autocracies in several ways. Firstly, throughout the 1990s, it was assumed that transition to democracy was inevitable and irreversible, and thus the debate was mainly concerned with democratization. Secondly, the debate was overtly guided by a Western perspective and by the presumption that mostly – or sometimes even only – democratic Western countries, whether intentional or not, would affect regime type (in the direction of democracy) elsewhere. Only when the third wave of democratization dried up in the 2000s, did the focus of this debate shift to the study of authoritarianism and, more recently, it has started to pay more attention to the implications of the rise of authoritarian external powers.

In the post-Cold War debate, Whitehead (1996) was among the pioneers to develop a conceptual framework to analyse external influences on democratization. He differentiated between the categories of contingency and control (Whitehead 1996: 4) and these categories were reflected in the structure of the discussion that further evolved. While contingency referred to the diffuse spread of norms and practices, the notion of control described intended democracy promotion by major democratic powers.

Whitehead's notion of contingency lines up neatly with diffusion theory. Recognizing that democratization has appeared not only in temporary, but also in spatial waves where countries face significantly higher probability of undergoing regime change following transitions in neighbouring states, diffusion theory argues that ideas, norms, policies and political structures spread spatially throughout the world (Simmons and Elkins 2004; Levitsky and Way 2005; Gleditsch and Ward 2006; Brinks and Coppedge 2006). Theorizing on the causes of such democratic diffusion, Levistky and Way (2005) presented a framework of linkage and leverage, referring to the density of interactions with democracies and to the vulnerability of a government to external incentives provided by these interactions.[1] Nevertheless, a recent empirical investigation of the democratic domino theory, which tried to quantify the influence of neighbourhood effects, found that countries absorb, on average, only 11 per cent of the changes in democracy levels that their neighbours experience. This suggested that the effect of diffusion is rather small (Leeson and Dean 2009).

Whitehead's notion of control referred to intended democracy promotion. This debate on democracy aid has, however, not produced a theory of democracy promotion thus far, which reflects the difficulty of the discipline to come to a consensus on even basic concepts (Merkel 2010). But, as numerous democratic governments engaged in proliferating democracy in the world, a lively debate about the instruments and the effectiveness of external democracy promotion emerged (Carothers 1999; Grimm and Leininger 2012). Whether qualitatively or quantitatively, researchers found it inherently difficult to substantiate the effectiveness of democracy promotion. The fact that some studies have even discovered a counter-productive impact of more general external funding on good governance and democratization could indicate that the dissatisfying results in the aid effectivness research are not only due to various analytical problems (Knack 2001; Easterly 2002; Svensson 2003; Leeson and Sobel 2008; Keefer and Knack 2007).

Two important findings of this debate are particularly relevant here. Firstly, the argument that foreign aid can be seen as a form of non-tax revenue and, as such, has a stabilizing effect on governments. Secondly, the argument that the effect of aid on democratization depends on the initial institutional context in the recipient country. Accordingly, it does not matter how non-tax income is generated, but it has been found that non-tax revenue generally stabilizes democracies and autocracies alike (Morrison 2009). While it leads to less taxation of richer elites in democracies, non-tax revenue leads to increased spending on poorer citizens in non-democracies, both easing pressure from potentially regime-threatening subgroups of society. Moreover, the specific effect of foreign aid on democratization has been found to be greatly dependent on the initial political conditions in a country. Foreign aid is more likely to help autocratic leaders to democratize when they are relying on a large distributional coalition (Wright 2009), when democracy is already emerging (Nielsen and Nielson 2010) or when elites face the threat of being overthrown (Bueno de Mesquita and Smith 2009).

In the new millennium, the debate slowly shifted its research interest from democratization to autocratic persistence. However, it is indicative of the preoccupation with a Western democratic perspective that the discussion on the influence of autocratic external powers remained underdeveloped in the first part of the 2000s. The perceived ineffectiveness of development aid has usually been connected to the strategic objectives of Western donor countries (Zeeuw 2005; Emmanuel 2010). This view is also shared by those coming from the discussion on autocratic longevity. For example, Bellin (2004) attributed the longevity of Middle Eastern and North African autocracies to strategic Western interests in the region. 'Multiple western security concerns in the region guarantee continuous international support to authoritarian regimes in the Middle East and North Africa even after the cold war... Together, these factors reinforce the coercive apparatus' capacity and prevent democratic reform' (Bellin 2004: 152). Similarly, Magaloni and Kricheli (2010) suspected Western donors and the international financial institutions to have caused the observable spread of dominant-party autocracies in the post-Cold War period. Levistky and Way (2010) attributed persisting autocratic structures to low vulnerability and exposure to Western influence. The recognition that Western democracies may *nolens volens* have contributed to autocratic persistence is certainly in place. However, it is remarkable that, for a long time, the influence of autocratic external powers remained undiscussed, even though it was admitted that 'not all linkage is Western' (Levitsky and Way 2010: 50).

It was only with the (re-)emergence of Russia and China that the question was raised whether and how autocratic rule was protected and promoted by major autocratic countries (Carothers 2006; Gershman and Allen 2006; Burnell 2006, 2010; Diamond 2008). It was argued that, in their attempt to 'diffusion proof' their own regimes against democratization pressures from the outside, some autocratic powers, notably Russia, Venezuela and Iran, engaged in propping up other autocrats (Ambrosio 2009; Jackson 2010; Bader *et al.* 2010; Vanderhill 2013; Koesel and Bunce 2013). To date, the discussion on whether or to what extent autocratic powers pursue 'autocracy promotion' still remains much focused on conceptualizing and tracing this 'black knight' support. On the one hand, no consensus exists so far on how to define and distinguish autocracy promotion from other forms of external influences. On the other hand, most contributions emphasize the influence, rather than the impact, of authoritarian patrons (Ambrosio 2009; Tolstrup 2009; Jackson 2010; Vanderhill 2013). Even though many studies convincingly illustrate that autocratic powers have sought to promote and support autocracies abroad, they provide little assessment of the impact of such attempts. Thus, we do not know whether such black knight support makes a difference or not.

This cursory review of the current state of research illustrates that authoritarian major powers, China in particular, have received little attention when it comes to their influence on regime type elsewhere. In general, the debate on the external dimensions of regime type and regime durability has taken on a Western perspective and is driven by the question whether and how the industrialized Western democracies could promote democracy abroad. While authoritarian powers were assumed to have influenced the form and durability of political systems in the developing world during the Cold War (Easterly *et al.* 2008), their influence on autocratic longevity in the post-Cold War period remains under-researched. There are a few investigations into the external relations of emerging authoritarian regional powers such as Russia, Iran or Venezuela and their role as patrons for autocratic regimes (Ambrosio 2009; Tolstrup 2009; Jackson 2010; Vanderhill 2013; Reilly 2013; Bader and Kästner 2013). However, these studies tend to provide little assessment of the impact of such external autocracy support, and often do not cover China. As will become clear in the following, China's role as an emerging autocratic power is contested. There is a need, therefore, for more systematic comparative empirical investigation.

China as an emerging autocratic power

The above discussion on autocracy promotion is strikingly silent with regard to the role of China. It seems that this is partly due to a lack of understanding of the nature of China's foreign behaviour and the difficulty of establishing that China is actively, or intentionally, promoting autocracy. For example, in her comprehensive comparison of different autocratic powers, Vanderhill (2013: 9) left out China for this reason. Indeed, compared to Russia's offensive pursuit of its external interests, which often involves direct interference or coercion, China seems to pursue its interest more subtly (Bader and Kästner 2013). In contrast to Russia or Venezuela's observable interference in neighbouring countries, China's leaders deny any such intention. They frequently refer to the five principles of peaceful coexistence and non-interference, and are worried of being perceived as interventionist. At the same time, a number of studies on China's soft power, and on its engagement in Africa, suggest that China's activities on the continent have indeed contributed to autocratic stability (Taylor 2006; Kurlantzick 2007; Halper 2010). Similarly, its international engagement in the media sector, with the aim of promoting China's soft power, has been criticized for undermining freedom of expression with potentially negative consequences for political competitiveness in these countries (Puddington 2010; Farah and Mosher 2010). These studies have not been taken up in the autocracy promotion debate, largely due to a perceived lack of intentionality.

Though China has received much attention outside the autocracy promotion debate, there is no clear picture of China's impact on the political regimes in other countries to date. Evidently, China's increased external engagement from the late 1990s onwards is only a relatively recent phenomenon. In addition, while the Chinese presence is often widely visible and sensible, for example through the establishment of Chinese communities that follow Chinese investments, the effect of China's broader engagement in many countries remains difficult to assess. With respect to many aspects, the extent of China's presence in other countries remains opaque and intransparent: data on China's external engagement are generally difficult to access or not available at all. There are, for example, no published disaggregated statistics of Chinese development assistance as these are considered a state secret (Brautigam 2009). Chinese companies and state actors abroad are known to be hesitant in communicating to the public (Grimm *et al.* 2011). China's domestic structure with party dominance over state structures and a complex interdependence between party, state, private and state-controlled economic actors makes the analysis even more troublesome. The constellation and interdependence of players in China's foreign policy often remains unclear – not only to the outside observer.

For all these reasons, the first generation of studies examining the impact of China's rise in and on other countries has predominantly been descriptive, rather than systematically assessing the effect of China's rise. These studies have illuminated China's objectives, strategies and instruments (Alden 2007; Davies *et al.* 2008), mapped the various actors involved in Chinese foreign policy (Reilly and Na 2007) or reconstructed the amount of Chinese assistance, foreign direct investment (FDI) and financial flows to other countries (Frost 2004; Lum *et al.* 2008; Brautigam 2008, 2009; Cheung *et al.* 2012; Wolf Jr *et al.* 2013). Their explorative value aside, these approaches tend to be non-comparative and, as argued, they often remain unconnected to the above debate on the causes of regime type elsewhere. In short, they provide valuable insights on what China is doing elsewhere in the world – often in Africa – as well as how it does it and which Chinese state institutions and non-state actors are involved.

Yet hardly any research has attempted to systematically assess whether or to what extent China's behaviour is sensitive to the other's regime type or to characteristics that can be related to the latter. For example, research has been conducted regarding the extent to which China's aid allocation, its diplomatic leadership travels, its trade patterns, or its arms trades prioritize other authoritarian regimes (Berthélemy 2011; De Soysa and Midford 2012; Kastner and Saunders 2012; Dreher and Fuchs forthcoming). These few studies deliver a mixed picture: the allocation of Chinese economic cooperation or aid (defined in several complementary ways) is not determined by aspects of good governance or regime type in the recipient (Berthélemy 2011; Dreher and Fuchs forthcoming), but, when travelling, Chinese leaders stay systematically longer in authoritarian countries than in democracies (Kastner and Saunders 2012). To my knowledge, there is no systematic and comprehensive assessment of China's effect on regime type elsewhere.

Finally, China's rise has received much attention among scholars in the field of International Relations (IR). Given the recentness of China's rise to global power, it is not too surprising that the discussion in this field of research is also dominated by ambiguity about the nature of this rise. Here, scholars disagree on whether China's rise will be peaceful in the long run. For example, according to power transition theory, whether China's rise will bring peace or war is dependent on its degree of satisfaction with the existing international order. Proponents of power transition theory argue that dissatisfied rising powers challenge the existing hegemon when they approach power parity with the hegemon (Organski 1968; Lemke 2003). With regard to this debate, some scholars have claimed that the autocratic nature of China's political system necessarily puts its leaders in opposition to the current liberal international order (Naim 2007; Kagan 2006, 2008). Yet, others challenge this view and argue that China has been fairly well socialized into the US-led world order (Johnston 2003; Kang 2007; Chan 2008; Kastner and Saunders 2012). Whether China is a status quo or a revisionist power is partly a matter of interpretation. Given that there are still only a few systematic studies of China's recent foreign behaviour and even fewer assessments of its impact, the interpretation of China's foreign behaviour is overtly difficult.

Plan of the book

The remainder of this book is divided into three parts: Chapter 2 begins with a theoretical reasoning on why major powers are generally interested in system convergence, and why autocracies in particular seek to nourish other autocrats elsewhere. The main arguments are that it is beneficial to major powers if other countries share a similar regime type, and that autocracies are particularly vulnerable to exploitation from outside. This political economy argumentation is broadly based on the selectorate theory (Bueno de Mesquita *et al.* 2003) and builds on earlier theoretical work (Bader *et al.* 2010). At the end of Chapter 2, three hypotheses are derived from this theoretical framework. These hypotheses theorize under which circumstances one should expect to observe increased cooperation between autocracies and when this cooperation should lead to autocratic survival.

The book then proceeds by investigating the main empirical implications of the argument. Part II examines the core empirical implication, i.e. that small-coalition governments are more vulnerable to exploitation from outside. Furthermore, it explores whether countries with different regime types have different interactions with China. By the means of three comparative case studies, it is examined whether and how China has realized its interests in countries with differing degrees of democratization. This investigation begins with a description of the case study design in Chapter 3, in which the case selection of Burma, Cambodia and Mongolia is explained. This chapter also introduces three distinctive Chinese foreign policy interests (China's 'one China' policy, access to natural resources and geopolitical considerations), which later serve to compare China's success in realizing its foreign policy objectives in these different countries.

Chapters 4, 5 and 6 provide a discussion of each of these cases and each chapter consists of three main parts: firstly, a brief introduction of the country's relations to China from a historical perspective; secondly, a discussion of the current domestic political situation from the perspective of the selectorate theory as the main independent variable of interest; and thirdly, an investigation of the interaction between Chinese actors and their counterparts in the three countries. Finally, Chapter 7 compares the compliance of the three countries with these Chinese interests. It synthesizes and discusses the findings of the three case studies with regard to the observed patterns of compliance as well as the observed patterns of Chinese behaviour. The chapter provides a discussion of the scope conditions of the theory and the generalizability of the presented findings. It concludes this part of the investigation with some critical reflections on the theoretical framework.

In Part III, the remaining hypotheses are tested quantitatively. Chapter 8 focuses on the question of whether the Chinese government specifically targets autocratic regimes in its external behaviour by making use of data on the allocation of Chinese economic cooperation projects. Chapter 9 presents several survival regressions that investigate the effect of different forms of China's bilateral interaction on leadership survival elsewhere.

Finally, the book concludes with a summary of the analysis and some reflections on their theoretical and empirical implications in Chapter 10.

Note

1   In their more recent book, Levistky and Way (2010) shifted their focus from explaining democratization to explaining comparative authoritarianism. In order to explain comparative authoritarianism, another factor, the organizational capacity of autocrats, was introduced.

2 Why autocracies should have an interest in the prevalence of authoritarianism

This chapter presents a theoretical argumentation explaining why autocratic powers have an interest in the prevalence of other authoritarian states and how this preference for autocratic regimes translates into autocratic survival. As has become clear from the review of the existing literature, there is currently no comprehensive framework for the role of external players in promoting or supporting a specific regime type in other countries. Most existing studies on external regime type promotion are empirically driven and focus on democratic players and their impact in promoting democracy abroad. Only a few studies consider whether autocratic powers too could have an interest in promoting or preserving their own type of political regime elsewhere in the world. However, these are generally weak in assessing the impact of such an interest.

This chapter lays out a number of reasons why one should expect autocracies to be interested in the prevalence of other autocratic regimes in the world. By connecting these arguments to a number of existing theoretical approaches on the logic of domestic politics, on the interplay between domestic politics and foreign policy, and on the interaction between regime type, interaction at the international level and political survival, an integrated framework is presented regarding why and how the preference for autocratic persistence of major powers may lead to autocratic longevity.

The domestic logic of political survival

This section presents some basic considerations on the principles of power and politics that are widely acknowledged in literature and that are important for the further argument as they define the incentive structures for political actors. Proponents of a political economy approach believe that political actors play a crucial role in determining political outcomes (Olson 1965, 1982; Gilpin 1996; Milner 1999; Bueno de Mesquita et al. 2003; Lake 2006). Fundamentally, they assume political actors to be rational and to be office-seekers. Political actors, whether conceptualized as individuals or collectives (in their function as government or opposition, for example), seek to attain power and, once power is achieved, seek to remain in office (Downs 1957; Wintrobe 2001; Lake and Baum 2001; Bueno de Mesquita et al. 2003).

Furthermore, it is assumed that in their struggle to achieve and preserve power, political actors are reliant on the loyalty of the population – or, more precisely, of specific societal groups – to accept and support the government in office. A political leader can create loyalty by distributing resources among a targeted constituency and so bind the welfare of this constituency to his own political survival in office. Therefore, in the view of political economy theory, the political process is understood as a political game in which the government offers targeted concessions or privileging policies to specific constituencies in exchange for political support (Wintrobe 1990; Bueno de Mesquita *et al.* 2003).

At the same time, a leader can use repressive means to coerce opponents and repress segments in society that could potentially challenge his rule (Wintrobe 1998; Bueno de Mesquita *et al.* 2003). Thus, 'the use of violence by governments is a strategic choice' (Vreeland 2008: 73).[1] Repression is a strategy that is carefully weighed against other strategies to respond to challenges to the ruling coalition, even though it is not entirely clear when and under what circumstances repression is actually the most attractive strategy (Gartner and Regan 1996; Moore 2000). However, for the sake of simplicity, one can argue that repression is closely related to, or even determined by, a leader's distributive policy. This is because the distribution of privileges influences the loyalty to the regime; that is, the willingess of individuals to act against or in favour of the autocratic regime. Thus, when some individuals benefit from a given leadership more than others do, they are less likely to protest against the regime as it is in their interest that the regime prevails in order to maintain their privileged situation. By the same token, one should assume that, lacking any personal gains, individuals are less willing to carry out oppression against others in the name of the regime unless they are forced to do so.

The existing literature focuses on different societal actors as the main threat to political leadership. In contrast to Wintrobe (1998), who assumed the whole population has the potential to challenge a leader in power, Bueno de Mesquita *et al.* (2003) differentiated between two societal subgroups, the selectorate and the winning coalition, which they considered to be most important. According to Bueno de Mesquita *et al.* (2003), the selectorate is the subset of all residents 'that has a formal role in expressing a preference over the selection of the leadership that rules them, though their expression of preference may or may not directly influence the outcome' (Bueno de Mesquita *et al.* 2003: 38). Later, Bueno de Mesquita *et al.* further qualified the argument and came up with the distinction between the 'nominal' and the 'true' selectorate. 'Fundamentally, the nominal selectorate is the pool of potential support for a leader; the real selectorate includes those whose support is truly influential; and the winning coalition extends only to those essential supporters without whom the leader would be finished' (Bueno de Mesquita and Smith 2011: 5). They continue to argue that the winning coalition is the most important of the three subsets. 'These are the people whose support is essential if a leader is to survive in office' (Bueno de Mesquita and Smith 2011: 5). This latter subgroup, which is critical to keeping a government in power, can consist of educational, economic or military elites, bureaucratic actors or a combination of these (Olson 1965; Bueno de Mesquita *et al*. 2003). As a consequence of this distinction, a government is specifically inclined to offer preferential policies to the collective actors of its winning coalition. The concept of the winning coalition is a useful tool to explore the logic of political survival. According to this political economy approach, governments, as rational political actors, pursue their overriding interest of preserving their power by distributing resources to specific constituencies and, if necessary, also to a repression machine such as special police forces, militaries, thugs or secret services.

According to Bueno de Mesquita *et al*. (2003), it is the size of the winning coalition in relation to its selectorate that incentivizes government behaviour. However, the authors often use the terms democracy and large-coalition system or autocracy and small-coalition system interchangeably (Bueno de Mesquita and Smith 2011). For the sake of simplicity and convenience, I will refer to common regime classifications such as democracy and autocracy. In line with the concepts of winning coalition and selectorate, the understanding of what a democracy is relates to minimal definitions of democracies. Such understandings focus on 'contestation open to participation' and minimal procedural requirements such as free and fair elections, political equality of all citizens, a free press and the freedom of association (Dahl 1971). When a distinction is made between democratic and autocratic regimes, all regimes that fail to meet the minimum standards of such democratic institutions are considered non-democratic. Hence, whenever reference is made to non-democracies or autocracies, this includes hybrid regimes with some democratic institutions.

One important structural difference between the different regimes identified by scholars of regime theory, proponents of political economy and scholars in the field of authoritarianism, is the difference in size of the winning coalition. Whereas in democracies, through the mechanism of regular elections, leaders must repeatedly compete to win the majority's favour, autocratic elites usually come to power on the basis of the support of narrow elite circles (Olson 1993; Lake and Baum 2001; Bueno de Mesquita and Root 2002; Faust 2007a). Winning coalitions tend to be relatively large in democracies and small in autocracies (Olson 1982).

It seems obvious that these differing mechanisms for acquiring power have far-reaching consequences. The first important consequence, which stems from different winning-coalition sizes, is that, in democracies, political actors are more inclined to respond to the demands of wider parts of the population, while leaders in autocracies can afford to be responsive to only a small subset of the society. If support is generated by privileging the respective winning coalition, then the bigger the winning coalition becomes, the more expensive it becomes to pay off every single member of the winning coalition. Thus, the bigger the winning coalition gets, the less effective the provision of private goods to generate support becomes. Eventually, it is more efficient to provide public goods, thereby making the whole population better off. For this reason, democratic governments tend to rely heavily on the provision of public goods, whereas autocratic governments focus more on the privileging of a small and exclusive group by providing their coalition members with private goods in order to generate support. This view is supported by the empirical fact that democracies produce more public goods and tend to be more resilient to the interests of the population as a whole (Lake and Baum 2001; Bueno de Mesquita *et al*. 2003; Faust 2007a; Blaydes and Kayser 2011).

Second, in addition to the fact that the larger winning coalitions in democracies require efficiency in the distribution of resources, the nature of democratic institutions also establishes a minimum of accountability to the electorate with regard to how leaders allocate these limited resources. Even though democrats are by no means perfectly controlled, the most basic democratic institutions, such as elections and press freedom, impose a certain degree of transparency on the government. This makes democrats accountable for their behaviour and constrains their discretionary power to allocate benefits. Autocratic governments, in contrast, are generally much less accountable to their citizens. Lacking a mechanism of regular evaluation in combination with restricted information flows through the repression of free media, autocratic governments generally benefit from a much larger discretionary leeway for the allocation of resources. Autocrats are incentivized to accumulate substantial personal wealth not only because their winning coalition is small (Bueno de Mesquita *et al*. 2003), but also because they can do so, as it is much more difficult for political challengers and the public at large to get information on government behaviour. Empirical evidence shows, for example, that democratic governments are more willing to report and publish data related to government performance such as unemployment rates or inflation (Rosendorff and Vreeland 2006). Moreover, it appears that the adoption and spread of new communication technologies, such as the Internet, is often delayed in autocracies. This, it has been argued, is not because of lower socioeconomic development, but because ruling elites fear that a better informed population will cause instability (Milner 2006). Consequently, autocratic governments are generally more self-determined in allocating their budgets than democratic leaders.

Third, the process of regular elections in democracies is not only an incentive for the incumbent government to convince with good performance, but also a chance for the opposition to regain power. In non- or weakly institutionalized autocracies, where a clear mechanism for the alternation of governments is missing, losing office is connected to insecurity about future possibilities to regain power. Because political power most often involves material advantages, it is generally also economically costly to the incumbent government. Therefore, losing power has more dramatic consequences for autocratic governments, especially if it would additionally expose purged leaders to being held responsible for the economic, political or societal crimes that the unrestricted monopoly of power allows them to commit (Tullock 1987). Consequently, in fear of an uncertain and most likely unpleasant future, autocratic leaders face much stronger incentives and far fewer restrictions in making use of every means, including repressive ones, to cling to power. This finding is supported by the Law of Coercive Responsiveness, according to which state authorities generally tend to employ repression when the status quo is challenged, but that in highly democratized countries repression is diminished (Davenport 2007).[2]

To clarify, the argument here is not that democracies are always good and autocracies are always bad. Instead, the argument reasons that the underlying incentives for actors in autocracies and democracies systematically differ and this leads to systematically different behaviour with regard to 1) the production of public goods in relation to private goods; 2) the extent to which leaders are accountable to the wider population; and 3) in the degree to which they cling to power and thereby possibly use repressive means. Relative to democracies, the composition of private and public goods in autocracies is such that targeted policies, on average, outweigh public goods. Democrats tend to be more accountable and less discretive than autocrats, and they tend to rely less on the use of repression.

However, this is not to say that autocratic leaders are entirely insensitive to the broader population, never seek to provide public goods, or always rely on repression. Many autocratic governments are eager to gain the favour of the broader population and some, such as Singapore, even excel in the provision of public goods. Indeed, research on authoritarianism has pointed out that within the category of autocracies, there is a wide variance with regard to their behaviour, performance and stability (Geddes 1999; Gandhi and Przeworski 2007; Wright 2008; Escribà-Folch 2012). While much of the contemporary research in the field of authoritarianism attempts to better understand the underlying causes of these differences largely by classifying and investigating different types of authoritarianism, proponents of selectorate theory focus on the variety in terms of winning-coalition size and selectorate prevalent in autocracies. Hence, the variance within autocracies by no means contradicts the selectorate theory, but reflects variance in a regime's ability to ensure the exchange of privileges against political support.

However, while it is relatively straightforward to connect large-coalition, large-selectorate regimes with democracies, it is much harder to envision how other configurations of these two variables relate to real-world regime types. In other words, what exactly does it mean when a regime has, for example, a small winning coalition and a large selectorate? The concept of winning coalition and selectorate theoretically allows for a more fine grained distinction than broad regime classifications (Bueno de Mesquita *et al.* 2003). Nevertheless, there are some generalizations that one can make to meaningfully connect the size of winning coalitions and selectorates with regime types with which the reader may be familiar.

Without denying that there is considerable controversy among scholars in authoritarianism research about the criteria that decisively characterize a given authoritarian regime (Alvarez *et al.* 1996; Hadenius and Teorell 2006; Geddes *et al.* forthcoming), two broadly known authoritarian regime types stand out for typically having small winning coalitions and small selectorates: military regimes and monarchies (Bueno de Mesquita *et al.* 2003). Military regimes in particular are considered to rely on very small, exclusive winning coalitions; they are often only weakly institutionalized, more repressive and inherently unstable (Geddes 1999). Regimes that are based on dominant political parties to institutionalize the interaction between citizens, elites and rulers tend to have large nominal selectorates, and winning coalitions that, although still small in comparison to those of democracies, are often considerably larger than in military regimes or monarchies (Wright 2008). Single-party regimes have thus been found to have better economic performance, and to be significantly more stable, more inclusive and less repressive than other forms of authoritarianism (Wright 2008; Magaloni and Kricheli 2010). Finally, regimes which rely neither on the military, nor on a royal court, nor on a party organization to moderate the interaction between ruler and ruled, but which instead rely heavily on patronage networks and personalized leadership, tend to take a middle ground with rather small winning coalitions and selectorates that are broader than those in monarchies and military regimes, but often considerably smaller than in dominant party regimes. Again, while this correlation between different regime types and different-sized winning coalition systems can help us to think about different-sized winning coalitions in a meaningful way, it is by no means a perfect correlation.

Before deriving the foreign policy preference for a specific regime type that follows from these structurally different incentive systems in democracies and autocracies, I briefly turn to a second existent approach that connects domestic politics to the international context as well as to regime type and regime survival.

Domestic politics, international cooperation and leadership survival

The second piece to link autocratic domestic structures to external autocracy promotion or support for autocratic survival is the literature on regime type and international cooperation, and international cooperation and leadership survival, respectively. These approaches are located at the conjunction of the fields of International Relations and Liberal Foreign Policy Analysis, which usually perceives foreign policy as an instrument to achieve domestic objectives (see, for example, Milner 1997; Moravcsik 1997). The logic of political survival as a barter between preferential policies and support is automatically extended to international politics as soon as one assumes that different policy fields are used in an instrumental way to satisfy a leader's desire to stay in power. Consequently, governments assess their external relations according to the degree to which they serve their interests, thus their utility to remain in power.

Putnam has developed the notion of a 'two-level game' where governments play at a domestic and an international level simultaneously.

> At a national level, domestic groups pursue their interests by pressuring the government to adopt favourable policies, and politicians seek power by constructing coalitions among those groups. At the international level, national governments seek to maximize their own ability to satisfy domestic pressures, while minimizing the adverse consequences of foreign developments.
>
> (Putnam 1988: 434)

Putnam's two-level game is a useful approach to think about the interplay between domestic and international politics and has been used as a starting point to model interaction at the international level (McGillivray and Smith 2000, 2004, 2006; Bueno de Mesquita and Smith 2007; Smith 2009). The basic assumption here is that leaders are often confronted with requests from other governments to adopt a specific policy that is not necessarily in their own interest. However, when asymmetries in power relations exist, leaders face additional incentives to comply with these external interests. For example, they are confronted with the threat of sanctions or the promise of a reward from the stronger player in order to comply with the external interests. When external powers threaten to punish non-compliance of a given government with sanctions against that government, the political survival in power of that specific government can be directly linked to its compliance with external interests (McGillivray and Smith 2004). Unlike traditional liberal approaches which view states as unitary actors and are, there-fore, blind to leadership turnovers, leader-specific approaches perceive sanctions and rewards to be targeted at a specific government. This conceptualization not only allows for the restoration of cooperation after the removal of non-coopera-tive leaders, it also implies that external powers can target international cooperation to specific actors in another country and withhold it from others.

Based on the selectorate theory presented earlier, Smith (2009) provided a formal model in which he showed that selective international cooperation disturbs the domestic balance of power and impacts on the survival of competing political actors in a country. Recall, the selectorate theory argued that the redistribution of resources to crucial societal subgroups is necessary to succeed in the domestic competition over power. Assuming that international cooperation is, in principle, beneficial to a government, external actors can influence the distributional capac-ity of domestic actors by cooperating or interacting only selectively. In other words, when external actors decide to cooperate with only a specific actor in a country, and not with another, they support the former and disadvantage the latter. This is because the former gains from interaction and can redistribute these gains among his constituency, while the latter cannot.

Extending Smith's model, I argue that the effect of such selectivity by external actors on the distribution of power in a given country should be dependent on the existing institutional setting that shapes the competition between political oppo-nents. That is, if external interaction creates private benefits to leaders, whether and how much these benefits advantage one opponent over the other should largely depend on the degree of competitiveness and the domestic institutional constraints that define how freely actors can use these benefits. External interac-tion and the benefits it creates should be most supportive to leaders with few constraints and great flexibility in terms of how they reinvest these resources. Accordingly, unconstrained, small-coalition leaders should benefit most from such interaction.

Unlike some studies in the field of IR, which assume that dyadic interaction is shaped by similarity in political regime types (Leeds 1999; Mansfield *et al.* 2000; Russett and Oneal 2001; Milner and Kubota 2005), this approach would suggests that dyadic interaction is the cause, rather than a consequence, of regime stability. Within the democratization debate, a similar point has been made by diffusion theory (Gleditsch and Ward 2006; Brinks and Coppedge 2006). Levitsky and Way's (2005) notion of linkage similarly theorizes that intensive interaction between countries leads to a convergence in political systems. However, as already mentioned, the focus in these works was predominantly on the spread of democracy.

Foreign policy – preferences for regime convergence and autocratic stability

The previous sections first illustrated the domestic logic of political survival and the different incentive systems in autocracies and democracies. Second, they connected foreign policy behaviour and international cooperation with domestic political survival. If foreign policy, as a policy field, is assumed to be used in order to achieve a government's overriding goal of securing its position in office, the domestic logic of maintaining power determines foreign policy decisions. Accordingly, foreign policy is designed to realize the decision-maker's desire to stay in power and tends to follow the domestic strategies to do so.

From this starting point, three arguments can be derived that suggest that governments are not indifferent to the regime type of others, especially not to that of their neighbours. The first consideration is related to the distributional means of preserving power. While democratic leaders, in order to satisfy a rather broad coalition, are more reliant on the provision of public goods, it is more important for autocratic governments to selectively distribute private goods to their relatively small coalition and to respond to specific vested interests. In turn, democratic governments face strong incentives to exploit international relations in order to improve their performance in the provision of public goods. In many ways, the provision of public goods goes beyond domestic borders and often international cooperation can contribute to their creation. For example, it has been shown empirically that democratic governments are less likely to go to war with each other and are more willing to open their domestic markets for international trade because peace and free trade primarily favours a large part of the population (Russett and Oneal 2001; Milner and Kubota 2005). Moreover, environmental degradation, which can seriously affect the provision of a healthy living environment, does not stop at national borders. In short, democratic incentive structures elsewhere ease the provision of transboundary public goods and, therefore, are in the interest of democratic leaders.

This argument becomes even stronger when authoritarian states cause negative externalities, which are counterproductive to a democratic government's efforts to perform well in the provision of public goods. As the performance of democratic leaders is evaluated in elections by the masses, they are more vulnerable than authoritarian governments to falling as a result of crises, even when these are caused by others. Autocratic leaders, in contrast, are relatively immune to external influences, as long as they can shield their narrow support groups against negative effects. For democratic leaders, there are two strong reasons why one would expect them to favour other countries to be democratic as well: first, the fact that cooperation in order to produce public goods is more likely to materialize between democracies because they are equally interested in their production; and second, the fact that negative externalities are more likely to be provoked by autocrats.

But, which preference would one expect for autocratic leaders? The very same distributional incentives also deliver an argument for why leaders in powerful autocracies should be interested in others being autocratic too. According to the domestic distributional logic, autocratic leaders are likely to use foreign policy to increase the resources that they can redistribute among the winning coalition. Instead of producing public goods, this often involves the distribution of private goods. Again, this is not to say that autocratic governments have no interest in the creation of transboundary public goods per se. Since remaining in power is easier with the support of broader segments of the population than without it, the production of public goods may create legitimacy and be generally beneficial for autocratic governments, too. However, given that their winning coalitions are generally much smaller, they are faced with less pressure and fewer incentives to actually produce these public goods. Ultimately, they maintain the loyalty of their winning coalition by ensuring that this group is better off than the rest of the population.

Moreover, as has been argued, a democratic government's spending and decision-making is often scrutinized more thoroughly. The requirements concerning accountability and transparency in democracies are generally higher. Therefore, it is relatively difficult to influence democratic decisions from outside. In autocracies, however, the circle involved in decision-making is small, accountability to the population is low and the interests of the decision-makers tend to be narrow. Therefore, it is comparatively easy to manipulate an authoritarian government's decision-making. In relative terms, it is easier for external players to exploit authoritarian states than democratic ones (Bueno de Mesquita *et al.* 2003). Exploitation, in this sense, refers to the realization of economic, political or geo-strategic interests, such as the extraction of natural resources, the acquisition of land concessions, the agreement on transit rights or the establishment of strategic military bases on foreign territory at relatively low costs.

Clearly, this exploitation argument is theoretically also valid for major democratic powers. However, as argued above, democracies are also more vulnerable to negative externalities produced by autocracies. So, for democracies the preference order may be less clear than for autocracies. Since the incentives for democratic leaders to prefer democracies or autocracies are ambiguous, making a general prediction about which type of regime a democratic power would prefer is not straightforward.

Just as autocracies are likely to produce negative externalities for democracies, democratic spillover effects from democracies are a cause of concern for autocratic leaders, especially when democracies are in their immediate neighborhood (Ambrosio 2009). On the one hand, being less reliant on the use of repression, democracies are more likely to pressure others about human rights abuses, while authoritarian governments are more likely to share similar attitudes regarding the means of repression to stay in power. Since autocrats are principally more reliant on repression to maintain power, they are less willing to criticize and to interfere in the domestic affairs of others (Burnell 2010). Moreover, the liberal atmosphere in democracies, with better access to information, more open debates and less human rights abuses, forms a potential cause of unrest if this diffuses into autocracies and inspires a demand among the population for the same rights and freedoms enjoyed by democratic neighbours. Even when such calls do not succeed in mobilizing enough support to overthrow the dictator, they are costly for the autocrat, because of the need to respond with increased repression or co-optation.

At the core of this potential to destabilize autocracies is the vulnerability of autocrats to the question of legitimacy. Because this legitimacy question is typically posed when people realize that autocracy is not inevitable,

> autocrats have a stake in ensuring that additional countries do not 'fall' to democracy. For instance, from a regional perspective, the ability of a country to withstand democratic pressures benefits all authoritarian regimes in the region. If a pattern of democratic transitions is halted, this would undermine a sense of momentum and reverse any belief that the overthrow of autocratic leaders is inevitable.
>
> (Ambrosio 2009: 29)

This domino effect became evident in Latin America, where almost all countries democratized within one decade during the 1980s, and then in the states of the former Soviet Union after 1989. The 'Arab Spring', the 2010 wave of popular upheaval in the Arab world, provides a new and vivid example of the strength of neighbourhood effects in inspiring attempts to overthrow authoritarian governments.

From the perspective of the autocrat, having a dictatorial neighbourhood is desirable, not only because it reduces the risk of subversive democratic spillover effects, but also because it reduces the likelihood of being punished for using repressive means, thereby reducing the cost of repression.

It follows, then, that governments should, with good reason, favour similar regimes, especially in their neighbourhood. There are clear incentives for democratic leaders to favour other democracies relating to the performance orientation of democratic governments. In contrast, autocratic leaders benefit from authoritarian neighbours because it is easier to extract vital assets from them. While this incentive is, in principle, also valid for democracies, being in an autocratic neighbourhood is a mixed blessing for democracies as democratic leaders may suffer from the negative externalities caused by authoritarian neighbours more than their authoritarian counterparts. Finally, autocracies have a strong incentive to favour other autocracies when it comes to their reliance on repression to enforce their position in power.

Bringing together the different approaches that have been presented, political economy provides a micro-foundation for foreign policy preferences. Accordingly, democrats are expected to use the game at the international level to make others more willing to contribute to the creation of public goods, while autocrats are expected to make use of the international level to acquire private goods to maximize their own ability to satisfy domestic pressure. At the same time, the adverse consequences that governments seek to minimize also differ: for democrats, this is the negative externalities created by autocracies, while autocrats perceive the democratic diffusion effects and interventionist intentions from democracies as a threat. From this perspective, a country's interest in a specific regime type elsewhere is purely instrumental.

Autocratic leaders simply seek to survive in power and while it is beneficial for their own longevity when others are also autocratic, this does not necessarily imply that a specific regime type is actively promoted elsewhere. Empirically, one can distinguish between the inducement of transition from a democratic to an autocratic type of regime and the support or stabilization of existing autocratic leaders. This study focuses on the latter. It should be noted that the exploitation argument as an instrumental motivation for supporting the persistence of autocracies already implies the very mechanism that stabilizes autocracies; namely, by addressing the autocratic leader and his winning coalition with targeted private goods. The erosion of democratic institutions or the inducement of transition from a democratic to an autocratic type of regime, on the other hand, would refer to a qualitatively different process. Whether and how far democracy is undermined when, for example, democratic leaders are addressed with targeted goods in order to achieve policy concessions, is a valid question. However, it is not addressed here.

Theoretical expectations

The previous sections have layed out my theoretical thinking on the foreign policy preferences of governments in different political regime types. I have discussed why leaders are benefiting from specific regimes elsewhere and how, or under what conditions, international interaction can stabilize existing structures. The remainder of the book will investigate whether this theoretical approach can be applied to the case of China. To this end, this theoretical chapter concludes by formulating my theoretical expectations in terms of three hypotheses.

It is not difficult to establish that China's political system has autocratic features; thus, it serves as a case for the investigation of autocratic foreign preferences and behaviour. Characterized by a socialist political system with the monopoly of power in the hands of a single party, China is consistently rated as highly authoritarian by the most common political indices. One common measure of the level of democracy, Freedom House, ranging from 1 (most democratic) to 7 (least democratic), rated China with 6 from 1972 until 1987 and with 7 from then on. On the other frequently used dataset, the Polity index, ranging from 10 (most democratic) to -10 (least democratic), China has scored -7 since 1975

(Marshall and Jaggers 2013). Certainly, with the change in leadership from Mao Zedong to Deng Xiaoping, China's political system has undergone considerable changes. These, however, mark a shift from a totalitarian to an authoritarian system,[3] rather than a step towards democracy. And while economic liberalization since 1978 has been successful, it was not particularly conducive to fundamental regime change. Attempts at political reforms and liberalization remain limited.

The first theoretical expectation to be investigated relates to the very root of the political economy argument, which assumes that small-coalition governments are easier to exploit from the outside. Hence, external players should find it easier to realize their foreign policy interests in autocratic small-coalition systems. Being the external actor, the Chinese government should thus be more successful in realizing their foreign interests vis-à-vis small coalitions than vis-à-vis large winning coalitions. This is my first hypothesis.

Hypothesis 1: China is more successful in realizing its interests in small-coalition (autocratic) systems than in large-coalition (democratic) systems.

One implication of this first theoretical prediction is that external actors are not entirely indifferent to the domestic political structure of others and, specifically, not to their winning-coalition size, because this crucially affects the ease with which a government can be influenced from the outside. This fact can act as a powerful motivation to prefer small-winning-coalition systems to large winning coalitions, especially in countries in which one has strong foreign policy interests.

Moreover, as small-coalition governments strongly rely on the targeting of goods towards their specific supporters to remain in power, the logic would suggest that this finds reflection in their interactions with the outside world, and especially in interactions with other small-coalition governments. This is because, driven primarily by their own domestic interests, both sides will seek to find an agreement. Thus, small-coalition leaders will only be willing to make policy concessions to the external actor when what they receive in return strengthens their own survival in power. The rationale for giving in to such demands for the external player, in contrast, depends on the salience of the foreign policy interest, which, in turn, is primarily shaped by his domestic considerations.

It has been argued that one strategic tool to purchase or reward policy support from other countries (Bueno de Mesquita and Smith 2007, 2009) is development aid. Indeed, several studies find that development aid allocation is driven partly by the self-interest of donor countries (Schraeder *et al.* 1998; Hook and Zhang 1998; Alesina and Dollar 2000; Weder and Alesina 2002). Against this background, it is expected that the Chinese government also transfers resources, for example, in the form of development assistance or financial aid, to other governments in order to make these more responsive to Chinese interests.

If small-coalition regimes are easier to exploit from outside, and if the transfer of resources can be interpreted as an attempt at external influence, one would expect that, all else being equal, small-coalition regimes are more likely to be targeted by external actors. Therefore, my expectation with regard to the attempt to specifically target small-coalition systems is that the Chinese government is more likely to target small-coalition (autocratic) systems than large-coalition (democratic) systems.

> *Hypothesis 2: China is more likely to target small-coalition (autocratic) systems than large-coalition (democratic) systems.*

Finally, my third theoretical expectation is that the effect of external interaction on the domestic distribution of power is dependent on the pre-existing power distribution and institutional constraints. Therefore, hypothesis 3 suggests that external interaction is more beneficial to less constrained small-coalition (autocratic) leaders than to more constrained large-coalition (democratic) leaders.

> *Hypothesis 3: International interaction is more beneficial for small-coalition (autocratic) leaders than for large-coalition (democratic) leaders.*

In this section, three hypotheses concerning China's foreign policy behaviour and its effects have been derived from the overall argumentation. These predictions are investigated in the subsequent chapters. The comparative case studies in Part II of the book provide an examination of hypothesis 1. Part III will quantitatively examine hypothesis 2 and hypothesis 3.

Notes

1   For a comprehensive overview of this literature see Davenport (2007).
2   However, democratization itself does not necessarily lead to decreased repression. 'The road to political openness is thus paved with political coercion but the arrival is generally pacific' (Davenport 2007: 11).
3   For the distinction within the category of authoritarian systems, see for example Linz (2000) or Brooker (2009).

Part II

External exploitation

Who, how and when?

3 How external exploitation materializes

From the theoretical framework posited in Chapter 2 one can derive a number of theoretical expectations, three of which have been articulated in the form of hypotheses at the end of Chapter 2. The remainder of this book explores the validity of the theoretical argument by investigating whether or to what extent these theoretical expectations hold true empirically. This part of the book tries to shed light on the mechanism of autocratic interaction and investigates hypothesis 1 – that China is more successful in realizing its interests in autocracies than in democracies. As this involves a great deal of exploration, this is done by the means of three comparative case studies.

This chapter is designed to lay out the logic of the case studies. It elaborates on the comparative design of the case studies, presents a clearer definition of the notion of 'winning coalition', and explains how 'exploitation' can be measured. Then, it presents and discusses the selection of cases which is one of the most critical decisions of this part of the analysis. Chapters 4, 5, and 6 present the actual case studies and Chapter 7 concludes this part of the book by presenting a structured comparison of the three cases. This comparison serves to assess the validity of hypothesis 1.

Purpose and design of the case studies

The following three comparative case studies have two objectives. First, they attempt to provide better insights into the interaction between elites in and outside China and, thus, to investigate the mechanism of external exploitation and autocratic stability, respectively. Second, they seek to investigate whether small winning coalitions – where the winning coalition is expected to be easier to co-opt – are easier to exploit from the outside.

Starting with the latter objective, the case studies simply seek to provide a substantiation of hypothesis 1, which relates to the very root of the theoretical argument. Recall the basic theoretical consideration, which assumed that the domestic political structures of a state or, more precisely, the size of its coalition, is of interest to the Chinese government, because it affects the ease with which a government can be influenced. The core of the argument is, therefore, that small-coalition governments are easier to exploit from outside. Consequently, if the theoretical argument is right, China should be more successful in exploiting small winning coalitions than large winning coalitions. Hence, the outcome to be explained with regard to this part of the comparison is China's success in realizing its interests elsewhere. A country's coalition size is suspected to be a main determinant of a country's compliance with China's interests and, thus, is the explanatory factor of interest.

The other objective of the case studies is to provide a better understanding and substantiation of the causal mechanisms at play. In this regard, the object of investgation is the interaction between the Chinese government and other governments. In terms of the causal mechanism, the theoretical reasoning assumes that exploitation works through a mechanism of exchange. When asked to make policy concessions to external players, governments tend to ask for something that suits their specific needs in exchange. External players with their own interests in extracting policy concessions from other governments make use of this incentive system in counterparts when they are knowledgeable about the size and composition of the winning coalition elsewhere. Therefore, one expectation of the theory is that external players specifically target a government and the members of its winning coalition with goods that suit the specific needs of this group. In autocratic small-coalition systems, targeting the dictator and his coalition is the most effective way to make the dictator comply with external interests. A similar approach in democracies, in contrast, would be less effective, because the democratic leader has fewer incentives to accept targeted goods in exchange for such policy concessions. This is because the democratic leader is often forced to make his decisions transparent and needs to make the policy concession acceptable to a wider part of the population if he wants to be re-elected. Consequently, targeted goods are assumed to be beneficial to the survival of the autocrat, because he can redistribute them among his supporters.

In light of the theory, the interaction and exchange between Chinese actors and their counterparts is also of particular interest. The Chinese government is expected to address small-coalition leaders primarily with goods or policies specifically targeted to the needs of the leader and his coalition. The needs of the population at large are expected to play a role when the coalition is large. Accordingly, a democratic leader should be approached by China with goods or policies that help him to be re-elected.

Unfortunately, with regard to this objective of the case studies, there are many obstacles to a rigorous comparison of the interaction between Chinese and outside actors with the aim of revealing the degree to which exchanged goods are targeted and towards whom. To start with, information on the volume, the nature and the recipients of exchanged goods or policies is difficult to obtain. With regard to overall information on such interaction, the suspected nature of the interaction suggests that there is an incentive to either cloud or misrepresent it in order to make it appear beneficial for a broader constituency. If bilateral exchanges are really beneficial for only a small elitist group, the beneficiaries should not disclose this out in the open to the public. However, if leaders want to make the broader society believe that bilateral relations with an external partner are beneficial to the country, they will selectively emphasize aspects with high visibility that may or may not be representative of the overall relationship.

There are a number of difficulties with regard to defining the nature of such exchanges. On the one hand, it is often hard to assess the identitiy of those who provide the goods. This involves assessing the degree to which the Chinese state is involved as the lines between economic assistance tied to Chinese State-owned enterprises (SOEs) and state commercial investments, and between state and private actors, are blurred. Often, it is difficult to establish whether, for example, Chinese companies act as private or state actors and to what extent they are, in fact, controlled or backed by state institutions. On the other hand, in many instances, it is impossible to define the targets and the true beneficiaries of such provision of goods, especially with regard to infrastructure projects. Finally, the nature of exchanged goods may be different, depending on whether one considers their production or their consumption. That is, even if an infrastructure project provided by China is untargeted with regard to its end users, it is a targeted project with regard to its production. Ultimately, the (Chinese) construction company is the beneficiary of the fact that such projects are provided by Chinese authorities.

Hence, this first part of the investigation, which is presented in the Chapters 4, 5 and 6, is more descriptive and explorative than explanatory in nature. Each chapter examines the interaction and exchange between Chinese actors and their counterparts in one of the investigated countries. For the sake of simplicity, in the following, the focus lies on the actors in the targeted countries, rather than on the Chinese side. A systematic investigation of the political economy of the involved actors on the Chinese side would doubtless be a valuable undertaking and is needed to complete the picture. Even though the case studies, at times, give some insight into this question, an in-depth analysis of how the Chinese government uses foreign policy to satisfy its own domestic winning coalition is beyond the scope of this study.

In order to scurtinize whether membership in the winning coalition matters in terms of being addressed by the Chinese, the broader structure of this investigation follows the question of whether specific actors are included in or excluded from the winning coalition. More specifically, each case study in Chapters 4, 5 and 6 is structured in four parts, beginning with a brief presentation of the political developments in the country from a historical perspective. This necessarily includes a special focus on the historical link between a country's political developments and China. Section two then turns to the domestic political structure in the post-Cold War period (the independent variable). This section describes the domestic political structure through the lens of the selectorate theory and defines the members of the winning coalition. Section three builds a descriptive bridge between the domestic winning coalition (the independent variable) and a country's compliance with Chinese interests (the dependent variable). This section specifically illustrates the links between Chinese actors and their counterparts in other countries, thereby shedding some light on the causal mechanisms that lead to compliance. Against the background of section two, it describes the targets and instruments of China's external relations from an actor-centred perspective and tries to illustrate how leaders exchange policy concessions against material and political benefits from China. Occasionally, this section also illustrates how this exchange relates to the political survival of elites in the target countries. Finally, each case study chapter concludes with a brief summary and reflection on the findings of the examination.

Chapter 7 is dedicated to the second objective of the case study analysis. It investigates and compares whether and how well the Chinese government can realize its foreign policy interests in each of the three countries and so puts hypothesis 1 to a test. In this part of the investigation, the focus lies entirely on the compliance of a government with Chinese objectives (the dependent variable). As will be explained in more detail below, three different Chinese foreign policy objectives are investigated. Accordingly, this chapter is divided into different parts, each concentrating on one Chinese foreign policy interest. The findings of this comparison together with the evidence of the three previous case studies are then compared and discussed in the concluding section of Chapter 7. It is here that the validity of hypothesis 1, that China is more successful in realizing its interests in small-coalition than in large-coalition regimes, is assessed.

How to measure winning coalition size and exploitation

How can one distinguish between members and non-members of the winning coalition? And how can the degree of exploitation be measured and compared? To begin with, a definition and measurement is needed to distinguish between small- and large-coalition systems and to define who the members of a winning coalition are. Regime type and the size of the coalition will be measured here qualitatively. Recall from Chapter 2 that the selectorate was defined as the subset of all residents with a formal role in choosing the leadership, regardless of whether or not their choice influences the selection of leadership (nominal selectorate), and those whose support is truly influencial (true selectorate).

Furthermore, the winning coalition was defined as 'a subset of the selectorate of sufficient size such that the subset's support endows the leadership with political power over the remainder of the selectorate as well as over the disenfranchised members of the society' (Bueno de Mesquita *et al*. 2003: 51) 'without the support of which the leader would be finished' (Bueno de Mesquita and Smith 2011: 5).

In sum, the authors of the selectorate theory remain rather vague regarding which groups are in or out of the coalition in a concrete case. This decision is basically left to the plausibility of argumentation: the size of a coalition in a given regime depends on the 'qualities required for membership' – which can vary from lineage to arms to party membership – 'and on the degree to which those qualities relate to lumpy or broadly distributed characteristics within the selectorate' (Bueno de Mesquita *et al*. 2003: 51).

Against this background, each case study provides a discussion of the qualities on which membership of the winning coalition is based and of the subgroups of society constituting the winning coalition. As the selectorate's formal role is usually defined *de jure* in a country's constitution, the definition of the nominal selectorate is the starting point of the analysis. But, to put the constitutional provisions in their right perspective, the de facto validity of the constitutional framework will also be discussed, thereby discussing membership of the true selectorate.

Having established how the winning coalition of a country can be identified, I now turn to the question of how to assess a country's compliance with external interests or its 'exploitability'. External exploitation can be understood as the degree to which outside actors succeed in realizing their own interests elsewhere. Thus, in order to assess the degree to which China is able to exploit others, the degree to which China is successful in furthering its interests in a country is measured. Measuring China's success in realizing its interests in a country and comparing the compliance of target governments requires a definition of China's most important foreign policy goals. Subsequently, the terms 'interest', 'goal' and 'objective' are used interchangeably. Three interests are defined as key foreign policy objectives by the Chinese government: the 'one China' policy and China's territorial integrity; China's access to primary resources in a given country; and a country's compliance with context-specific Chinese geopolitical interests and its behaviour towards the US in particular.

Firstly, the 'one China' policy refers to China's territorial integrity and is here related exclusively to the Taiwan question and Tibet. Both Taiwan and Tibet are non-negotiable Chinese interests (Nathan and Scobell 2012) and, according to a Chinese government spokesperson, they rank among China's most important and sensitive core interests (Chinese Government 2009). This is because they are not only economically valuable, but also are crucial to China's security (Nathan and Scobell 2012). As the Taiwan problem 'has been an obsessive focus of much of Chinese diplomacy' (Nathan and Scobell 2012: 361), a country's dealings with Taiwan is a formidable indicator of the realization of Chinese interests. Moreover, in a press release, the *China Daily* threatens that '[Western] nations should recognize that Tibet is an inalienable part of China and stop intervening if they want to remain on good terms with China' (*China Daily* 2009). This is explicitly linked to the question of how countries treat the Dalai Lama; thus, a country's dealing with the Dalai Lama serves as another good indicator of compliance with Chinese interests.

Secondly, economic 'growth has been at the top of the Chinese Communist Party (CCP) policy agenda ever since the 1980s and especially so after the end of the Cold War' (Wang 2005: 682). Since Deng Xiaoping's policy of economic reforms, the provision of economic development and prosperity to the Chinese population and party elites was the key to political stability in China. Thus, the Chinese developmental model has been extremely resource intensive. 'With about 6 per cent of global GDP, China consumes 31 per cent of the world's coal, 30 per cent of iron, 27 per cent of steel, 40 per cent of cement, 20 per cent of copper, 19 per cent of aluminium and 10 per cent of electricity' (Jiang 2009: 586). While the CCP's leadership has corrected its focus on economic growth at all costs for a more balanced socio-economic development, which pays more attention to environmental and social aspects and income equality, this does not alter the underlying need to maintain economic growth in the first place. Accordingly, economic and energy insecurity were explicitly identified in China's 2004 and 2008 Defence White Papers as non-traditional security threats (State Council 2004, 2008), while the government's 2003 White Paper on Mineral Resources promised the active promotion and protection of investments in mineral resource exploitation outside of China (State Council 2003).

Thirdly, China's geopolitical interests in Asia mostly relate to the US's containment policy in Asia, to the regional security architecture and to the strategic importance of China's regional environment for China. On the one hand, many Chinese analysts believe that the US seeks to contain China's rise by the means of strategic encirclement (Nathan and Scobell 2012). On the other hand, many of China's neighbours were highly suspicious of China when bilateral relations normalized in the early 1990s. This was because of earlier Chinese interventionism, resulting in Chinese support for insurgencies, and in efforts to influence Chinese ethnic communities in those countries (Harris 2005). In view of this, China has sought to strategically reassure, politically engage and economically integrate with its neighbours in order to 'hedge against downturns in Sino-U.S. relations' and to ensure that its neighbours do not 'fall within the ambit of another power antagonistic to China' (Goh as cited in Li 2007: 10; Yunling and Shiping 2005). Thus, it is the Chinese government's objective to prevent its neighbours from bandwagoning with the US or Japan against China (Harris 2005). For this reason, the way in which countries position themselves in security issues vis-à-vis China and the US – and, to a lesser degree, to other regional competitors such as India – is a useful indicator.

Leaders in all case study countries are confronted with these Chinese interests and have to respond to them. The success of Chinese engagement in realizing these interests can thus be measured in terms of the 'responsiveness' of the countries under investigation. One can differentiate between three degrees of compliance along a spectrum of compliance reaching from one extreme of 'refusal' to the other extreme of 'eagerness'. 'Reluctance' denotes a middle position. Figure 3.1 visualizes this spectrum of compliance.

According to the responsiveness of the respective targeted country, one can classify China's success in three broad categories on a continuum from

Figure 3.1 Spectrum of compliance

unsuccessful to very successful. Accordingly, a government can refuse to comply with Chinese interest, show formal compliance, or actively promote Chinese interests. Each reaction corresponds to one of the three types:

1   Refusal: a government publicly disagrees with the Chinese position and disregards Chinese interests. This means China is unsuccessful in realizing its interests in that country.
2   Reluctance: a government formally gives in to Chinese interests by responding on the base of a lowest common denominator; i.e. coming up with a diplomatically appropriate solution. This is a face-saving solution for both sides and can, from the Chinese perspective, be considered a nominal success in realizing its interests.
3   Eagerness: a government publicly promotes the Chinese position and proactively pursues the Chinese interests. As this goes beyond nominal compliance with Chinese interests, it exceeds Chinese expectations. Accordingly, China is very successful in implementing its interests.

With regard to each of the three specific Chinese foreign policy goals, a particular reaction in the spectrum of compliance is possible. In the following, I briefly elaborate on the nine combinations. Table 3.1 provides an overview on which particular reaction corresponds to which position in the spectrum of compliance.

First, with respect to the interest of territorial integrity, the 'refuser' frustrates the Chinese request to adhere to the 'one China' policy and diplomatically recognizes Taiwan. The 'reluctant' type of reaction is to recognize the People's Republic of China (PRC) as the sole Chinese state, but to simultaneously maintain unofficial relations with Taiwan. This is the mainstream reaction of countries to the 'one China' policy. 'Eager' countries, in contrast, do not even unofficially cope with Taiwan and proactively support the Chinese position in international fora.

Regarding interaction with the Dalai Lama, reactions are similar. Whereas the 'refuser' gives the Dalai Lama attention and seeks contact with him, the 'reluctant' responds to the Chinese interest by dealing with the Dalai Lama on a low profile basis, but not particularly avoiding contact. He is also willing to interact with the Dalai Lama as a private person, as opposed to a state guest. Again, the

Table 3.1 Different degrees of compliance by issue area

Issue area	*Degree of compliance*		
	Refusal	*Reluctance*	*Eagerness*
Taiwan/ Dalai Lama	Diplomatic recognition/ Welcoming	Unofficial relations/ Unofficial interaction	No relations/ Persona non grata
Resource access	Marginalization of Chinese investors	Equal treatment of Chinese investors	Favouring of Chinese investors
Geopolitics	Balancing China	Hedging	Bandwagoning

'eager', irrespective of the Dalai Lama's diplomatic status, treats him as persona non grata, not providing him a platform at all.

When it comes to the Chinese interest of acquiring raw materials, I compare how successful Chinese companies are in accessing natural resources. Here, the three categories describing the Chinese success refer to the following: the 'refuser' marginalizes or even fends off Chinese attempts to gain access to natural resources. The middle position is one in which Chinese companies are treated as any other investors, resulting in a fair share of Chinese companies active in the resource sector. An 'eager' government favours Chinese companies over other investors and, therefore, heavy Chinese engagement in the resource sector is stimulated.

Finally, with respect to China's geopolitical objectives and a country's behaviour towards the US in particular, I refer to the concepts of balancing and bandwagoning to describe a government's behaviour when dealing with the two competing powers, China and the US (Waltz 1979). Accordingly, the 'refusing' type adopts a strategy of balancing. Balancing describes a behaviour of containing the rise of the PRC as a challenging power. Hedging is, then, the typical reaction of the 'reluctant' compliant. Hedging describes a strategy that seeks to be neither dominated by a rising China, nor to antagonize it (Chung 2009). The 'eager' pursues a strategy of bandwagoning. This can include either siding with China for profit-sharing and rent-seeking, or joining the emerging Chinese nation in an effort to counter the dominance of US hegemony (Chung 2009).

Why Burma, Cambodia and Mongolia?

As we are interested in studying whether the size of winning coalitions impacts on a country's compliance with China's foreign policy interests, and whether the Chinese government interacts differently with governments of different coalition sizes, a comparison is sought between countries that are different in coalition sizes yet similar in terms of other characteristics that may possibly affect compliance. This most-similar system design allows for exploiting divergence with respect to political systems in order to check whether compliance differs with varying coalition sizes. At the same time, similarity with respect to other factors that may possibly shape compliance patterns seeks to 'control' for alternative causal explanations (Gerring 2006).

Burma, Cambodia and Mongolia are the result of a selection procedure that tried to account for the selection criteria of a most-similar system case study design. With respect to their political systems, Mongolia is the most open case with a large coalition and a large true selectorate. In contrast, the governments in Cambodia and Burma are based on small coalitions. Cambodia and Burma differ, however, in the sizes of their selectorates. Cambodia features as a hybrid case in the middle; it has a large nominal selectorate, but a relatively small true selectorate. At the time I started working on this book, Burma had no nominal selectorate and the winning coalition formed the true selectorate. Its recent political reforms, however, offer some additional insights through within-case comparison over time. The three political orders will be discussed in more detail in the respective chapters on the cases. In 1989, the Burmese government changed the name of the country from Burma to the Union of Myanmar. For practical reasons, I continue to refer to the country as Burma.

The selection of these three cases also accounts for other factors that may plausibly influence a country's compliance with China's interests. First, all countries are located in China's regional neighbourhood, which ensures that the intensity of China's interests are roughly similar and the threat of coercive means to enforce compliance is equally credible. In addition, all countries are continental Asian countries and none of them is involved in territorial disputes with China, which would most certainly influence their compliance with regard to China's geostrategic interests. Furthermore, world regions often share similar historical experiences and cultural characteristics. With Buddhism as the major religion, all three countries have more or less comparable cultural and religious patterns. Historically, all countries have – at different points in time – been under Chinese influence (or, in the case of Mongolia, the other way round). Much later, all three countries were under communist rule until the end of the 1980s, before they embarked on different political paths.

Second, all three of the nations are poor in terms of national income, but rich in natural resources that have the potential to increase the countries' wealth. With respect to their income, all countries belong to the poorest nations in Asia and classify comparably as lower middle (Mongolia) and low income (Cambodia and Burma) countries in the ranking of the World Bank.

Third, in terms of resource endowment, all three countries have at their disposal easily extractable natural resources. Certainly, Mongolia with its abundance of high quality minerals leads the list. Mongolia's treasures include minerals such as copper, tin, nickel, zinc, fluorspar, gold and silver. Most notably, the country has the world's largest untapped copper and gold resources, the world's largest untapped deposits of fine quality coke coal and the world's largest uranium reserves. Cambodia and Burma, in contrast, are rich in timber and precious stones, and both have a high hydropower potential. Cambodia has an estimated untapped reserve of 2 billion barrels of oil and 10 trillion cubic feet of natural gas (Lum 2007). Burma's oil reserves are almost depleted, but its proven natural gas reserves were estimated at 10 trillion cubic feet in 2010 (US Energy Information Administration 2010). Most importantly, one can safely assume that resource deposits in all three countries may be of interest to China, because their exploration in all three countries only started during the 2000s and a considerable part of known reserves are still to be developed for exploitation.

In sum, all three cases are continental Asian, Buddhist, post-communist countries with low economic income, but rich in raw materials or natural resource deposits. This relative similarity attempts to increase the comparability of the cases. Unfortunately, this comes at the cost of narrowing down the scope of the investigation. What the selection of these cases means in terms of the generalizability of this investigation will be discussed in Chapter 7.

One caveat is in place here, however. Despite their similarity and comparability in various aspects, the case selection is far from ideal, as some of the countries' characteristics cannot be controlled for. For example, the countries still differ with regard to the degree to which the three countries are integrated into the international community, to which they are exposed to other major powers, or to the strength of state authority in these states. Moreover, even though they are culturally similar and share some historical experiences, there remain variations; for example, with regard to the presence of Chinese minorities, a country's Cold War alignments, or its type of Buddhism. Whenever these differences appear to be plausible alternative explanations, they will be addressed in the cases studies or in Chapter 7.

The case studies cover the post-Cold War period until the end of 2012. The starting point for each case study is chosen individually in accordance with their domestic transformation in the post-Cold War period. In Burma, it starts with the 1988 military coup and the elections in 1990. The investigation of Cambodia focuses on the period after the peace settlement brought about by the Paris Peace Agreement and the subsequent United Nations Transitional Authority in Cambodia mission (UNTAC, from May 1992 to November 1993) and looks at the Kingdom of Cambodia under the 1993 constitution. In Mongolia, the period under examination covers the country after the 1992 constitution was adopted.

The case studies are based on the analysis of secondary literature, but also on interviews and conversations with academics and political actors in these countries. These interviews and conversations took place during a period of three years from mid-2007 to the end of 2010. During this period, I conducted more than 80 semi-structured interviews and conversations with academics, political actors, administrative staff and international experts in Beijing, Shanghai, Ulaanbaatar, Phnom Penh, Hanoi, Singapore, Berlin and Bonn.

It should be noted that data collection was not equally feasible in each of the countries. Whereas in Mongolia it was easier to gather information through direct contacts with government officials, in Cambodia I was forced to rely on interviews with NGOs, members of the opposition, emigrants and international agencies. For Burma, finally, the analysis is mostly based on secondary literature and a few expert interviews. In addition, existing literature discusses Mongolia's relations with China very much from a strategic point of view, frequently taking on an academic IR perspective. This perspective is less apparent in the literature on Sino-Cambodian or Sino-Burmese relations.

It is unfortunate that such differences in reporting and documentation may partly be produced endogenously by the different degrees of political openness of these countries. However, rather unexpectedly, such endogeneity also worked in the opposite way: in some respects, it was more difficult to gather information on China's actions in Mongolia than in Cambodia or Burma. Different from Cambodia and Burma, in particular Chinese economic engagement in Mongolia remains largely unexplored.

4   Burma

Neither puppet, nor pawn

During most of the period under investigation, the Burmese political system can be characterized as a military regime in which power was concentrated in the hands of a few powerful generals who formed the extremely small winning coalition and, at the same time, the selectorate. Consequently, the military's rule excluded the broader Burmese citizenry and the organized democratic opposition from political life. At the same time, the junta's control over power was far from absolute: several of the country's ethnic minorities effectively resisted subjugation under the central government's control. The territories of these ethnic rebel groups were ruled by local leaders who, competing with and challenging the central government, had their own winning coalitions.

Towards the end of the period of this study, Burma's political system underwent considerable change with the introduction of a new constitution in 2008 and the subsequent 2010 parliamentary elections. However, only in early 2011, with the generational turnover of the military leadership, did the dynamics in Burma's domestic politics start to affect the constellation of actors and the distribution of power between them. Hence, most of the investigation of the Sino-Burmese relationship described in the second part of this chapter assumes a small-winning-coalition system. Nevertheless, the dynamics in Burma's domestic politics allow us to investigate the Chinese reaction and adaptation to a gradual opening of Burma's domestic winning coalition.

This chapter describes, in detail, the investigation of China's interaction with the diverse Burmese actors. This investigation shows that throughout the period under investigation, the focus of the Chinese government has been on state-to-state relations with the military junta. This included military and economic support and protection against international diplomatic pressure, sanctions or interventions. This interaction was beneficial to the winning coalitions of both sides. While the Burmese military junta could upgrade its military capacities and pursue its domestic development strategy, Chinese SOEs in a variety of sectors, including the military, profited from lucrative state procurement contracts.

Nevertheless, China's state actors also reached out to the junta's competitors. On the one hand, the Chinese provincial governments, against the will of the Burmese central authorities, also maintained relationships with some of the ethnic rebel groups that challenged the junta's monopoly of power. Collaboration of local authorities on both sides of the border ensured the survival in power of local Burmese war lords who, in exchange for weapons and hard currency, offered opportunities for Chinese exploitation of the land, natural resources and people under their rule. The Chinese central government only recently intervened in this symbiotic relationship when it realized that the interests of Chinese local and provincinal officials could not be aligned with those of the Chinese central government and the broader national interest. On the other hand, even before the introduction of Burma's new constitution, the leaders of Burma's democratic opposition movement were targets of Chinese intelligence gathering and co-optation. Given the Burmese central government's difficulties in establishing and maintaining its rule domestically, the Chinese cooperation with individuals in the junta and its collaboration with the ethnic rebel groups have irritated the Burmese central government.

Finally, those excluded from power received much less attention from Chinese state actors. The interests of the broader Burmese population were not only ignored by the Chinese government, but bilateral agreements between Burma and the PRC have often been harmful to Burma's local populations. Interestingly, China's sensibility to the grievances of ordinary Burmese has shifted dramatically in response to Burma's domestic opening up.

The following investigation begins with a brief presentation of the political developments in Burma from a historical perspective. Then, the domestic political structure is layed out from the perspective of the selectorate theory. Finally, the interaction between Chinese and Burmese actors is scrutinized, and so the causal mechanism that is suspected to lead to compliance is investigated.

Historical background

Sino-Burmese history goes back to imperial China when the Burmese kingdom formed part of China's tributary system. Contemporary relations after the end of the Second World War were troubled by Chinese efforts to pursue troops of the Kuomintang, which had retreated into Burma, by supporting communist insurgencies in Burma and by Mao Zedong's attempts to export the Cultural Revolution to Burma. This history of attempted interference in Burma's domestic politics, which is briefly outlined in this section, is still evident in Burma's leaders' mistrust of China today.

The visit of the Pyu delegation to Chang-an (the capital of the Tang dynasty) in 802 AD is considered the first confirmed diplomatic contact of the Burmese kingdom with China (Tin 2003). During the centuries that followed, the kingdom of Burma was invaded by Chinese empires several times. In the thirteenth century, Burma was occupied by the Mongol Empire for 15 years, and in the seventeenth century, 'hostilities between the Ming emperor and the Manchus spilled over into Myanmar for a short while' (Tin 2003: 190).

In the nineteenth century, Burma fought three wars against the British (1824–26; 1851–52 and 1885–86) and for half a century it was a 'province' of British-ruled India. In 1937, it became a separately administered British colony.

During the Second World War it was invaded and occupied by the Japanese, later to be recaptured by the British (Baily 2007). Eventually, it regained its independence from the British in 1948.

The British legacy left Burma with a parliamentary democracy oriented along the lines of a socialist development agenda. 'Not widely favoured in the West after independence due to its choice of polity, it was, however, expected to have a bright economic future due to an education system that was, at that time, deemed the best in Asia, and its bountiful agricultural production' (Baily 2007: 1–2). But what was lacking was a common national identity in a multi-ethnic society (Dukalskis 2009). Right from the start, the independent state of Burma suffered ethnic and communist insurgencies.

The internal threat of communist insurgency and ethnic rebellion was aggravated by the retreat of the defeated Chinese Koumintang troops into Burmese territory (into the Shan State) in 1949. Relations with the newly founded PRC thus became delicate and Burma's Premier U Nu tried to prevent an adverse Chinese reaction by cultivating his personal diplomacy with Chinese leader Zhou Enlai (Tin 2003). These friendly relationships with the PRC were maintained throughout the 1950s, despite several changes in government in Burma, Chinese incursions into the north of Shan State and Chinese support for the rebels of the Communist Party of Burma (Tin 2003). However, during China's Cultural Revolution, these good bilateral relations between Burma and the PRC cooled.

In 1962, against the background of multiple ethnic insurgencies which threatened the nation's unity, General Ne Win staged a coup (Clapp 2007a). The subsequently established military Revolutionary Council abolished the constitution and introduced socialist state structures with the hierarchical rule of a single party, the Socialist Programme Party (Tin 2003; Baily 2007). During ensuing years, Chinese residents were perceived a threat to the well-being of ethnic Burmans and were expelled from Burma. Anti-Chinese riots also evolved in the late 1960s when ethnic Chinese tried to extend the Chinese Cultural Revolution to Burma (Clapp 2007b; Hongwei 2012). Moreover, 'Burma's ruling generals earned their first medals fighting Chinese-supported communist insurgencies along the border between 1968 and 1978' (Clapp 2007a: 12).

In 1974, under the rule of General Ne Win, the Socialist Programme Party established the Socialist Republic of the Union of Burma with a new constitution and a highly centralized state; but the socialist programme failed badly. In reaction to economic failures and harsh repression of dissent, public unrest emerged. In 1988, after the government's decision to demonetize large-denomination kyat bills, student-led mass protests broke out (Clapp 2007b). The students were brutally repressed by the military causing an estimated 3,000 casualties (Bünte 2008). With the promise to restore law and order, the military finally took control over the government that was, by then, on the verge of collapse (Tin 2005a: 76). A new military junta under the name of the State Law and Order Restoration Council (SLORC) emerged.

After the 1988 coup, bilateral relations with China were rapidly re-established with the visit of General Than Shwe, then SLORC second in command. This rapid re-establishment of relations was facilitated by the fact that the Chinese support for the Burmese communists had been phased out in 1985. In 1989, the SLORC changed the name of the country from Burma to the Union of Myanmar.

With the intention to return the country to a military-controlled parliamentary government, which had prevailed under General Ne Win, the military junta, i.e. the SLORC, held elections in 1990. Those were, however, won with a landslide victory by the oppositional National League for Democracy (NLD). The military was unwilling to fully transfer power to the NLD and limited the elected representatives' authority to drafting a new constitution – an unacceptable proposal to the election winners (Bünte 2008). Any agreement 'on the terms of national reconciliation and the modalities of democratization' failed (Tin 2005a: 78). This failure has dominated Burma's domestic politics since then.

Burma's domestic coalition: A military junta

In fact, from 1988 to the early 2010s, the political system in Burma was based on the rule of a military junta. For a significant period of time, there was no constitutional framework: in 1988, the 1974 constitution was suspended and a new constitution was introduced only in 2008 (Englehart 2012). Lacking any constitutional framework until 2008, the domestic politics in Burma – in terms of selectorate and winning coalition – were heavily dominated by the Burmese military. The prevalent military leadership had no formal selectorate. As the military junta had seized power forcefully by the means of a coup, it is evident that the armed forces formed the true selectorate that put this leadership in power. With regard to its survival in power, the government was equally dependent on the military in its function as the winning coalition. The military took control of all state organs, the bureaucracy and the economy, while, over time, a new class of business tycoons emerged on the basis of their strong ties to the military. Those who were not in the armed forces were generally excluded from the coalition, reducing the coalition to a very exclusive, small-sized elite. Also expelled from the coalition were the armed ethnic rebel groups who did not accept the rule of the military junta and who had managed to bar the central government from their regions.

From 1992 to 2011, i.e. during most of the period under investigation, General Than Shwe was the strongman in Burma's central government. In 1997, the SLORC reconstituted itself as the smaller and more unified State Peace and Development Council (SPDC) (Tin 2003; Hlaing 2005; Dukalskis 2009). After the removal of several corrupt senior military officers, only 12 high-ranking militaries remained in the SPDC (BBC News 2007). The political system remained highly personalized around SPDC Chairman, Senior General Than Shwe, who had 'managed to acquire unquestioned sway over the country's military and government structures' (Clapp 2007a: 4). Than Shwe and this leadership circle were, first and foremost, reliant on the armed forces for remaining in power – not only with regard to external opposition, which challenged the military rule as such, but also with regard to competitors or rivals from within the military. Thus, at the level of individual members of this leadership circle, the rise to power of single junta members and their ability to remain in a powerful position was based on the support of factions within the armed forces. From the perspective of individual junta members, these factions formed winning coalitions that needed to be satisfied as a protection against challengers from within the military organization.

Even though it has been argued that, in general, the military leadership in Burma was surprisingly coherent (Bünte 2008; Dukalskis 2009), this lack of trust was characteristic of Than Shwe's rule. It was mirrored in his governance style, which has been described as manipulative and unpredictable, 'keeping potential rivals off balance with sudden, unexpected decisions made after little if any consultation with his colleagues' (Clapp 2007a: 4). His desire to insure himself against internal competitors and external challengers will become relevant again in the later analysis of the junta's engagement with China. To further illustrate this point, the purge against General Khin Nyunt, third in the hierarchy of the leading circle until 2004, is briefly investigated in the following.

This purge sheds some more light on the inner workings of the junta and the fragile power balance between different competing factions within the military. Khin Nyunt, chief of the Defence Intelligence Organization and former prime minister, was considered the most open and most moderate of the leading triumvirate until he was arrested and sentenced to 44 years in jail and house arrest in 2004. Officially, he was detained because he disregarded the hierarchies of seniority and did not sanction his subordinates in the intelligence corps when they challenged a regional commander loyal to General Maung Aye, strongman number two and a competitor to Khin Nyunt (Hlaing 2005). Observers reason, however, that the incident was only a pretext for Khin Nyunt's detention and that, in reality, he was ousted for fear of his growing power acquired through his leading role in the political reform process (Clapp 2007b) and his pro-Chinese policies (International Crisis Group 2009). He was in charge of negotiating the conditions for the establishment of a multi-party system with the opposition and managing the opponent ethnic rebel groups (both will be discussed below). Consequently, after he was purged, his power base, the secret service, was dismantled and the agreements he had reached with domestic opposition groups were dismissed (Clapp 2007b). Following his detention, 'more than 30,000 military forces were discharged, demoted, or sentenced to long jail terms. Several ministers were fired and threatened with punishment. Many members of the business community, who had profited from Khin Nyunt's patronage were disenfranchised' (Clapp 2007b: 8). Intelligence units became integrated under the control of regional commanders and several younger generals loyal to Than Shwe were promoted into the leading circle (Hlaing 2005). Hence, personal loyalties to Than Shwe were rewarded and thus strengthened.

In addition to its role as an insurance against internal competitors, the armed forces were also the backbone of the state and its economy and thus formed the winning coalition of this leadership with regard to external challenges to power. Rather than co-opting the existing important societal groups, the military leadership seized control of all relevant structures in the state, the bureaucracy and the economy by positioning military personnel in these institutions. Several hundred high-ranking military officers and their families formed the body of the ruling elite around the leadership circle (Niksch 2007: 13). These controlled the bureaucracy and the economy.

Moreover, the mass of soldiers and low-ranking officials served as an instrument to carry out the junta's orders and, specifically, to repress the population and the opposition. Given its illegitimate grip on power, the junta's rule rested, to a considerable extent, on the use of force. Thus, the armed forces constituted the crucial instrument to maintain the government's power. This was reflected in the massive military apparatus, which, with its almost 500,000 members, belonged to the largest in Southeast Asia and in military expenditures reaching as high as 30 per cent of the national budget (Bünte 2008). The members of the Tatmadaw, the Burmese military, also enjoyed privileged treatment: whereas higher-ranked members of the armed forces enjoyed lucrative positions, the military as a whole was eligible for separate health and educational systems (Clapp 2007a). It was, therefore, described as a kind of caste with privileges.

> In a wholly peculiar way, the armed forces have become a kind of 'caste' in Myanmar society, comprised almost completely of BaMa [the ethnic group of Bamar] soldiers... A soldier's entire family (remarkably, up to 60 people) is technically part of an ancillary militia, obliged to undergo some form of fundamental infantry training. With approximately four million Burmese associated with the SiTat [Tatmadaw] (both personnel and family members), this represents a significant sector of the population with an interest in seeing itself empowered and with continuing access to perquisites.
>
> (Matthews 2006: 213)

Rather than co-opting existing elites into its winnning coalition, Burma's military government brought all vital state functions directly under its control. With regard to the administration, for example, the military leadership abolished the meritocratic system inherited by the colonial rule of the British and positioned members of the armed forces in central ministries. Many civil servants were forced to leave in the aftermath of the 1988 coup for political reasons, and another wave of militarization of ministries at all levels was observed in the mid-2000s (Clapp 2007a).

Control over the state apparatus not only ensured control over decision-making, but also offered rent-seeking opportunities for supporters. The highest-level military officers enriched themselves lavishly from their positions in government, both at the national and the regional level (Clapp 2007a: 9). In principle, salaries in the public administration and the military, however, were meagre; thus, in order to make a living, office-holders needed to abuse official positions by rent-seeking and corruption. Perry (2005: 193) described corruption as the core component, even a core value for individual and official decision-making in Burma. Corruption massively increased after 1988. In international comparison, Burma was the third most corrupt country in the world in 2009, exceeded only by Somalia and Afghanistan according to Transparency International's Corruption Perception Index (2009).

The ruling military elite also established a thorough grip on the economy. The SPDC reformed the plan economy after it came to power in 1988. However, instead of fully liberalizing it, the SPDC established new ways to keep control over the economic activities in the country. A distorted and over-regulated economy proved a valuable means to generate revenues. Control over exchange rates and the banking sector, a complex system of licencing, and several trade monopolies created direct and indirect subsidies to members of the military and state officials or directly served to pay off loyalists. To pursue the military's business interests, it set up conglomerates, such as the Union of Myanmar Economic Holdings Limited and the Myanmar Economic Corporation (Bünte 2008). These state corporations were managed by high-ranking military officers and often formed joint ventures with foreign investments (Niksch 2007). In addition to the capital and the technical know-ledge that these foreign investors brought into the country, the 'signing bonuses' for contracts in the oil and gas sector swept millions of dollars into the pockets of the military (Perry 2005).

The control over the economy produced strong vested interests in the clien-telist networks based on membership in the armed forces. As a result, 'nepotistic practices, which involve patronizing only the army-bred, ex-military officers and business-minded civilians who have unquestioningly embraced the primacy of the military class' ensured a strong loyalty towards the military junta (Zarni 2010). Major parts of the economy were controlled by 15 to 20 individuals (International Crisis Group 2012). Accordingly, the majority of the country's rich-est and most influential businessmen were army-bred or the offspring of the regime's highest ranking generals (Zarni 2010), while only a handful of non-military businessmen also received concessions because they were useful to the junta (International Crisis Group 2012). These clientelist networks continued to reproduce themselves when, in preparation of the new era heralded by the 2008 constitution and the 2010 elections, a mass sell-off and handover of public assets to businessmen close to the generals took place under the pretext of privatization. This has been interpreted as an act of uncertainty with regard to post-election rent-seeking opportunities (Turnell 2011).

Challengers to power from outside the winning coalition: The democratic opposition and the ethnic rebel groups

Thus far, the junta's winning coalition, which consisted primarily of the armed forces, has been discussed. Beyond the winning coalition, there is the broader population and some oppositional forces that the military junta needed to deal with. In a nutshell, the broader population outside the Tatmadaw was not only excluded from the privileges that coalition members enjoyed, but it was also marginalized and often repressed. While organized opposition, i.e. the activists of the 1988 protests and the members of the NLD, were prime targets of state repres-sion, systematic violence, human rights violations, rape, forced evictions and state-forced labour were also used to deter the population from upheaval.

Political activity was repelled by repressing civil and political freedoms and by media censorship. Many NLD intelligentsia was arrested during the 1990s. Most famously, opposition leader Aung San Suu Kyi spent almost 15 years under house arrest from 1989. In 2002, she was released; but, in 2003, when she embarked on a tour of the ethnic areas to consult with local NLD leaders and ethnic representatives, this journey ended in a violent clash between government mobs and the NLD. Following this 'Dipeyin incident' a renewed crackdown on the opposition ended her newly achieved freedom and a general decline in political activism among students and monks was observed (Hlaing 2005). This has changed since the 2010 elections, when Aung San Suu Kyi was released from house arrest, a number of other political prisoners were freed and some political rights were restored.

When necessary, the junta has not shied away from using pure violence, as the brutal repression of the 'Saffron Revolution' in 2007 demonstrated. Initially, protests broke out because of an increase in fuel prices, which caused high inflation. But, after a violent incident between security forces and protesting Buddhist monks dressed in orange, objectives changed from the economic to the political. After a month of growing support for the protestors among ordinary citizens, the 'Saffron Revolution' was brutally knocked down by the military (Clapp 2007a).

However, in addition to pure repression, the junta has also tried to co-opt and increase control over the population by less violent means. The creation of the Union Solidarity and Development Association, a mass organization comprising more than 24 million members, is a good example of this. With its community development and educational components, it sought to make membership attractive and especially tried to co-opt the youth. Nonetheless, this was not a participatory and inclusive organization as it also relied on conscripted membership, which suggests that the organizational goals also aimed at increasing control over its members. Indeed, on several occasions, the mass organization was mobilized to harass democracy activists or to disturb anti-government protests (Bünte 2008). In 2010, the Union Solidarity and Development Association was transformed into the Union Solidarity and Development Party under the leadership of Prime Minister Thein Sein in order to participate in the elections (BBC News 2010).

So far, the struggle for power has been described in terms of the distinction between in- and outsiders of the coalition. It is important to note that this perspective fails to grasp the full complexity of Burma's domestic politics. In addition to these lines of conflict between the members of the military and the oppositional forces, a second cleavage along ethnic lines is important. While the former was a struggle between the powerful and the powerless within the society of ethnic Burmese, a second dimension of conflict arises between the majority ethnic group of Bamars and several ethnic minority groups. A number of these ethnic minorities effectively challenged the rule of the military junta and were, therefore, excluded from the coalition too. In fact, these ethnic rebel groups can be understood as local power centres alongside the central government, each of them with its own local winning coalition.

Burma is inhabited by 135 officially recognized indigenous ethnic groups. Around 65 per cent of the population is Bamar. Today, the country is divided into 14 administrative regions comprising seven states, which are named after the major ethnic groups in that area, and seven divisions with Bamar majorities. Due to topography as well as differing political, economic and socio-cultural practices, a supra-ethnic Burmese identity has never evolved (Tin 2005a: 69). Consequently, several ethnic groups have been seeking independence from the Union of Myanmar ever since its independence in 1948.

Since 1989, the central government has successfully reached a level of understanding with 27 of these ethnic groups which pushed them to collaborate. After the coup in 1988, the Communist Party of Burma split along the lines of ethnicity into four groups. With the ceasefire agreements these groups transformed into legal organizations. Far from being able to control these rebel groups, the central government granted them wide autonomy in exchange for their collaboration, including the maintenance of military forces and the permission to produce gems, lumber and narcotics under a profit-sharing agreement. As a result, some of the minority areas are effectively ruled by patriarchal organized armed rebels relying on drug production (Hlaing 2005). In 2002 alone, the Wa minority military forces earned an estimated US$250–US$300 million from heroin smuggling into Thailand and another US$300 million from methamphetamine production (Niksch 2007: 9).

The road map to democracy, which is described in more detail below, fuelled the issue of ethnic separatism because the new constitution attributed all competences of national defence to the military – hence requiring the demilitarization of the armed groups that were in power after the ceasefire (henceforth referred to as ceasefire groups). Only some smaller groups accepted the SPDC's request to disarm and to transform into lightly armed border guard militias under Tatmadaw command in 2009. But, given the lucrative business interests at stake, and given that the 2008 constitution does not recognize the authority of the ceasefire groups, three of the largest groups, the Wa, Kachin and Shan, refused to do so. In 2009, in an attempt to consolidate control over the entire country before the elections, and under the pretext of cracking down on illegal narcotics and arms production, the central government launched military attacks against several separatist groups, including the Karen National Liberation Army and the Myanmar National Democratic Alliance Army, along the Thai and the Chinese borders. In particular, the attacks against the Chinese-speaking Kokang ceasefire group triggered a wave of more than 4,000 refugees into Thailand and some 37,000 refugees into China's Yunnan province (Storey 2009; Seekins 2010).

However, the strongest opponent to the border guard proposal was the United Wa State Army with more than 20,000 troops and great guerrilla potential. In order to increase its leverage over the ceasefire groups, the junta tried to enforce compliance with the border guard force plan by closing the border to Thailand, thereby disrupting cash flows from border trade (Weng 2010). It also started to build a railway from southern to eastern Shan State to ease the mobilization of military equipment into the Wa territory (Moe 2010a).

Burma under the 2008 constitution

Finally, I turn to Burma's new constitution and briefly elaborate on its implications for the political landscape in Burma and for my further investigation. Even though the larger implications of Burma's reforms for its prospects to democratize cannot be assesssed yet, my elaborations on the new constitution and Burma's most recent liberalizations illustrate that these only started to affect Burma's domestic politics significantly in early 2011.

After earlier attempts to draft a new constitution in the 1990s had failed, it was not until 2008 that a new constitution was adopted. This constitution was drafted by the National Convention, consisting of 1,076 hand-picked representatives with connections to the Tatmadaw, the Burmese military and to its mass organization, the Union Solidarity and Development Association. The National Convention and the subsequent referendum to adopt the constitution (which became famous for being held just days after Cyclon Nagris had devastated the country killing tens of thousands) were both part of a seven-point roadmap to democracy. This roadmap was a reform plan introduced in 2003 under General Khin Nyunt and aimed at a gradual transformation to 'disciplined democracy'.

With the elections in 2010, the nominal selectorate was extended to include all eligible voters. However, this did not challenge the position of the true selectorate because despite formally introducing multi-party elections, the constitution also formalized the military's position in power. A quarter of seats in legislative bodies were reserved for the military and control over a new powerful security council was assigned to the commander-in-chief, who also controlled key security ministries and received other extraordinary powers (International Crisis Group 2010a: 1). In addition, the military gained the privilege to choose one out of three elected presidential candidates (Aung 2009; Englehart 2012). Because it entrenched the military's position in power, the constitution was boycotted by the main opposition party, the NLD (Matthews 2006).

Following the introduction of the new constitution, parliamentary elections were held in November 2010. Clearly, the constitutional framework ensured the military dominance over the country in the future, while the elections – though not free and fair (Englehart 2012) – were designed to dress the regime with legitimacy. In 2010, in preparation for the elections, the military leadership deposed many generals and replaced them with a younger generation, while the leadership itself tried to appear more civilian. However, after the elections, the generational shift continued within the military junta. It remains unknown why General Than Shwe finally removed himself and General Maung Aye from consideration for the presidency (Callahan 2012), but when the newly elected government resumed office in early 2011, power was transferred to Burma's new president, Thein Sein, who had held the post of prime minister under the old regime (Turnell 2011). This stipulated a transfer of power to a civil government.

It has been noted that the reforms that followed this leadership turnover have been more far-reaching than many, including its architects, had anticipated (Callahan 2012). After the new government resumed power, some political liberalization took place, restrictions on press freedom were eased and a number of political prisoners were freed from detention. In late 2010, opposition leader Aung San Suu Kyi was released from house arrest. In 2012, her party NLD swept to victory in parliamentary by-elections (Holliday 2013).

Whether the constitutional reforms mark the beginning of a new era under autocratic rule with electoral features (Diamond 2012; Croissant and Kamerling 2013), or the first steps towards democratization, still remains to be seen, but the country has seen dramatic changes and is no longer isolated from the international community. At the time of writing, Aung San Suu Kyi aspires to run for presidency. This, however, would require amending the constitution on the basis of a 75 per cent parliamentary majority – a difficult task given its built-in protection of the military's power (Turnell 2012). Another critical aspect is that more than two years into the new constitution, Burma is far from solving its problems with its diverse ethnic minorities.

Important for further analysis of the case of Burma is that most of the implications of these reforms for the leadership in Burma, the composition of its winning coalition, and the selectorate, only became effective after 2010. This is despite the fact that some preparations to transform the military's grip on power into a more civilian form of dictatorship materialized in the latter part of the 2000s; for example, the establishment of mass organizations and the privatization of state assets. Therefore, while taking into consideration the most recent developments in Burma's domestic politics, the focus of my further analysis of China's success in realizing its interests in Burma lies in the period from 1988 to 2010. It is assumed that during this period Burma's domestic reforms had no significant effect on the country's compliance with Chinese interests.

On a final note, it remains intriguing why these domestic reforms were initiated in the first place, and why at this point in time? As previously mentioned, plans to change the political situation have lingered for many years, and the seven-point roadmap to 'disciplined democracy' was incrementally implemented from 2003 onwards. But why did General Than Shwe and General Maung Aye finally step down and why did their successors push the reforms way beyond any prior expectations? At the time of writing, these questions remain unsolved, even though there is speculation that a combination of several factors may have contributed to this outcome: disagreement within the junta over the use of force to repress the Saffron Revolution, the country's desolate economic situation, the need to reconcile with the democratic opposition in order to achieve the lifting of Western sanctions and the generational shift within the ruling circle (Bünte 2008; Zin 2012). Interestingly, observers also view over-reliance on China and the Burmese generals' desire to balance China's economic presence in the country as an important factor (Bünte 2008; International Crisis Group 2009; Zin 2012). Chapter 7 will reflect on this important aspect in more detail.

Without delving into the details, from a theoretical perspective the junta's move to establish a regime type with a larger selectorate does not necessarily contradict the selectorate theory, as a regime with a small winning coalition and large selectorate promises to stabilize a leader's position in power by increasing the loyalty of those included in the winning coalition (Bueno de Mesquita *et al.* 2003). As this perspective presupposes that reforms are understood as a mere tool of power preservation, the assessment of whether and to what extent Burma's domestic changes are indeed in line with this theoretical expectation is greatly dependent on how one wants to interpret the nature of these changes; and whether one views these reforms as a mere attempt to transform military dictatorship into another form of authoritarian rule, or as the first steps of a transition to democracy. To the extent that the process is ongoing, it may simply not be possible to judge this question yet.

China in Burma

Having discussed the constituencies of the Burmese winning coalition, it becomes clear that Burma had a very small winning coalition, which relied heavily on support from the armed forces. At the same time, however, the SPDC never fully succeeded in subduing all oppositional forces under its rule, either by co-optation or by repression. A number of Burma's ethnic minorities in the border areas did not submit to the rule of the military junta and have managed to continue to exist as local power centres alongside the central government.

Against this background, we will now take a closer look at the nexus between Chinese and Burmese actors. First, we focus on China's engagement with the ruling generals and their military supporters and investigate China's approaches towards those who are outside of the winning coalition, the democratic opposition, the ethnic rebel groups and the broader population.

Focus on the Burmese government and its coalition

The relationship between the Chinese leaders and the Burmese junta is rather complicated. In part, the complexity of this relationship has historical roots. It stems partly from spillovers of China's own civil war and the subsequent attempts by the Chinese communists under Mao Zedong to spread the revolution and to support communist insurgencies in Burma. As mentioned earlier in this chapter, the CCP started incursions into Burma's northern Shan State during the 1950s in pursuit of Kuomintang fighters who had retreated into Burmese territory after their defeat. Later, during the Chinese Cultural Revolution, the relations with the CCP were severely disrupted. In 1954, Chinese Premier Zhou Enlai reassured the Burmese government under Prime Minister U Nu: 'Revolution cannot be exported, and any attempt to export revolution must suffer defeat' (Guo 2007: 30). Yet, a decade later, Chairman Mao Zedong actively encouraged regime change abroad (Hongwei 2012). The Chinese support for the Communist Party of Burma was covert because both sides had previously signed a treaty of non-interference. The support materialized in the form of training for Communist Party leaders, the supply of modern weaponry, infrastructure support, several hundred advisors from the People's Liberation Army (PLA) and thousands of Chinese soldiers (Guo 2007). When ethnic Chinese, encouraged by the Chinese embassy, tried to spread the Cultural Revolution further into Burmese society in 1967, violent anti-Chinese riots were unleashed in response. Subsequently, diplomatic relations between the two governments nose-dived in the period thereafter (Guo 2007). Only in 1985 was CCP assistance to the Burmese communists phased out (Guo 2007). It is beyond doubt that this record of attempts to export the Cultural Revolution created mistrust among the Burmese government towards China that persisted even after the end of the Cold War (International Crisis Group 2009; Hongwei 2012).

In the late 1970s, under the rule of Deng Xiaoping, Sino-Burmese relations formally normalized, but it is often emphasized that it was primarily the international unpopularity of the Chinese and the Burmese governments in the wake of repression of democratic upheavals that helped to consolidate their relationship in the late 1980s (Tin 2003). In 1989, General Than Shwe first visited Beijing. In 1994, then Prime Minister Li Peng, outlawed in the West for his hard stance with respect to the Tiananmen suppression, visited Burma. A common approach vis-à-vis their domestic oppositions was the foundation on which a convergence of interests developed between the leaders of the two countries in opposing Western values that threatened interference in their internal affairs (Tin 2003). The international isolation of the Burmese junta and its dire need for modern arms to 'ensure its continuing grip on political power', as well as the immediate threat of economic collapse, made Burma's leaders accept 'immediate diplomatic protection... arms, project aid, technical assistance and finance' from China. Against this background, Selth argues that it was 'a simple matter of survival' for the Burmese generals to alleviate the immediate crisis and gain time to consolidate power by accepting Chinese aid (Selth 1996: 222).

Since then, the Chinese government (along with the Israeli government) has become the largest supplier of weapons and military equipment to the Burmese government. Between 1989 and 1995, the Burmese junta increasingly invested in the military sector, trippling the national defence spending while the country experienced economic stagnation (Guo 2007). In 1990 and 1994, arms deals with China, involving weapons and military equipment with an estimated value of between US$400 million and US$1.2 billion, were reported. As a result of this supply of Chinese weapons on favourable terms, the junta was able to expand and improve its military capability (Tin 2003). High-ranking PLA officials often visited Burma and the Chinese military has been involved in improving and upgrading existing light equipment. It also provided the Burmese army with training in the technical use of weapons and weapon systems (Guo 2007; International Crisis Group 2009; Chenyang and Fook 2009).

In light of the theoretical framework, the close link between the two militaries in China and Burma appears to constitute an illustrative example for the exchange of private goods between the two small winning coalitions. Ultimately, the Chinese provision of military equipment strengthened the position of the military junta by increasing its capacity to fend off domestic competitors and to distribute targeted goods to their coalition members. One can object, as some Chinese analysts have pointed out, that the Chinese arms sales were focused on missiles, aircraft and other heavy weaponry designed for national defence, and not on light weapons that could possibly be used to suppress the population (Chenyang and Fook 2009; Ruisheng 2010). However, this is not only contested in the literature, but it has also been argued that, with Chinese military assistance, the Burmese generals could satisfy the corporatist interest of the military and so improve the status of their supporting winning coalition, despite the country's desolate economic situation (Tin 2003; Bünte 2008).

During the high-level meetings between Chinese and Burmese officials, a number of bilateral agreements on cooperation in a wide range of issues were announced, frequently, however, without publishing further details. In 1994, a trade agreement relating to bridge and railway equipment worth US$50 million was reached. In 2003, a major agreement on US$200 million of preferential loans for a hydropower plant was published, and a partial debt relief was announced in 2006 (Liu 1994; Liu 2003; Maung 2007). An analyst in Singapore has calculated, on the basis of Burmese data, that between 1989 and 2006, the PRC government provided in total over Yuan 2.15 billion and US$400 million in various forms of loans.[1] In addition, debt relief of Yuan 10 million and Yuan 200 million in grant aid was awarded by the Chinese (Maung 2007: 19). Maung also found that major development assistance was only paid after General Than Shwe's 1996 state visit to Beijing.

The Chinese cooperation focused on projects on the development agenda of the Burmese authorities (Tin 2003). They focused on agricultural technology, agricultural machinery manufacturing, fertilizers and power plants, but also included the renovation of the Yangon National Cultural Theatre and communications projects.

> Through bilateral development assistance, since 1988, China helped the Myanmar government build eight out of nine new sugar mills [US$158 million], 20 new hydroelectric power plants [US$269 million], 13 out of 45 new factories under the Ministry of Industry-1 [US$198 million], and 12 out of 21 new plants under Ministry of Industry-2 [US$137 million]. In addition, China also upgraded six factories under the Ministry of Industry-2 [US$346 million], supplied six ocean-going vessels, and built a dry dockyard [US$25 million]. In 2006, Chinese firms are building 7 out of 11 new hydroelectric plants in Myanmar [US$350–400 million].
>
> (Maung 2007: 23)

From 2003 onwards, hydropower projects gained importance. Several infrastructure projects, such as the dredging of the Yangon and the Ayerwaddy Rivers, several railway connections and a number of roads, were realized with Chinese assistance. Finally, China's interests in Burma's natural resources are reflected in a US$200 million loan in 2006, part of which was designated for the procurement of drilling materials for oil drilling rigs.

In general, this assistance was uniquely channelled through the SPDC, another factor that directly strengthened the position of the military junta. In the industrial sector, the Chinese assistance mainly helped to establish Burmese SOEs (Maung

2007). For example, the Burmese Ministry of Industry-2 increased its number of factories from nine to 21 during the period from 1988 to 2006. All of these factories were financed through grants, loans and bank guarantee notes from the Chinese government (Maung 2007). At the same time, the Chinese state export subsidies played a crucial role in penetrating the Burmese market, which became heavily dependent on its economic ties with China. It is believed that the no or low interest on commercial loans and suppliers' credits from Chinese SOEs and state banks were, in reality, added to the cost of the project (Maung 2007). As such, the strong motivation to promote Chinese exports with its loans and grants was reflected in China's dealings with Burma.

Because the industrial projects constructed with the help of Chinese funds were allocated under the direct control of the Burmese military authorities, it can be argued that the goods provided or financed by the Chinese were targeted at the Burmese leadership and its winning coalition and were private in nature. This allowed the military government to reap the profits of these investments, if necessary extract assets, and redistribute these gains to its winning-coalition members. Again, the exchange between the two small-winning-coalition governments in Burma and China helped to satisfy the crucial coalition members in Burma, thereby increasing the political stability of the small winning coalition.

The military also heavily relied on the extraction of natural resources to fill its coffers and, as will be shown in Chapter 7, Chinese energy companies have been among the beneficiaries of Burmese gas exploitation. In 2001, natural gas became Burma's top export item, and it accounted for around 40 per cent of total exports in recent years (International Crisis Group 2012). As oil and gas investments legally required a 50 per cent joint venture with the state-owned Myanmar Oil and Gas Enterprise, resource extraction has directly propped up the military regime. Foreign investors received exploration rights for oil and gas and brought in the capital and expertise that the junta lacked. Usually, Myanmar Oil and Gas Enterprise stepped in only at the production phase to collect revenue after a commercially viable discovery was made, thus avoiding any risk in the process (Smith 2007). However, since, in the past, almost all of the natural gas was exported, the economic concessions given by the Burmese government to foreign companies did not improve the domestic energy supply, but were directly transformed into monetary resources at the junta's discretionary disposal (Clapp 2007b). At the same time, foreign investments were often heavily protected by the Burmese military forces, which is why oil and gas companies in Burma have frequently been accused of being involved in and responsible for serious human rights abuses, including forced relocation, forced labour, killings or rape in relation to oil and gas projects.

But the Chinese shore-up of the junta went beyond military and economic support and also materialized in high-level diplomacy. In 2000, on the occasion of the 50th anniversary of bilateral diplomatic relations, Chinese Vice-President Hu Jintao paid a visit to Burma, only to be followed by President Jiang Zemin in 2001 (Guo 2007). Premier Wen Jiabao visited Burma in 2010. In fact, the Burmese generals have been visiting Beijing almost every year; they were officially received by the Chinese presidents and premiers in 2003, 2004, 2006 and 2010. The leaders of both countries met on numerous occasions during multi-lateral conferences in Asia and countless high-ranking Chinese delegations visited Naypyidaw, including Chinese State Councillors, members of the Political Bureau of the CCP Central Committee and high-ranking PLA staff. China's foreign minister Yang Jiechi visited Burma twice in 2008 (International Crisis Group 2009).

Importantly, the Chinese government has also protected the regime against external pressure from the UN. In early 2007, the Chinese government, together with Russia, vetoed a UN Security Council resolution on Burma's human rights situation tabled by the US and Britain on the grounds that the issue was an internal Burmese matter (Zhao 2007). This veto clearly protected the regime with the intention of prolonging the political survival of the generals. However, since the Chinese government was not the only force to act in favour of the junta, it is easy to argue counterfactually that Russia's opposition meant that the generals would not have been harmed by the UN resolution anyway, because it could not have materialized.

Despite this protection and support from the Chinese government to the Burmese junta and the public praise of their close ties, it seems that both the Chinese leadership and the SPDC under General Than Shwe did not have a very cordial relationship. Analysts interpreted the fact that the Burmese generals never travelled to China for medical treatment as an indication of their continuing distrust. Supposedly, dozens of Taiwanese intelligence agents working in Burma had been co-opted by the regime to provide the generals with information on China (Moe 2010b). More strikingly, in several instances the Chinese government found itself confronted with decisions taken by the junta without being informed in advance. It was taken by surprise by the relocation of the capital to Naypyidaw in 2005, the military offensive in Kokang and the dismissal of former Prime Minister General Khin Nyunt (Jagan 2009; Holliday 2009; Moe 2010b). At the same time, one of the suspected motivations for purging General Khin Nyunt was his pro-Chinese stance; hence the Chinese were subsequently deprived of a link to the SPDC and the gap between the Chinese and the Burmese government widened further (International Crisis Group 2009: 32).

From the Chinese perspective, the SPDC's rule, its economic mismanagement and its intransigent dealings with the domestic opposition was highly unsatisfying. It created much international attention and criticism which, in turn, often fell back on China. China has a strong interest in political stability in Burma, but it recognized the need for better governance and a more legitimate government.

Therefore, the Chinese government called for improved governance and reconciliation on the international stage by explicitly supporting visits of UN special rapporteurs and the UN Good Offices Mission. In 1993, the Secretary-General obtained the mandate to use his good offices to help implement several UN resolutions on Burma. China assisted the visits of the UN's special envoys and rapporteurs by, among other things, arranging visas and urging the junta to grant access to the leadership, the democratic opposition groups and ethnic minorities.

Despite having prevented the 2007 UN resolution on Burma, the Chinese government did not prevent a critical presidential statement from the UN Security Council later that year; this was interpreted as a break with the Burmese government (Holliday 2009).

At the national level, in order to achieve domestic stability in Burma, the Chinese government envisioned some policy adjustments *within* the existing structures, with a strong central government, rather than federalism or liberal democracy (International Crisis Group 2010b). This essentially meant a continuation of the small winning coalition, but under a regime with a more civilian appearance and with some form of participation of the varying domestic oppositional players. Domestic reconciliation should ensure that the domestic opposition be involved in the political process in the future, that the central government finds a more sustainable solution with respect to the ceasefire groups, and that it has more legitimacy among the broader population (Chenyang and Fook 2009). Thus, the Chinese government hoped that the seven-point roadmap to democracy and the 2010 elections would increase the domestic and international legitimacy of the regime and so serve its strategic and economic interests in the country. It did not perceive these domestic reforms as a challenge to its own interests in Burma, especially as it was not expected that they would lead to a democratic government (International Crisis Group 2010b). Therefore, even though the Chinese government was unwilling to mediate between both sides, it encouraged the military junta to enroll in a process of domestic reforms and reconciliation and called on the junta to hold direct talks with the opposition (International Crisis Group 2009: 5).

Behind the scenes, the Chinese also tried to push for the reconciliation of the central government and the armed rebel groups in order to increase the government's legitimacy. Given the close relations to the ethnic Chinese rebels in Burma, which will be discussed in the following, the Chinese government was reluctant to cut its support to these groups and its pressure only gained momentum after 2009 (International Crisis Group 2010b). In 2009, in what became known as the 'Kokang incident', the Burmese military junta triggered a massive flow of Burmese refugees into China's Yunnan province when they attempted to disarm and attack the Chinese-speaking Kokang ceasefire group. China did not close the border as the SPDC had hoped, but allowed the rebels along with the population to flee into Chinese territory. The Chinese government was 'extremely upset' because of the instability along its borders and subsequently deployed PLA units to stabilize the region (Storey 2009; Seekins 2010; International Crisis Group 2010b). The government was also cited as being 'furious' that it had not been forewarned by the Burmese central authorities about this military operation (Jagan 2009). Bilateral relations between the Chinese and the Burmese central governments reached an all time low.

As a consequence, after the Kokang incident the Chinese government increased its pressure on both the SPDC and the ceasefire groups to engage in negotiations. While pressuring the rebel leaders to participate in negotiation talks, it urged the SPDC to guarantee the safety of the representatives participating in negotiations (International Crisis Group 2010b). To the irritation of the SPDC, the Chinese government insisted the issue should be settled with peaceful negotiations, rather than force (International Crisis Group 2010b). This is important because, together with the direct and indirect support the ceasefire groups received from Beijing, it partly explains the SPDC's doubts about China's true intentions to back the Burmese central government. In late 2010, during a state visit by General Than Shwe, the Chinese government declared that it did not support any group that carried out anti-government activities along the Sino-Burmese border, thereby giving its approval for the SPDC's initiative to disarm the rebel groups (The Associated Press 2010b). However, it was only after the 2011 power transition to President Thein Sein that the Chinese stance with regard to the ceasefire groups shifted from maintaining the status quo towards promoting reconciliation in the sense that it increasingly considered the SPDC's attempts to unify the country as legitimate (Sun 2012).

Attempts to co-opt the democratic opposition

Even though it was the Chinese ambassador who was the first to welcome the oppositional NLD party to power after their election victory in 1990, Burma's democratic opposition movement, and the NLD leader Aung San Suu Kyi in particular, did not enjoy clear approval from the Chinese government (Ruisheng 2010). The NLD was considered too Western-oriented. Moreover, a democratic political order, in general, was expected to enjoy much support from and probably be much more susceptible to Western influence, which was generally not in the Chinese interest.

The Chinese government stayed away from providing the democratic opposition with the kind of support that it had granted to the SPDC. In 1988, opposition leader Aung San Suu Kyi called on the Chinese ambassador to Burma to exert pressure on the military junta by closing border trade with the Burmese military under the pretext of technical problems. In his personal reflections, the former ambassador acknowledged that he did not consider this request at that time, even though he confronted the military government with a call for national reconciliation between the military and the democratic opposition (Ruisheng 2010).

At the international level, China's backing of the UN Good Offices Mission significantly helped the UN and thereby also promoted the cause of the opposition. However, before approving Security Council statements or UN resolutions, China has often pressed for significant softening of such statements. The Chinese government approved a Security Council statement and a UN Human Rights Council resolution after the violent crackdown on the Saffron Revolution in 2007, but urged the removal of several demands from the initial draft, including the release of opposition leader Aung San Suu Kyi. Moreover, when Aung San Suu Kyi was sentenced to another 18 months under house arrest in 2008, the Chinese representation initially agreed to a press statement by the Security Council, but later opposed a draft presidential statement condemning the verdict and only agreed to a watered-down version.

Nonetheless, even before Burma's 2011 liberalization, direct interaction between the Chinese government and the Burmese democratic opposition, including the NLD, existed. These contacts, which were said to have increased after the renewed detention of Aung San Suu Kyi in 2003 and the purge of Khnin Nyunt in 2004, were described as 'a mix of intelligence gathering, reassurance and relationship building' (International Crisis Group 2009: 9). Accordingly, the Chinese government used these contacts to gather information on the groups themselves, including their funds, their links to the West and the NLD. They also served to better understand their position on a number of issues with the government, their perception of China's engagement in Burma, and on US and Thai policies towards Burma. At the same time, the Chinese agents tried to convince the groups to engage with the military government and to participate in the 2010 elections.

Hence, it appears that the Chinese government's approach to Burma's democratic opposition, at least before Burma's opening up, was one of co-optation, rather than of material support. The exchange between Chinese officials and these groups reportedly took place in Thailand or at the Sino-Burmese border, but also in Beijing or in Yunnan's capital Kunming to which the representatives of some oppostion groups were invited. Reportedly, the groups were treated very well during these trips, were hosted in top hotels and treated to visits to tourist attractions (International Crisis Group 2009: 10).

China's dealings with Burma's democratic opposition reflected its support for the prevalent small winning coalition and its desire to stabilize the regime through gradual reforms. Not only did the Chinese try to convince the opposition to participate in the elections, reportedly they also asked Aung San Suu Kyi whether she 'could be flexible and whether she might be able to accept a role less than head of state, in which she could exercise influence but could also be reconciled with the army's position' (International Crisis Group 2009: 10). Obviously, this approach sought to negotiate a power-sharing agreement whereby the opposition would be convinced to relinquish its aspirations to replace the government and instead accept its inclusion in the extant winning coalition. It is, therefore, not surprising that no transfer of resources from China to the Burmese opposition has been observed. The Chinese strategy targeted at increasing the incentives and gains for the opposition for participating in the given coalition, rather than increasing its capability to reward its own loyalists.

Decentralized exploitation of the ceasefire groups

In addition to the democratic opposition, some ethnic ceasefire and rebel groups challenged the power of the SPDC. As stated earlier, the relationship between the Burmese ethnic rebel groups and the Chinese communist leadership dates back to the 1960s when the CCP actively supported communist revolutions elsewhere. The umbrella of the Communist Party of Burma, at that time, united several ethnic minority groups. Several of these groups are of Chinese ethnicity and are located along the Sino-Burmese border. After China had stopped its assistance to the Communist Party of Burma, the party disintegrated into ethnic rebel groups that financed themselves through poppy cultivation, opium trade, and lumber and gem production. These armed militias have never submitted to the Burmese central government, but negotiated ceasefire agreements in which they were granted a high degree of autonomy.

More than a dozen minority nationalities that also dwell in neighbouring Vietnam, Laos and Burma, live in China's south-western Yunnan province (Guo 2007). The Chinese Dai nationality, for example, is connected to Burma's Shan nationality, and the Chinese Jingpo nationality has kinship ties to Burma's Kachin nationality. In both countries, there are Miao, Yao, Yi, Wa, Hani and Lisu nationalities, who share the same origins and speak the same languages. Some parts of the Burmese Shan State, in particular the Wa-controlled territory and Kogang, have a closer relationship with China's Yunnan province than other parts of Burma because of geographic proximity and kinship ties (Guo 2007: 51). As these minorities strived for autonomy, Chinese officials and companies had better access to some of the ceasefire areas than the Burmese central government, which sometimes needed Chinese help to access these areas (International Crisis Group 2009: 11). Given China's own problems with separatist minorities, it was, and remains, not in the interest of the Chinese central government to see the Burmese ethnic minorities achieving independence. To the contrary, the Chinese government considers stability in its border regions a top priority (Sun 2012).

Before the Kokang incident, in order not to trouble its relations with the Burmese central government, the Chinese government claimed to maintain no direct relations with the ceasefire groups. It officially pursued a 'Four No's' policy towards the ceasefire groups, constituting no political recognition, no military support, no organizational exchanges, and no economic aid (International Crisis Group 2010b). However, by controlling its borders to Burma, the Chinese government had an effective leverage to decide upon the survival of the ceasefire groups along the borders. In the past, it allowed cross border trade and supplied many Burmese cities along the Chinese borders with electricity, water and telecommunications, even though the ceasefire groups targeted some of their illicit activities, such as drug trade and gambling, at Chinese consumers (International Crisis Group 2009).

Moreover, the Chinese authorities reached out to the ceasefire groups via the Yunnan provincial government and intelligence agents. Contrary to its official statements, China also supplied the Wa minority – which had the closest contact with China and was also the most powerful among the ceasefire groups – with arms. Observers asserted that the Wa had been furnished with heavy weapons from China. The Chinese government has never prohibited its own SOE from selling arms to the Wa, and while 'officials deny that it is China's policy to sell weapons to the Wa, they admit that a few "rogue elements" from the People's Liberation Army (PLA) have done so' (International Crisis Group 2009: 11). After the Kokang incident, this changed. Realizing that it could not trust Yunnan's provincial government, which had its own interests in Burma and refused to align these with the broader Chinese national interest, the Chinese central government stepped up its own intelligence and began to engage in direct contacts with the ceasefire groups (International Crisis Group 2010b).

Even before the Kokang incident, observers already pointed to the diverging interests of the governments in Beijing and in Yunnan's provincial capital of Kunming. Yunnan's interests were primarily economic, with the provincial government of Yunnan and its businessmen mainly being interested in the economic development of their province and the private profits they could make from business relations across the border. Entrepreneurs and officials from Yunnan specifically profited from the chaotic situation in Burma's border regions, because they could achieve business agreements with local warlords that circumvented the Burmese central government – often without Beijing's knowledge.

The illicit collaboration of local elites on both sides of the border was particularly striking in the logging business, which was opposed by both central governments in Beijing and Naypyidaw. Even though illegal according to Chinese law, Chinese companies from Yunnan were heavily involved in logging and exporting timber from Burma to China (Chenyang and Fook 2009). Despite a domestic logging ban, China evolved as a major exporter of timber products with the wood-processing industry located along the Burmese border. Low prices for imported wood were attributed to the fact that 98 per cent of China's imported timber from Burma was estimated to be illegally logged (Global Witness 2005; Maung 2007). In reaction to a critical report by Global Witness[2] which urged the Chinese central government to rein in Chinese companies more actively, Chinese imports of wood across the land border from Burma fell by more than 70 per cent between 2005 and 2008. However, more than 90 per cent of the remaining imports continued to be illegal (Global Witness 2009a). This illegal timber trade directly involved Yunnan authorities, regional army commanders and ethnic ceasefire groups. Local businessmen admitted that Chinese companies had 'special cooperation and consensus with the local ethnic groups' (International Crisis Group 2009: 40).

Moreover, the exploitation of Burma's border regions by Chinese companies was further stimulated by China's regional anti-narcotic policy. In response to the growing drug and HIV/Aids problem in Yunnan province, and under pressure from the Chinese government, opium bans were enforced throughout the Kokang and Wa regions in 2003 and 2005. Because up to 80 per cent of the population was living on poppy cultivation in these areas, many subsistence farmers faced serious loss of income and a worsened food security situation as a consequence of the prohibition on growing poppies. To mitigate these effects, the Chinese government adopted an anti-narcotic policy that included an alternative crop project, targeted at farmers in the poppy-growing ethnic rebel groups regions in 2006.

However, instead of directly addressing local farmers, the Chinese government provided Chinese companies with soft loans through a national alternative development programme for investment in agriculture in these regions (Kramer 2009; Chenyang and Fook 2009). By so doing, instead of mitigating the negative effects of the opium ban on the livelihood of Burmese farmers, the Chinese government promoted and encouraged Chinese investment in rubber, tea or sugarcane monoplantations in Burma (Kramer 2009: 1). Many Chinese companies made arrangements with the local warlords to provide seedlings, fertilizer, pesticide, expertise and payment for labour, while the Wa authorities promised to provide land and labour. As a result, forced evictions, relocation of people and forced labour were spurred on. While creating many undesired effects, these projects did not significantly profit the population. Reportedly, Chinese businessmen also charged farmers for the road construction to the fields and forced the farmers to sell their crops back. Farmers reported that they were forced to work on plantations or to grow specific crops on their land without clear agreements on payment, let alone contracts (Kramer 2009: 9).

Clearly, from the perspective of China's southern Yunnan province, a weak central government in Burma appeared very attractive because it allowed local authorities and entrepreneurs to negotiate projects for the depletion of Burmese timber, mineral resources and land for agri-business directly with the ceasefire groups and sometimes against the will of the SPDC. The collaboration at the local level put the bilateral relations between the two central governments at risk. However, while the Chinese businessmen involved, for example in the crop substitution programme, acknowledged that their actions contradicted Beijing's goals, they argued 'that Myanmar is a source of plentiful raw materials and cheap labour that is begging for Chinese investment and technology' (International Crisis Group 2009: 41).

Insensitivity to popular grievances

It has already been mentioned that China's economic assistance was uniquely channelled through the Burmese government and, despite the provision of some philanthrophic assistance, it seems that the Chinese government did not make any further attempt to reach out to the broader Burmese society.

China's philanthrophic aid was mainly related to disaster relief after the 2004 tsunami and Cyclon Nargis. In early 2005, different Chinese state organizations, through the Chinese embassy in Burma, donated more than US$300,000 of disaster relief. However, US$100,000 of this was directly handed over to the Ministry of Defence of the Union of Myanmar. This assistance was thus filtered through the junta's redistributive networks. In the aftermath of Cyclon Nargis, the Chinese government also sent a 50-member medical team and donated some US$31 million of disaster relief (Xinhua 2008a; Chenyang and Fook 2009).

Moreover, at the time of writing, a student exchange programme and regular exchanges between art troupes between China and Burma were ongoing (Embassy of the PRC 2012). However, given that only 50 students were reported to be involved in this exchange annually, in a country with more than 48 million inhabitants, this programme seemed very limited and was probably targeted at selected students.

Even though China has invested considerably in Burma and provided loans to the Burmese government, few benefits accrued to the population. As mentioned before, most of the extracted natural resources were to be exported and, therefore, their exploitation did not improve domestic energy supply, while the negative externalities of extraction were to be borne by local communities. For example, intransparent land acquisitions, environmental impact and displacement caused by Chinese investments in hydropower, mining, oil or gas alerted environmental groups, while Chinese infrastructure and construction projects were often directly connected to increased military presence, large scale forced labour, forced evictions and other human rights violations (International Crisis Group 2009: 23).

This has caused widespread resentment among the local Burmese population towards the Chinese; indeed, even Chinese businessmen 'openly admit[ed] that what they are doing is not better than previous colonial powers' (International Crisis Group 2009: 23). However, according to Chinese analysts, before President Thein Sein's abandonment of the gigantic Myitsone dam project in 2011, public opinion in Burma was never considered to constitute a critical challenge to China's economic projects, because support from the SPDC could always 'be acquired using the "powerful lubricant" favoured during the junta era – bribes' (Sun 2012: 90). Moreover, according to a Chinese analyst, as Burma's biggest investor and international patron, 'China believed it deserves certain privileges in Myanmar' (Sun 2012: 91). As it expected Burma to remain dependent on Chinese investment and protection, 'China intentionally ignored public opposition to Chinese projects and the anti-China sentiment on the ground, believing that an isolated Myanmar would not dare to challenge Chinese projects and jeopardise future economic patronage' (Sun 2012: 91).

No wonder, then, that China's leaders were alarmed by the suspension of the Myitsone dam project in 2011 and reacted with increased sensitivity to anti-China sentiments in Burma. Chinese academics and leaders were taken by surprise by the domestic developments in Burma, and especially President Thein Sein's suspension of the Myitsone dam project, a bold move designed to profile him as a leader who listens to his people and stands up to exploitation by the Chinese (Sun 2012; *The Economist* 2012). A professor of IR at Peking University analysed China's mistake in Burma as being too focused on government-to-government relations, while paying no attention to the 'domestic political nuances' and shifting political climate in Burma. By doing so, the Chinese overheard dissenting voices and missed crucial shifts in Burmese policies, discourses and political ideas (*The Economist* 2012).

According to *The Economist*, in response to the suspension of the construction of this dam contracted to Chinese companies, the Chinese encouraged Chinese businesses, and specially SOEs, operating overseas 'to be more respectful of local customs and people'. This also led to the construction of many schools along China's oil pipeline through Burma (*The Economist* 2012). Moreover, the Chinese embassy in Burma emphasized the increase in people-to-people interaction between China and Burma in 2012 and praised a series of Chinese-Burmese 'Deep Fraternal Friendship' activities, such as free eye surgeries for cataract patients, a joint establishment of an eye-care centre, donations of equipment to schools, and a donation of US$50,000 to the Myanmar Red Cross Society on behalf of the Red Cross Society in China (Embassy of the PRC 2012). In August 2013, in the framework of a newly established China-ASEAN youth exchange programme, eight Burmese students were sent to China (*People's Daily Online* 2013).

Summary

Since the Burmese military took power in 1988, it has been heavily propped up by the Chinese government. The Chinese leadership maintained good state-to-state relations with the military government in Burma and protected the junta against international diplomatic pressure, sanctions and interventions.

In economic terms, the Chinese government has primarily targeted the military junta and its cronies. It provided no or low interest loans and grants to the Burmese military junta, and so enabled the junta to both upgrade its military capacities and to pursue its domestic development strategy. State industries under the control of the military and strategic infrastructure were constructed. In this way, the exchange between the Chinese and the Burmese leaders was beneficial to the winning coalitions of both sides. Chinese SOEs in a variety of sectors, including the military, profited from this policy as they received lucrative state procurement contracts to provide infrastructure, equipment, training or arms.

At the same time, the Chinese government, directly or indirectly, maintained relationships with the two challengers of the SPDC, the democratic opposition and the ceasefire groups. It is noteworthy that the ethnic rebel groups enjoyed a close relationship with Chinese state actors, albeit not at the central, but at the provincial government level. Between the leaders of the ceasefire groups and the Yunnan provincial government a convergence of interest similar to that between the two central governments evolved.

With respect to the opposition groups, the relationship appears to attempt to co-opt individual Burmese opposition leaders without involving material support, in an effort to make these groups more willing to collaborate with the central government.

Finally, the Burmese population at large received little to no attention from Chinese decision-makers as it was not part of the coalition and therefore had no power to push for its collective interests. It was not specifically addressed by the Chinese government; indeed, agreements between the two governments have often been harmful to the local population. It is also indicative that the Chinese government has allowed Chinese business interests and the leaders of the rebel groups to hijack its crop substitution policy, which was the only policy directly targeted at the population.

In sum, the cooperation between the two small-winning-coalition governments in Burma and China helped the Burmese government to stabilize its position in power in various ways. While the Burmese government was able to monopolize interaction with China, the Chinese government sought to focus the provision of material benefits selectively on the Burmese central government. Thus, the military junta was able to redistribute the benefits accrued from this external interaction or could extract externally provided assets from industrial or agricultural production sites to its cronies. The military equipment provided by China on preferential terms directly addressed the needs of the Burmese coalition members and increased the junta's capacity for fending off domestic challengers.

As will be seen in Chapter 7, China has been extremely successful in the exploitation of Burmese natural resources. The willingness of China's leaders to shield the Burmese government from international pressure and its attempt to co-opt Burma's domestic opposition by raising their gains from collaboration with the existing regime can both be interpreted as a reflection of China's interest in the prolongation of the Burmese small-coalition government.

Note

1   Before 1988, Burma had received Chinese development assistance loans of US$64 million in 1979, US$15 million in 1984 and Yuan 80 million in 1987 (Maung 2007).
2   Global Witness is a non-profit organization dedicated to uncovering the economic networks behind conflict, corruption and environmental destruction.

5   Cambodia

Rocking in China's soft underbelly

Cambodia's political system can be described as a party-based authoritarian regime with a relatively small winning coalition. While the country is formally a constitutional monarchy, in reality, the political system is dominated by informal structures in which the electorate has no decisive power and does not form part of the true selectorate and the winning coalition. Prime Minister Hun Sen, who was in power throughout the period of this investigation, has relied heavily on personal ties and on his Cambodian People's Party (CPP) to establish and maintain his monopoly of power.

This chapter investigates China's interaction with different actors in Cambodia. Historically, the Chinese government had close relations with the Cambodian Khmer Rouge party as well as the Cambodian royal family. The investigation of bilateral relations between China and Cambodia after the end of the Khmer Rouge regime, however, reveals that while the focus of Chinese cooperation has formally been on government-to-government collaboration, it has adapted pragmatically to the reality of power distribution in Cambodian domestic politics. Hence, it has shifted in favour of Prime Minister Hun Sen, who initially came to power under the Vietnamese. Since the late 1990s, China's military and economic assistance to Cambodia has de facto bolstered Hun Sen's grip on power. The investigation finds the re-emergence of Cambodia's Sino-Khmer elite with close relations to the Cambodian government and interests in business opportunities with Chinese investors to be an important factor in channelling Chinese interests to the Cambodian decision-makers. As such, Chinese assistance and investments have also promoted the Sino-Khmer elite's inclusion in the Hun Sen winning coalition.

Those excluded from the winning coalition have not been primary targets of China's external relations: Chinese attempts to reach out to members of opposition parties are limited to the few moments in Cambodia's post-civil war history when there appeared to be a chance for government turnover. China's development assistance projects in Cambodia are rarely altruistic and have always followed the priorities of the Cambodian government.

The structure of this chapter mirrors that of the previous case study of Burma. It begins with a brief discussion of Sino-Cambodian relations from a historical perspective. Cambodia's political structure is then presented against the background of the selectorate theory. Finally, interactions between Chinese and Cambodian actors are examined.

Historical background

As the impressive remains of the ancient capital in Angkor testify, Cambodia's monarchy is over 1,200 years old. However, the empire declined in the sixteenth century and the country was subsequently invaded by its Siamese and Vietnamese neighbours. Historians argue that Cambodia would have disappeared without an agreement between King Norodom and the French to place the country under French protectorate (Tully 2005). From 1863 to 1953, Cambodia was ruled by the French. During the Second World War, Cambodia was occupied by the Japanese empire, but it continued as a French protectorate after the war.

In the brief discussion of Cambodia's history after the Second World War it becomes clear that China's role in Cambodian domestic politics was highly ambiguous and mainly preoccupied with combating the influence of Vietnam over Cambodia. In 1953, Cambodia gained independence from France and transformed to a constitutional monarchy under Prince Sihanouk. In the years that followed, Cambodia's politics were dominated by turmoil and violent struggles for power. In 1970, Sihanouk was ousted by a military coup led by Prime Minister General Lon Nol. As a result of the friendship that Sihanouk had developed with the Chinese Prime Minister Zhou Enlai, whom he had met at the Bandung Conference in 1955, he was exiled to Beijing. The US supported Lon Nol's coup because Sihanouk, who officially started out with a policy of neutrality in the Vietnam War, increasingly began to support Viet Cong fighters along Cambodia's northern borders. In order to fight these, the US bombed Viet Cong bases and strategic infrastructure in Cambodia. These bombings caused hundreds of thousands of civilian casualties, which, in turn, played an important role in generating support among the population for the communist Khmer Rouge rebels.

China, in opposition to the newly established US-backed regime in Phnom Penh, pursued a two-track policy of supporting two competing Cambodian factions, Sihanouk and the Khmer Rouge (Hood 1990). Both Sihanouk, the internationally recognized leader of Cambodia, and the Khmer Rouge, who had the stronger military capabilities, formed the National United Front of Kampuchea in order to fight Lon Nol. When the Khmer Rouge besieged Phnom Penh in 1975, Sihanouk returned to the capital. However, shortly thereafter the coalition broke and Sihanouk was taken hostage by the Khmer Rouge. From 1975 to 1979, during the reign of Pol Pot, Sihanouk was kept under house arrest. Throughout the 1970s, Beijing not only delivered military support to the Khmer Rouge, but also sent more than 15,000 advisors to the country (Storey 2006).

The Khmer Rouge's rule of terror was brought to an end in 1979 by the invasion of Vietnamese troops together with Khmer Rouge defectors who had fled to Vietnam. In response, and motivated by the ideological competition with Vietnam and the Soviet Union, China then invaded Vietnam, but could not stop the defeat of the Khmer Rouge (Ross 1992). The Vietnamese installed a new government, the State of Cambodia, which was led by the Kampuchean People's Revolutionary Party, their Cambodian comrade-in-arms. Due to support from Vietnamese troops, the State of Cambodia was able to control around 90 per cent of the Cambodian territory.

Meanwhile, the three resistance factions of Sihanouk nationalists, the Khmer Rouge and the Khmer People's National Liberation Front, again agreed to collaborate and to form a Coalition Government of Democratic Kampuchea in opposition to the Vietnamese puppet government in Phnom Penh. King Sihanouk re-emerged on the political stage as a popular anti-Vietnamese symbol but, lacking military capacities, he was unable to marginalize the Khmer Rouge. Again, the coalition was supported from outside by China, but also by Thailand, Britain and the US. While Shinanouk's inclusion in the coalition legitimized international support for the Khmer Rouge (Hood 1990: 980, 987), the continued arms supply to the Khmer Rouge weakened Sihanouk's diplomatic efforts and strengthened the Khmer Rouge's bargaining position.

Efforts to solve the civil war in Cambodia did not really take off until the international context had dramatically changed after the end of the Cold War. In October 1991, the Paris Conference on Cambodia resulted in a comprehensive peace settlement signed by the four warring factions. The Paris Peace agreement was negotiated by the permanent members of the UN Security Council and included the establishment of a 12-member Supreme National Council comprising all four Cambodian warring factions. The UN was given a mandate to enforce a ceasefire and to deal with refugees and disarmament. The United Nations Transitional Authority in Cambodia (UNTAC), one of the UN's most complex peacekeeping operations to date, was also given the mandate to implement free and fair elections for the constitutional assembly (An *et al.* 2008: 8). It was expected that the constitutional assembly, after having approved the constitution, would transform into a legislative assembly that would then form the first government (Brown 1992: 91). Accordingly, in 1991, Vietnam's puppet government, led by Hun Sen, dissolved and the Supreme National Council was established. Also in 1991, Prince Norodom Sihanouk, the Cambodian king, returned to Phnom Penh after 21 years of exile in Beijing.

Initially, China did not want UNTAC to become a political force in Cambodia (Richardson 2010: 162), but the settlement that brought the civil war in Cambodia to an end turned out to be beneficial in terms of furthering China's strategic interests. It diminished Soviet influence in Vietnam and increased Chinese influence in a 'balkanized Indochina' (Ross 1992: 54). Moreover, the agreement did not criticize the Chinese backing of the disastrous Khmer Rouge regime, and even legitimized the Khmer Rouge's participation in the new government (Ross 1992: 54). China thus participated in the UNTAC peacekeeping mission.

In 1992, 15,900 peacekeeping troops, 3,600 civilian police and approximately 3,000 civilian administrators were working under the UNTAC mandate (Brown 1992: 84). Apart from the intimidation and political killings that kept being reported, a serious limitation of the UNTAC mandate was that it did not include any democratic institutional engineering beyond the elections (Croissant 2008). In addition, UNTAC's inability to dismantle the Kampuchean People's Revolutionary Party – which had, by then, transformed itself into the Cambodian People's Party (CPP) – control over the bureaucracy, caused critical opposition. But despite the Khmer Rouge's withdrawal from their commitment to participate in the elections, in 1993, the Constituent Assembly elections were held under UNTAC's auspices. A new constitution was then drafted, along the lines of UNTAC's mandate.

Cambodia's domestic coalition: Dominant-party rule

This section presents Cambodia's domestic politics from the perspective of the selectorate theory. It begins by briefly discussing how both the Cambodian nominal selectorate and the winning coalition are formally defined in Cambodia's 1993 constitution before contrasting the constitutional framework with the reality on the ground.

Cambodia's constitution stipulates that the country is a constitutional monarchy. The king as Head of State, however, has rather representative duties, mostly becoming active only after approval by the parliament. He appoints the head of government, the prime minister, but does so according to the parliamentary majorities. Furthermore, even though he must be a member of the royal family, he cannot choose his own heir, who is picked by the Council of the Throne, which consists of the prime minister, the presidents and vice-presidents of the bicameral legislative, and the chiefs of two Buddhist orders. Article 7, stating that the King of Cambodia shall reign but shall not govern, underlines the limited role of the king in daily politics (Kingdom of Cambodia 1993).

According to the constitution, legislative competence lies in the bicameral parliament consisting of a lower and an upper house, the 123-seat National Assembly and the 61-member Senate, respectively. Intitially, before the establishment of the Senate, the National Assembly was the only state organ with legislative competences; it approves the government budgets and it can dismiss the government, which is formally responsible to the National Assembly with a two thirds majority. The National Assembly, which is elected for a five-year term, can only be dissolved upon the proposal of the prime minister and with the approval of the Chairman of the National Assembly, but only when the government has proven to be highly disfunctional by being twice deposed within a year. Cambodia's constitution stipulates that all Cambodians aged 18 and older have the right to vote for the National Assembly.

Judged on the basis of the constitution, Cambodia's electorate is formally involved in selecting the government and, hence, it forms the nominal selectorate. As the government is supposed to be formed on the basis of the directly elected parliamentary majorities, Cambodia's winning coalition, according to the constitution, consists of those voters who happen to vote for the winning party and whose votes are decisive, as specified by electoral law, to win the election. Moreover, while the prime minister, as the head of government, holds the most powerful position in Cambodia's politics, he is constrained by various checks and balances, and most notably by his accountability to the National Assembly.

However, it does not take much to realize that the political reality in Cambodia differs greatly from this constitutional framework. In the past, other factors, rather than the outcome of the elections, have been decisive for the formation of the government suggesting that the voters are, in reality, not crucial to installing the government in power. Hence, it appears that the Cambodian electorate does not form part of the true selectorate. Moreover, once in power, governments are by no means constrained by the publicly elected parliament. The constitutionally designed checks and balances are virtually non-functional: whereas the executive frequently rules by edict, laws are regularly drafted in the ministries leaving both parliamentary chambers powerless (Ear and Hall 2008). It is thus necessary to look beyond the Cambodian constitution to understand the logic of political survival in place.

As Cambodia's political system is, in reality, personalized around Prime Minister Hun Sen, one needs to investigate how he has managed to hold on to power in order to identify the true selectorate and his winning coalition. In the following, it is argued that Hun Sen's position in power relies on his ability to maintain control over the most important executive state actors, such as the armed forces, the police and the bureaucracy, on the one hand, and its ability to maintain loyalties among economic elites on the other (Cock 2010a). The CPP's party organization has been crucial in establishing and maintaining these controls and loyalties, but they have also been reinforced by kinship ties. In brief, government formation after the first elections was decided by military strength and, after a coup in 1997, Prime Minister Hun Sen managed to strengthen his position as the leader in a quasi one-party system. Since then, he has been holding the position of prime minister. Over time, political violence has decreased in Cambodia and political stability – that is, Hun Sen's grip on power – over the last decade was achieved by more subtle means (An *et al.* 2008: 13). Political challengers have either been co-opted or pressured by 'rule by law', while the ruling party's patronage networks ensured the generation of just enough legitimacy among the impoverished population to win the elections (Mydans 2008a, 2008b; Un 2012, 2013). As a result, with the exception of the most recent 2013 election, oppositional parties such as the Sam Rainsy Party or the Human Rights Party – which merged to form the Cambodia National Rescue Party in 2012 – did not succeed in seriously challenging the CPP's monopoly of power in the past despite considerable financial and moral support from Western donors and steady increases in their share of votes. The royalist Front Uni National pour un Cambodge Indépendant, Neutre, Pacifique, et Coopératif (FUNCINPEC), in contrast, has ceased to constitute a real challenge to the CPP, as it was co-opted into the CPP and was driven to self-dissolution in the mid-2000s.

During the 1990s, the remaining civil war fighters and the armed forces, respectively, formed a crucial constituency of the selectorate and the winning coalition. This is reflected in the fact that claims to power were decided by military capabilities in 1993 and by pure force in 1997. The first parliamentary elections in 1993 resulted in a 58-seat majority (45 per cent) for the royalist FUNCINPEC, against 51 seats (38 per cent) for the CPP. But the CPP, threatening that it would not accept the election results, forced the FUNCINPEC into a coalition government with two prime ministers (Lum 2007: 3). Prince Ranariddh (FUNCINPEC) became the first prime minister and former Prime Minister Hun Sen (CPP) became second prime minister, although the latter de facto managed to control the government on his own. At the time, the formation of this government was considered a reflection of the military reality of '100,000 soldiers and 45,000 police under SOC [the State of Cambodia and thus the CPP's] command in contrast to FUNCINPEC's 5,000-strong armed force' (Um 1995: 76), rather than the 1993 election results.

The subsequent coalition was doomed to instability and many conflicts erupted about the distribution of positions between supporters of each of the parties. The size of the government increased considerably in order to integrate the newcomers from the royalist party (Roberts 2002: 526), but the CPP successfully refused to dismantle its organizational advantage and to leave sufficient positions of authority for the nominal election winner. In this way, it deprived the FUNCINPEC leaders of patronage and the means to reward the loyalty of their followers. In July 1997, the conflict about distribution of state resources to their respective supporters finally erupted into armed conflict between both parties when FUNCINPEC leader Ranariddh tried to realign with marginalized Khmer Rouge fighters in order to oust Hun Sen. Ultimately, Ranariddh was exiled, some 80–100 people were killed and many FUNCINPEC members fled the country (Roberts 2002; McCargo 2005; Lum 2007).

In recent years, the violence with which political opponents have been neutralized in the past has gradually been replaced by political pressure or 'rule by law', meaning that political opponents are silenced non-violently by the selective application of law, especially anti-corruption legislation (Mydans 2008a, 2008b; Un 2012). This strategy is reflected in the gradual improvement in indicators of political repression, such as Freedom House's civil liberties and CIRI's Physical Rights (Wood and Gibney 2010).

While the military has become a less visible actor in politics in the 2000s, Hun Sen has several times threatened to instigate civil war should he lose power, most recently in the 2013 parliamentary elections (Heinrich Böll Stiftung 2013). There is also no doubt about the continuation of close ties between armed troops and specific political leaders, particularly with Prime Minister Hun Sen. According to a 'family tree' published by the English-language newspaper *Phnom Penh Post*, many of the key positions that secure political power and internal security are kept under the control of the party leaders by intermarriage between their children.

Emerging from civil war, the inclusion of the armed forces in the coalition is a necessity and the country's political stability rests, to a great extent, upon the integration of former rebel fighters into the Royal Cambodian Armed Forces (RCAF). This results in the disproportional size of the Cambodian military. Officially, the budget for national defence was stable during the 1990s, but, reportedly, the RCAF consumed 25 per cent of all government revenues. The RCAF has also been rewarded with tax holidays and many other large extra-budgetary revenues, such as 700,000 hectares of land designated as 'Military

Development Zones', which generate revenues, for example from logging concessions (Sok 2005; McCargo 2005).

In recent years, the government under Hun Sen has also sought to exploit the elections as a means to legitimize its rule domestically and internationally, thus strengthening the party's grip on power. This led to an evolution from outright violence and voter intimidation to more subtle methods of electoral manipulation, which allow the regime to create legitimacy based on a 'technically sound and peaceful Election Day process' (An *et al.* 2008: 13). Since the first elections in 1993, and with the exception of the most recent election in 2013, the CPP has steadily increased its share of the votes. After decades of civil war, peace and stability seemed enough of an accomplishment for many impoverished people in the countryside to vote for the CPP. Most importantly, however, Hun Sen has increasingly relied on patronage in order to gain legitimacy among the population at the local level and so win elections (Un 2013). He has relied on patronage networks consisting of party leaders, government officials and big businesses, through which resources 'used for gift giving and local infrastructure development' (Un 2013: 143) can be channelled and strategically targeted to districts with sufficient votes for the CPP.

The CPP's party organization is the backbone of this patronage network, but it would be significantly less efficient if did not also comprise the state bureaucracy. As the CPP controls the state bureaucracy at all levels, it can rely on state infrastructure to reach out to the broader population. This is especially helpful with regard to the elections; not only because it includes a monopoly over media outlets, control over voter lists, and the possibility to oblige officials such as the police or teachers to engage publicly for the party, but also because it offers a possibility to sanction communes in which the population voted for parties other than the CPP by withholding development assistance to the voting district after the elections (Heinrich Böll Stiftung 2013). The bureaucracy is thus another crucial constituent in Cambodia's current coalition, not only at the national, but also at the grassroots level in the villages.

At the lower level, the CPP's loyalties in the bureaucracy were built up during the early 1990s, but the general strategy of co-opting the bureaucracy in order to consolidate power dates back to pre-UNTAC times. They were initiated when Hun Sen anticipated diminishing material support from Vietnam and the Soviet Union and began to reform the party and the country's economy in the late 1980s (Gottesmann 2004: 279). Privatization strengthened the party's power position vis-à-vis local civil servants, who had earlier opposed recruitment for a regime imposed by Vietnam. In the late 1980s, the supply of luxury goods – such as cigarettes, detergent, soap, petrol and paraffin – from the Soviet Union, which, until then, had supplemented civil servants' meagre salaries, dried up. At the same time, inflation increased. Against the background of these worsening economic conditions and the decreasing ability of the regime to reward its supporters with goods supplied by the Soviet Union, the introduction of private economy offered officials new discretionary opportunities to amass wealth (Hughes 2003: 41).

In the early 1990s, while declaring an end to Communism and transforming the Kampuchean People's Revolutionary Party into the CPP (Brown 1992), the party leadership coerced civil servants into the party (Hughes 2003). In doing so, it bound the access to these material benefits and the well-being of civil servants to the survival of the party rather than the state. This has enforced civil servants' loyalty to the party. The UNTAC mission failed to fully control the administration (Brown 1993; Um 1994). UNTAC's inability to deprive the CPP of its control over the bureaucracy was a contentious issue, criticized by the other parties at the time, because control over the Cambodian bureaucracy would have been crucial to levelling the playing field of the competing Cambodian factions. In fact, the loyalty of the bureaucracy was and remains a crucial advantage in the political competition. This has not only been emphasized by CPP leader Hun Sen (Hughes 2003: 81), but was also reflected in the inability of many FUNCINPEC ministers to carry out substantial policies during the first coalition government.[1] Until today, the CPP's domination of the state bureaucracy remains a crucial pillar of its rule, which it tried to reinforce in the 2000s when it introduced a strategy of decentralization to replicate the political dominance enjoyed by the CPP at national, local, provincial and district levels (Hughes 2009).

Finally, business elites form a third constituency in Hun Sen's winning coalition. This constituency is important as it finances the CPP's patronage systems. As a result of the CPP's domination of state structures, the distinction between the ruling party and the Cambodian state is blurred and, hence, the nexus between politics and business in Cambodia is very tight. On the one hand, political positions are designed to open up business opportunities to followers and, given the weakness of political institutions and powerful hierarchical patron-client relationships, personal networks are indispensable for doing business successfully. On the other hand, the government's capabilities and its willingness to generate income through taxation is limited (Cock 2010a). Instead, it relies on non-tax revenues, such as foreign development assistance or private donations to the CPP (or the Cambodian Red Cross – which are subsequently channelled to the CPP through its chair, first lady Bun Rany). Consequently, a mutually beneficial relationship has evolved in which the political leadership is financially supported by a few super-rich party members who, in return, receive political support and economic concessions to increase their business imperia. As a consequence of the strong relations between politics and business, Cambodia is one of the most corrupt countries in the world, losing an estimated US$500 million due to corruption annually. Transparency International ranked Cambodia as 131 in 2005 and 158 out of 180 countries in 2009 (Transparency International 2009). An anti-corruption law was discussed for 15 years before it passed through parliament in 2010, only to then be applied selectively to political competitors.

Effectively, a few Cambodian families control large chunks of the most lucrative economic sectors, including tourism, logging and rubber plantations, exploitation of minerals, oil and gas, infrastructure and the communication and banking sectors. Many of these tycoons hold the title of '*Okhna*', a prestigious title awarded to generous donors who contribute to rebuilding the country. In

Cambodia, the system of certificates and titles has a historical tradition dating back to the fifteenth century; but, in 1994, it was revived by a decree from the two prime ministers according to which donations between US$500 and US$100,000 are rewarded with specific certificates and titles, including the title of *Oknha* for donations exceeding US$100,000 (Mengin 2007). Frequently, these *Oknhas* are very close to the government and act as counsellors or senators.

A vivid illustration of the collusion between business and politics is given by one of the richest and most powerful *Oknhas*, Lao Meng Khin, who is said to be the main sponsor of the Hun Sen faction. His company, Pheapimex, which he runs together with his wife – who is also engaged in the Cambodian Red Cross – has several joint ventures with international business partners. It holds a number of economic land concessions and land concessions for plantations, logging and mining, covering around 7.4 per cent of Cambodia's total area (Global Witness 2007: 77). The company and its branches have been criticized frequently by civil society organizations for, among other things, allegedly obtaining concessions in conflict with Cambodian land law and being involved in land conflicts and brutal forced evictions carried out by armed security or military forces (Heder 2011).

In respect of the analysis of China's interaction with the Cambodian leadership and its winning coalition that follows, it is important to note that a number of the powerful tycoons that have made inroads into Cambodian politics are of ethnic Chinese origin. Historically, the small ethnic Chinese minority has always played a substantial role in Cambodia's society. Many Sino-Khmer and Chinese were well integrated in society and have been organized in communities since the fifteenth century. Traditionally, they engaged in trade and were relatively well-off. In the twentieth century, however, this minority became a target of discrimination and prosecution. The ethnic Chinese were continuously discriminated against under the rule of Lon Nol, during the Khmer Rouge regime – when people of Chinese descent were mainly prosecuted for their urban life-style – and during the 1980s under the Vietnamese occupation (Mengin 2007). Ironically, they formed a prime target group for Khmer Rouge aggression, even though the regime was supported by thousands of Chinese advisors at the time.

Today, an estimated 2.5 per cent of Cambodia's population is of Chinese ethnicity (Burgos and Ear 2010). In 1990, the CPP government allowed the establishment of associations of ethnic minorities. Specifically, since its relations with the Chinese government had improved, the CPP 'allowed China to actively assist in the cultural and economic revival of the Cambodian-Chinese community' (Marks 2000). Sino-Khmer individuals like *Oknhas* play a key role in China's relations with Cambodia. As will be discussed in the following, driven by economic incentives, these elites exploit their political power to channel Chinese political and economic interests to the Cambodian decision-makers.

Summing up the discussion of the Cambodian winning coalition, survival in power crucially depends on a working party structure and deeply entrenched patron–client relationships. With the party organization of the CPP, Hun Sen is able to successfully co-opt and control those societal subgroups, which are of paramount importance to his government's grip on power. First, the integration of the bureaucracy into the CPP's networks enables the party to dominate state structures. Second, and hardly surprising for a post-conflict country in which the use of force or the threat to do so creates considerable authority, the military, i.e. the RCAF, also belongs to his winning coalition. Third, the country's business elites are an important constituency of the winning coalition; they play a prominent role in financing the party in exchange for political concessions to generate their income. With regard to this last group, it is noteworthy that some of these coalition members are of Chinese ethnicity.

Thus, there are persistent gaps between the constitutional framework and the political reality. According to the constitution, the winning coalition should include the electorate; but, in reality, the Cambodian political system is dominated by informal structures in which the electorate has no decisive power. Hence, the electorate is de facto excluded from the true selectorate and the winning coalition.

China in Cambodia

Having discussed the members of the Cambodian winning coalition, this section takes a closer look at the interaction between Cambodian and Chinese elites. It should be noted that the case of Cambodia delivers some outstanding insights into China's engagement. This is for two reasons: first, China's development assistance to Cambodia is more transparent than elsewhere, because the many international donors active in Cambodia have tried to integrate China into the donor harmonization process. As a result, the Chinese government committed to Cambodia's Official development assistance (ODA) database provided by the Cambodian Rehabilitation and Development Board (CRDB). Second, there is a great variety of NGOs operating in Cambodia that critically monitor and document what Chinese actors are doing in the country.

The domestic conflict over power in 1997 marked a turning point in China's approach vis-à-vis the different Cambodian political factions. This turning point coincided with a more active Chinese regional strategy, which encouraged Chinese state companies to invest abroad, including in Cambodia. In Cambodia, the implementation of this policy was greatly facilitated by the existing ethnic Chinese minority. In the following, I will look in more detail at the Chinese engagement of the Cambodian leaders and their coalition, before turning to the question of whether and how the broader population is addressed.

Embrace of the tycoons and the military

The 1997 conflict between de facto leader Hun Sen and his challenger Ranariddh clearly marks a turning point in Sino-Cambodian relations, and in China's focus on specific factions of Cambodia's ruling elite. As laid out earlier, in its attempt to push back the influence of Vietnam in Cambodia, China supported several, at times competing, Cambodian factions throughout the Cold War. In 1979, the PRC even invaded Vietnam to punish the latter's incursion into Cambodia. As Hun Sen had come to power under the Vietnamese-backed resistance against the Khmer Rouge regime, the Chinese government considered Hun Sen a representative of a Vietnamese puppet regime. This distrust was mutual. In 1988, the Cambodian prime minister accused China of being the root of all that was evil in Cambodia (Marks 2000).

In 2000, in marked contrast to these historical hostilities, Prime Minister Hun Sen declared China to be Cambodia's 'most trustworthy friend' (Storey 2006). How could this historic antagonism between both governments have been bridged? A shift in alliances was overdue as the power position of the two factions that the Chinese government had previously supported declined markedly during the 1990s. The Khmer Rouge were outlawed, King Sihanouk was bankrupt (Peou 2000: 220) and plagued by cancer, as a result of which he spent most of the time out of the country for medical treatment. His son, Ranarridh, who had taken over the FUNCINPEC, had driven the party to the edge of dissolution. Already in 1996, during a visit by Hun Sen to Beijing, an agreement on party-to-party relations between the CCP and the CPP was made (Richardson 2010), but Hun Sen's victory in the conflict with Prince Ranariddh delivered a good opportunity for the Chinese government to reconcile with the CPP.

Declaring the conflict an internal affair in which the Chinese government would not interfere, the Chinese government was quick to accept the new balance of power in Cambodia in which Hun Sen had prevailed over Prince Ranariddh. In the Western international society, however, the 1997 conflict was interpreted as a coup d'état by Hun Sen. Several donors put assistance flows on hold to express their disapproval. The US, for example, withheld its development assistance to the government for a decade. The Association of Southeast Asian Nations (ASEAN) also tried to push the CPP government to reconcile with Ranariddh (Möller 1998). Hun Sen was not prepared for this international pressure and the connected financial penalties (Ros 2000).

From 1997 onwards, visits between high-level Chinese and Cambodian leaders intensified and they were always accompanied by announcements of new Chinese aid provision or economic cooperation agreements (Osborne 2006: 30). China started to support the RCAF loyal to Hun Sen and the visibility of the Chinese-Cambodian friendship was further increased by ceremonies with high-level participation from both sides whenever a Chinese investment project in Cambodia was completed. In 2002, Zhu Rongji announced the cancellation of Cambodia's debts to China (Richardson 2010).

It is difficult to assess whether the support from and cooperation with the Chinese government was vital for Hun Sen's political survival, because other external players tried to mediate in Cambodia's domestic crisis, too. In fact, it was Japan's mediation efforts that eventually saved Cambodia. The Japanese government finally managed to convince the Cambodian parties to find an arrangement that allowed Prince Ranariddh to return and new elections to be held (Möller 1998; Ros 2000). Even though the Chinese support undoubtedly lifted the pressure on Hun Sen, the traditional donor community's pressure was still strong enough to push Hun Sen to allow Ranariddh to return to Cambodia (Ros 2000).

Eventually, the CPP managed to co-opt the remaining FUNCINPEC members into the CPP's patronage networks. When the 1998 parliamentary elections were won overwhelmingly by the CPP, Ranariddh refused to accept the election outcome. However, the stalemate was overcome with the establishment of a second chamber, the Senate. New positions were created to integrate FUNCIN-PEC members and to depose the head of the National Assembly, a member of the CPP, allowing Ranariddh to take this position despite his election defeat (Roberts 2002). The coalition between CPP and the remaining FUNCINPEC was renewed. Despite having only two delegates in Parliament since 2008, the party maintains several ministerial positions, albeit without portfolios (Heinrich Böll Stiftung 2013). FUNCINPEC continues to exist, primarily consisting of members of the royal family, but over time it effectively lost its political weight.

Interestingly, the Chinese government, while acknowledging Hun Sen's position as Cambodia's strongman, continues to cultivate its relationship with, and seems to avoid antagonizing, the royalists. For example, despite the FUNCINPEC's lack of political power in Cambodia's domestic politics, whenever the CCP's International Department reports on visits to Cambodia or interaction with Cambodia's leadership, it refers equally to both parties, the CPP and the FUNCINPEC (International Department CCP 2013c). In conversations with a former Cambodian ambassador to the US, a member of the FUNCINPEC, I was told that during the time of his mission in Washington he was invited to China once or twice a year on a tourist trip arranged by the Chinese Ministry of Foreign Affairs. When asked whether his visits were of a private nature, he explained that his personal relationship with Chinese officials dated back to their collaboration during the time of resistance against the Vietnamese and that the Chinese used the contact with him to gather information on issues of interest to them, for instance on the US's stance towards China.

The Chinese government also strengthened its cooperation with the RCAF. At the end of 1997, just a few months after the fighting ended, the Chinese government provided military equipment to Cambodia worth US$2.8 million, mostly to RCAF units (Storey 2006). It is claimed that this deal pre-dates the July 1997 fights and was officially given to the Cambodian national armed forces (Marks 2000). However, in the context of Cambodia's post-civil war history, the armed forces were not neutral. Military ability observably translated into political power after the 1993 elections. So, instead of increasing the capacity of national defence, this military support primarily helped Hun Sen to bolster his position in power against domestic competitors.

According to a Cambodian defence official, China was the biggest supporter of military aid to the RCAF in 2005, even though Vietnam upheld their strong ties with the armed forces via numerous training sessions. China's annual support to the Cambodian military between 1999 and 2005 amounted to approximately US$5 million (Rith and Cochrane 2005). It is noteworthy that, from 2005 onwards, Chinese military assistance specifically targeted the Cambodian naval forces to help safeguard projected offshore oil sites in which Chinese companies have considerable interest. The Cambodian government purchased six naval patrol boats from China in 2005 and, in 2007, the Cambodian government was given a preferential loan from the Chinese government to buy another nine vessels for an estimated US$60 million from China State Ship-building Corporation (*People's Daily Online* 2007; Burgos and Ear 2010). In 2010, shortly after the US suspended a military programme, including the delivery of some 200 military trucks, because of the deportation of 20 asylum-seeking Uighurs to China, the Chinese government stepped in and provided 257 vehicles to the Cambodian government (The Associated Press 2010a).

In a private conversation, a former Minister of Defence praised the arms trade with China, because China – unlike the US, which he accused of using such deals to dispose of second-hand equipment – delivers brand-new arms at 'friendship prices'. These are perceived as a fairly good offer and so create a win-win situation. They are beneficial to the Cambodian government, its military and, in particular, to the minister in charge, because these arms deals are usually accompanied by a commission for the government official who arranged the deal.[2]

Clearly, the Chinese decision to cooperate with the Cambodian government after the coup de facto improved the position of one of the two competitors for power, Hun Sen, and thereby stabilized his political rule. It helped to improve the equipment of the armed forces and to maintain their willingness to defend his rule against domestic competitors if necessary. But China's material support for the RCAF went beyond the mere provision of hardware: by providing construction materials for barracks, schools and hospitals (Storey 2006), the Chinese government also contributed to improvements in living conditions for Cambodia's military. Thus, the Chinese military assistance also increased Hun Sen's capacity to satisfy this subgroup in his winning coalition, thereby increasing its loyalty. Against this background, the provision of military support is better understood as the narrowly targeted provision of privileges to an important subgroup within Hun Sen's winning coalition, rather than a contribution to Cambodia's national defence as a whole, which would classify as a public good.

The rapprochement between Hun Sen's CPP and the CCP coincided with the emergence of a more active Chinese regional policy approach, as China's new public diplomacy with its specific focus on the Asian region was launched in the late 1990s. Its goal was to increase the Chinese government's attempts to improve its reputation among all its neighbours (Medeiros and Fravel 2003). Integrating the region economically was one strategy to this end, and consequently economic relations between China and Cambodia were built up steadily. In 2004, for the first time, FDI from China surpassed any other individual investing country (Burgos and Ear 2010). In the same year, in line with the Chinese 'go out' policy, Chinese Vice-Premier Wu Yi, while on a visit to Cambodia, further encouraged Chinese investments to Cambodia. Until then, Chinese investments had typically been concentrated in the garment sector, attracted by Cambodia's textile export quota to the US. Although numerous, these small and medium-sized investments in garments and retail were in no way comparable to the new type of large scale investments that were being promoted by the 'go out' policy and further stimulated by pledges from the Chinese government. According to the Council of

Development of Cambodia (CDC), a one-stop agency for investments directly under the control of the prime minister, these investments overtly target infrastructural projects, such as the construction of roads and bridges and in the energy and mining sector. Additionally, there was one big resort development project. From 2006 to 2010, the Cambodian investment board approved US$6 billion in Chinese investments, and China provided over US$2 billion more in grants and loans (Heder 2011).

The Chinese state-backed 'go out' policy, with interests in strategic sectors, sheds a different light on the re-emergence of the Sino-Khmer elites in Cambodia. These now gained a crucial role as facilitators of proactively pursued Chinese interests. Several Chinese business associations and the Chinese Chamber of Commerce, located in the Chinese embassy in Phnom Penh, offer an institutionalized network that facilitates investments by Chinese companies. However, individuals with sometimes shady connections to the underworld maintain a pivotal role in arranging business deals.

It is a common practice that these key persons with close ties to both the Cambodian government and officials of the CCP at various levels host business delegations from mainland China.[3] These facilitators are financially rewarded by the investors for arranging business. Therefore, it has been argued that economic assistance and investments from China have catalysed the accumulation of the Sino-Khmer elite's wealth (Mengin 2007: 28). In this respect, it is interesting to note that some of the Sino-Khmer *Oknhas* have also set up businesses in the PRC. Therefore, they have also become dependent on the Chinese authorities' support in China. In this way, a business deal made in Cambodia can also pay off in terms of business concessions in China.[4]

Clearly, on the Chinese and the Cambodian side, the line is blurred between when individuals act as state or as private actors. Or, to put it differently, abuse of public power to pursue private economic interests is common. Many powerful members of the Cambodian winning coalition are rewarded directly by Chinese actors for facilitating business interests in Cambodia with private goods, such as provisions or stakes in joint ventures (Cock 2010a).

Two such elitist joint ventures, involving the extraction of Cambodia's national wealth by Chinese companies against rewards for a few Cambodian individuals, are well-known: Wuzhishan L.S. Group Co. Ltd is a Sino-Cambodian enterprise and an offshoot of Pheapimex. It is directed by Mr Liu Wei, a representative of the overseas Chinese business community in Cambodia, Sino-Khmer *Oknha* Sy Kong Triv, and Sino-Khmer Lau Meng Khin who also owns Pheapimex (Fullbrook 2006; Mengin 2007; Cambodian Human Rights Action Committee 2009). Cambodian civil society organizations, among others, have criticized that Wuzhishan's total concessions exceeded the legal maximum size of 10,000 hectares by twenty times. The company was also accused of forced land evictions and forest clearance operations in an area that was six times bigger than the original 10,000 hectares that was covered by a concession for a pine plantation in Mondulkiri province (Cambodian Human Rights Action Committee 2009). In 2001, in a joint venture with Pheapimex, under the name of Pheapimex-Fuchan,

China Cooperative State Farm Group established a pulp plantation in Kompong Chhnang and Pursat provinces. The US$70 million investment was financed by a loan to the Cambodian government from China's Import-Export Bank (Fullbrook 2006; Mengin 2007).

It has also been argued that the Chinese government approached the Sino-Khmer elites not only in economic matters, but also in political issues. For example, during the 1990s, Sino-Khmer Theng Bunma, then-president of the Chinese Association of Cambodia – and a famous figure in Cambodia's under-world – was just such a facilitator of Chinese interests in the Cambodian government (Marks 2000). Theng Bunma was allegedly involved in drug traf-ficking. It is not clear, however, whether he was a real Sino-Khmer, given that his birthplace has been variously documented in Cambodia, Thailand, China and Taiwan (Mengin 2007). The Chinese government has reportedly asked Bunma, via the Chinese embassy, 'to intervene on several occasions with his senior contacts in the ruling Cambodian People's Party when Beijing does [did] not agree with the way the Cambodian government is [was] handling a particular issue' (Jeldres 2003). Accordingly, Bunma had been asked by the Chinese government to intervene in the context of the formalization of the Khmer Rouge tribunal (Jeldres 2003), but also to control Chinese triad gangs from the PRC, which had established themselves in Cambodia and were involved in human trafficking of Chinese illegal emigrants, drug smuggling, illegal capital flight and arms trade (Lintner 2002).

Opportunism and ignorance towards democratic opposition parties

Some empirical evidence suggests that the Chinese government is carefully observing the political developments in Cambodia and pragmatically adjusting its engagement with all those actors who could potentially become powerful. Reportedly, members of the oppositional Sam Rainsy Party, for example, explained that they were usually ignored by Chinese officials in Phnom Penh. However, for a short period in 2003, when the party emerged as a potential coali-tion candidate after the elections, they started to receive calls and invitations from the Chinese embassy. 'They'd invite us to banquet with them [at the Chinese embassy], they'd drop hints about how they could aid us' (Kurlantzick 2007: 47). At that time, Hun Sen finally succeeded in ending the political deadlock after almost a year by co-opting some of the Sam Rainsy Party's allies into his coali-tion. The Sam Rainsy Party remained excluded from government and, as a result, calls from the Chinese embassy immediately ceased (Kurlantzick 2007).

Provision of infrastructure to ordinary Cambodians

The Cambodia ODA database provided by the Cambodian Rehabilitation and Development Board (CRDB) of the CDC delivers insight into what is officially claimed governmental assistance to Cambodia by the Chinese government

(Council for the Development of Cambodia 2010). The Cambodia ODA database records details of project and programme assistance provided by all development partners. It has been developed in an attempt to achieve donor harmonization and to increase aid effectiveness. The information on Chinese projects is, almost certainly, neither fully correct, nor complete. The first projects enlisted only began in 2005 and the information on Chinese projects varied between two visits to the database, whereby some assistance that had been claimed in earlier years had been removed from the database in 2010. This concerned mostly in-kind donations (excavators, pumping machines, motor cycles, fire trucks and anti-malaria medicine), materials for elections, some donations to the royal family and a unit of a THSCAN Mobile Container System, worth Yuan 20 million, which was transferred to the Cambodian government in 2006.

Several features of Chinese development assistance to Cambodia strongly suggest that the Cambodian population is not the primary target group. Firstly civil society and non-state actors, in general, are not partners for cooperation for the Chinese government. All of the 41 Chinese development projects reported in 2010 were implemented by Cambodian state institutions, not a single one by a civil society organization or a non-state actor (Council for the Development of Cambodia 2010). Likewise, none of the various foreign-funded development projects implemented by Cambodian non-governmental organizations received money from the Chinese government. Second, Chinese aid projects focused on the provision of financing for specific capital investment projects, rather than on human-capacity building. The majority of Chinese projects concentrated on the transportation sector and concern building roads and bridges. Only one project in the educational sector was listed: the provision of some US$80,000 for an electronic library to the Royal Academy.

Third, upon closer examination, most projects in the sectors of 'environment and conservation' and 'governance and administration' appeared to be prestige projects, beneficial to the Cambodian government or its cronies. They included the establishment of a botanical garden in the capital, the construction of a new building for the Council of Ministers (the Cambodian cabinet), and the provision of equipment and vehicles to the Senate as well as to the Ministry of Parliamentary Relations and Inspection. Given Cambodia's widespread corruption, one can interpret these projects as direct contributions to the living standards and social status of Hun Sen's winning-coalition members. As a visitor to the popular Waterfestival in Phnom Penh in 2007, I was overwhelmed by the huge number of luxury jeeps with government and military licence plates, lined up in front of the VIP stand; at the same time, public transport for ordinary Cambodians was very limited at best.

The Council of Ministers building was constructed and financed through a concessional loan from China worth roughly US$36 million. It was meant to accommodate the government. However, as it did not suit the taste of Prime Minister Hun Sen, upon completion he immediately started on the construction of a new building next to it (Burgos and Ear 2010). Against this background, the construction seems to be a complete waste of Cambodian (and Chinese) public resources, from which only the Chinese construction company profited.

The most prominent example of Chinese support for Cambodian prestige projects is one of the largest foreign investments in Cambodia; that is, the US$280 million Kamchay hydropower station in Kampot Province. It should be noted, however, that this project is not included in the CDC's aid statistics. It is currently being built by Sinohydro, a Chinese SOE that was fined for poor quality work and downgraded for its performance in 2005 by the Chinese government (Middleton 2008). The 'strong support for the project by the Chinese government appears to be more about gaining political points with the Cambodian government than Sinohydro making a large profit' (Middleton 2008: 48). In the past, several international investors rejected a proposal to finance the dam construction located in a national park, because they considered it a prestige project that was not economically viable. NGOs reckon that the project is financed as part of a 2006 US$60 million package from China, and most likely subsidised with low interest rates by the Chinese government. Electricity produced by the dam will cost considerably less than current electricity, although it is expected to be more expensive than imported electricity from Vietnam. The Cambodian government had to guarantee profits in case the project turned out not to be financially viable and it was reported that Hun Sen received loans from China well in advance to polish the facility's performance during the start-up phase (Fullbrook 2006).

Cambodian NGOs also criticize the intransparency around Chinese investments in Cambodia. The Cambodian government itself has no interest in allowing public discussion, let alone participation of civil society. Environmental impact assessments of major investment projects are required by law but are often done only after the government has already contracted a company.[5] The Cambodian government also badly communicates its plans to the general public, affected communities and citizens. Chinese investors and the Chinese embassy frequently also refuse to communicate with ordinary Cambodians or NGOs.[6] Even regional or local governments with formal responsibility for the polity are sometimes circumvented. For example, the district governor of O'Reang District stated that, although he believed Wuzhishan's plantation to be illegal, the level of political interaction between the national and provincial governments and the Chinese company was out of his reach, so he simply avoided those areas of his district. In a newspaper, he was cited as saying: 'I never went to the sites. The province never informs me about it. I don't want to be involved' (Plaut and Chan Thul 2006).

As the above makes clear, China's engagement is, in many aspects, targeted at the narrowly defined objectives of the Cambodian government and its cronies, rather than Cambodian society. The Chinese government has shown willingness to support Hun Sen by financing and constructing prestige projects, which he considers meaningful, in order to show his political power. This is not to say that local populations do not benefit from China's infrastrucure projects. To the contrary, given the poor condition of Cambodia's transportation system, infrastucture can be crucial for local economic development. However, the CPP's practice of instrumentalizing such projects in order to buy votes in the countryside, de facto turns such projects into a tool to support the CPP's position in power. It is noteworthy, however, that the CDC's database also contains a number of more recent projects in the agricultural sector. Most of these entries refer to irrigation projects, all of which were started in 2010 or later.

There is, however, one area, the field of education, in which China seems very keen to address ordinary Cambodians. Since 1998, more than 70 Chinese language schools opened up in Cambodia, the largest of which has more than 10,000 students and is bigger than any other Chinese school in any non-Chinese-speaking country (Marks 2000). These schools are usually run by Sino-Khmer communities and associations.[7] The Chinese schools are very popular among Cambodians, because they are cheaper than Cambodia's public schools. 'Because the Chinese-language schools in Cambodia receive this outside funding, they can charge less than many public schools, where impoverished (and sometimes corrupt) Cambodian teachers demand excess payments' (Kurlantzick 2007: 69).

It has been argued that these schools, when necessary, receive assistance from mainland Chinese governments or language associations (Kurlantzick 2007: 69). They are reportedly supported financially through teachers sent from China or in kind, through the provision of textbooks (Fullbrook 2006). The Chinese government has reportedly funnelled this assistance through the Cambodian-Chinese General Assembly, an umbrella organization of the Sino-Khmer associations. By supporting only those schools participating in these associations, the Chinese embassy has gained a certain degree of influence over the school boards. In my own conversations with members of these associations, I could not confirm the financial dependence of these schools on Chinese state money.

However, beyond promoting the Chinese language and culture, schools may still push China's strategic policy objectives by spreading Chinese interpretations of history and China's version of territorial distribution in Asia. Thus, the Chinese schools are also a gateway and instrument for promoting China's strategic interests. For example, after the bombing of the Chinese embassy in Belgrade by the US in 1999, a 'month-long campaign to "combat Western influences" among his pupils' was conducted by one of the school's principals; at the same time, Chinese investors in Cambodia were protesting in front of the US Embassy in Phnom Penh (Marks 2000).

Summary

The Chinese government has established good state-to-state relations with the CPP government in Cambodia. When it became clear that Hun Sen had won the conflict against his competitor Prince Ranariddh in 1997, the Chinese government accepted him as the de facto leader. It subsequently improved its party-to-party relations with the CPP. Over the years, a convergence of interests between members of the Chinese and Cambodian winning coalitions in the military, the economic and the political sectors has evolved and the needs of these elites are directly addressed by Chinese state or state-backed actors. Oftentimes, cooperation is in the best interests of the winning coalitions on both the Chinese and the Cambodian side. With its military aid to the RCAF, the Chinese government targeted a prime constituency of Hun Sen's winning coalition. This military assistance not only bolstered Hun Sen's military advantage over his domestic competitors, but also improved the living conditions for his supporters, thereby satisfying an important constituency of his winning coalition.

In the economic field, China's economic rise stimulated FDI and increased the demand for Cambodia's easily extractable raw materials. Chinese business interests were often channelled through Sino-Khmer tycoons who form part of the current government's winning coalition. The rewards these elites received from Chinese companies in return for their networking and facilitating services cemented the unbalanced access to economic resources. This, in turn, strengthened the CCP's domination of the political process.

Little is known about China's engagement with the opposition parties in Cambodia. Anecdotal evidence suggests that Chinese officials occasionally tried to co-opt opposition leaders when they perceived them as potentially powerful.

Relatively few efforts have been made to target the Cambodian public. Though ordinary Cambodians are excluded from the winning coalition, China's infrastucture projects can have tangible effects on the broader population. While these can have positive effects for ordinary Cambodians, they have also been used to further Hun Sen's political survival objectives to increase his votes in the elections. In addition, China's engagement in infrastructure may also be motivated as much by China' strategic objectives as by philanthropy as the Chinese government seeks to economically develop the Southeast Asian region and to construct region-wide transportation networks. China's support for the Sino-Khmer associations in promoting Chinese culture and setting up language schools, on the other hand, can be seen as an attempt to build on existing networks in order to improve China's reputation and soft power in the region.

In conclusion, support from the Chinese government has helped Hun Sen to overcome a period of political isolation after the coup and, later, to consolidate what Levitsky and Way (2010) called 'competitive authoritarian' structures. While the Chinese engagement has probably never been vital for the CCP's survival in power, financial assistance and development cooperation from China decreased Western leverage over his government and contributed to the skewed distribution of economic and political resources in the country. This enforced the dominance of informal structures over the constitutional order by further empowering the winning coalition consisting of entrenched business elites and members of the armed forces. The constitutionally defined selectorate, the electorate, has further lost the potential to be decisive in appointing the government.

Moreover, a convergence of interests between members of the winning coalition in China and in Cambodia has evolved. The exchange of goods and policies between the two governments and their cronies was not only helpful to stabilize Hun Sen's power, but also to achieve China's strategic interests while being directly beneficial to some commercially active members of the Chinese winning coalition.

Notes

1 Private Source, Phnom Penh, 19 November 2009.
2 Private Source, Phnom Penh, 10 November 2009.
3 The same practice has been reported for Taiwanese business delegations that are promoted by a mafia boss from Taiwan (Lintner 2002: 220).
4 Private Source, Phnom Penh, 17 November 2009.
5 Private Source, Phnom Penh, 19 November 2008.
6 Private Source, Phnom Penh, 19 November 2008.
7 There are 13 family clan-based (based on common Chinese family names), and five region-based (based on origin from the same region in China) associations in Cambodia, some of which have a history of more than 2,000 years. These associations are usually funded by donations and they function as a network and forum to nourish cultural heritage, but also to provide assistance to each other. For example, often the association has a temple and some property that can be used for funerals or to run Chinese language schools. Rich association members usually generously donate in order to help out other members. These family clans are also connected to communities in other Chinese-speaking countries, for example Singapore or Malaysia. (Conversations with several associations in Phnom Penh, November 2009).

6 Mongolia

Between a rock and a hard place

Mongolia is a parliamentary democracy with a large selectorate that forms part of the comparatively large winning coalition. Despite a number of shortcomings, such as unstable voting laws, high corruption levels, and the oligarchization of Mongolia's politics, the electorate has considerable influence on domestic politics. Thus, the Mongolian public is particularly concerned with China's influence over Mongolia's economy. As a result, Mongolian politicians have used populist Sino-phobia for their own cause while, at the same time, finding it difficult to propose policies in China's favour.

The investigation of Sino-Mongolian relations that is presented in this chapter finds that China's approach to Mongolia reflects the Mongolian logic of political survival. That is, in a system where governments can change frequently, the Chinese attempt goes beyond good government-to-government relations and is keen to establish party-to-party relations with all of the competing Mongolian parties, including Mongolia's oligarchs. Most interestingly, the Chinese government has shown considerable concern for Mongolia's popular Sino-phobia and has tried specifically to charm the Mongolian electorate by providing philantrophic aid, educational programmes and by rewriting the disputed Sino-Mongolian history.

The investigation is structured in the same way as the two previous case studies. After a brief introduction to Mongolia's history, the selectorate theory is applied to Mongolia's domestic political structure. The second part examines how China's leadership interacts with Mongolia.

Historical background

Mongolia shares a long history of common statehood with China as both territories were governed commonly for several hundred years. The fact that Chinese leaders have long considered Mongolia to belong to Chinese territory still resonates in contemporary Mongolian fears of being annexed by China or demographically outnumbered by migration from China.

During the Yuan Dynasty, from 1271 to 1368, China was under Mongol rule. Under the Qing Dynasty, both China and Mongolia again belonged to the Manchurian Empire for more than two hundred years. It was the Manchus, a

Tsungun tribe originating from North East Asia, who, after having subjugated the numerous independent Mongolian princedoms, divided the Mongolian territory into Outer and Inner Mongolia. This division still separates today's Mongolia from the Autonomous Region of Inner Mongolia that belongs to the PRC (Agwaandorjiin 1999).

When the Qing Dynasty fell apart in 1911, Mongolia declared its independence, seeking protection from Russia. During the decade that followed, Mongolia fell into chaos. It was affected by struggles between Red and White Russians, and then the Chinese and the Japanese (Green 1986). In 1919, China tried to re-establish its rule over Mongolia by military force. Both the Kuomintang and the CCP considered Mongolia a lost territory that was to be re-integrated into the Chinese territory. Although Russian forces had helped to defeat the Chinese military in 1921, three years later, when Mongolia declared its independence as the Mongolian People's Republic, Russia signed an agreement with China acknowledging that Outer Mongolia was an autonomous but integral part of China.

In 1945, under pressure from the US, China was forced to relinquish its legal claim to Mongolia for the first time as the country's independence was a Russian condition in the Yalta agreement to enter the war against Japan (Green 1986). During the Cold War, the Mongolian People's Republic developed close ties with the Soviet Union. 'Mongolia was so completely integrated both politically and economically with the Soviet Union that it acquired the label "the 16th republic"' (Pomfret 2000: 150). Under President Choibalsan, Mongolia shared Moscow's Stalinist policies, such as the destruction of the nomadic economic structure in the course of socialization, and the elimination of roughly 38,000 members of the country's intellectual and religious elite. Mongolia became a member of the UN in 1961, but most countries fully recognized the country only after they had suspended their diplomatic ties with Taiwan (Green 1986), which, until 2002, constitutionally considered Mongolia as belonging to the Republic of China (Campi 2004: 8).

Mongolia's transformation started in March 1990 when the 1989 demonstrations for the end of single-party rule eventually provoked first a generational change within the incumbent communist Mongolian People's Revolutionary Party (MPRP) and later its final resignation. In 1990, a first parliamentary election was held and a new constitution was introduced in 1992. With the new constitution, the Mongolian's People Republic adopted the new name Republic of Mongolia.

Mongolia's domestic coalition: Voters and oligarchs

I begin the discussion of Mongolia's selectorate and its winning coalition by looking at the constitution that brought into existence the Republic of Mongolia. The constitution of 1992 set the foundation of the new political order, 'a mixed political system, resembling a semi-presidential regime loosely modeled on France's Fifth Republic' (Batbayar 2003: 46). It established a division of power between the executive, the parliament and the judiciary.

Most importantly, with regard to political leadership, the executive consists of the government, which is headed by the prime minister, and a directly elected president, the head of state. Though the president enjoys a strong position, the constitution comprises a complex mechanism to check and balance his powers: the president, whose incumbency is limited to two terms, has a veto power that can, however, be rejected by a two thirds majority of the parliament. The president also nominates a prime minister, but must pick him from the majority party in parliament. Finally, the president can propose to dissolve the parliament, but this then needs to be approved by a two thirds majority of the parliament. The legislature, Mongolia's 76-member parliament, which is called the Great State Hural and elected for a four-year term, in turn, has the power to remove or relieve the president and to appoint or replace the prime minister (Batbayar 2003).

The nominal and true selectorates: Voters

According to the constitution, the Mongolian president has a wide range of powers; at the same time, the constitution prescribes a complex system of checks and balances between different state organs, and especially between the president and the parliament on the basis of which the government is formed. Therefore, both institutions are considered crucial when it comes to the question of how the leadership is selected. Thus, both presidential and parliamentary elections are considered relevant mechanisms. However, while it could be argued that it is the president who ultimately holds power in his hands, the following analysis of the selectorate and the winning coalition would still hold.

According to its constitutional order, all Mongolians of 18 years or older are entitled, by universal suffrage, to participate in presidential and parliamentary elections, and this electorate forms the nominal selectorate. Since 1990, six parliamentary (in 1992, 1996, 2000, 2004, 2008 and 2012) and six presidential elections (in 1993, 1997, 2001, 2005, 2009 and 2013) have been held and Mongolia saw several turnovers of governments and presidents in accordance with the election results. This suggests that the selectorate is effectively engaged in choosing the leadership.

Whether or not a voter belongs to the true selectorate depends on his vote: the number of votes a candidate receives is decisive for whether he or his party wins the elections and, subsequently, becomes president or forms the government, respectively. Therefore, those voters who chose to vote for the winning candidate or party form the true selectorate.

Over the years, a multi-party system has developed in Mongolia with the more conservative former communist Mongolian People's Revolutionary Party (MPRP) and the more liberal Democratic Party (DP) as the two major rivals, the latter being a merger of several opposition parties that emerged from the democracy movement in 1989.[1] In 2010, the MPRP split into two parties, one dropping and one keeping the 'revolutionary' in its name (Dierkes 2011). Smaller parties such as the Civil Will Party (since 2011, the Civil Will-Green Party), the National New Party, and the Republicans have also been successful in gaining seats in the Great State Hural.

The fact that several power turnovers occurred in accordance with the election results testifies to the relevance of the elections for putting the leadership in power and underlining the importance of the selectorate identified above. Nevertheless, there are a number of shortcomings in the functioning of Mongolia's democratic institutions. Mongolia's election rules, for example, have been very unstable. Moreover, observers reported numerous irregularities in the 2004 parliamentary elections, including 'illegal use of state property and civil service workers', police intimidation, fraudulent ballots, multiple voting, the rejection of political party and foreign observers from polling stations, or ballot box stuffing. Also, 'transfer voter' provisions, which allow Mongolia's nomadic population flexibility in polling stations, can easily be exploited by shipping mobile voters to the many very scarcely populated districts (Landman *et al.* 2005: 28). Moreover, in the aftermath of the 2008 parliamentary elections, riots seemed to bring the country to the brink of political chaos. Though international observers had declared the elections largely free and fair, the frustrated opposition questioned the election results, referring to much more optimistic forecasts. Subsequent demonstrations spiralled into violent riots during which the MPRP party building was burnt, one of the country's art museums looted and five civilians died (Bulag 2009). The events, which led to a four-day state of emergency, have not entirely been investigated and no-one has been held accountable (Amnesty International 2009; Freedom House 2011). Finally, because of technical problems, some contestation of the vote count arose even after the parliamentary elections of 2012, despite the use of electronic voting machines (Narangoa 2012b).

Before the 2008 riots observers have never questioned the positive political and public attitude towards democracy in Mongolia (Landman *et al.* 2005; Freedom House 2006). The 2008 riots were interpreted as an expression of frustration with corruption and the political process. However, in the end 'Mongolia's parliamentary, semi-presidential democracy survived' and 'the boundaries of acceptable political protest were re-established' (Sneath 2010: 255). Despite the firm competition between the political parties and their occasional attempts to manipulate the election results, voters play a crucial role in installing the government and the president. The executive is formed on the basis of elections, meaning that the role of voters is crucial in both the true selectorate and the coalition.

The majority of the electorate

Those voters whose vote translates into the winning of the election form part of the winning coalition. Usually, the rules of how votes are translated into power are defined by election law. With regard to the parliamentary elections, the majority system adopted in Mongolia's 1992 constitution set the minimum requirement for the winning coalition to represent 50 per cent of the electorate. As in many other majoritarian systems, however, this legal requirement repeatedly produced election results in Mongolia in which the victorious party in parliamentary elections could heavily capitalize from what was, in reality, only a small electoral advantage. For example, 57 per cent of the votes translated into 93 per cent of parliamentary seats in 1992 and in 2000, 51 per cent of the votes into 72 out of 76 seats. Since only an absolute majority in the Great Hural is required to form the government, the coalition can even be considerably smaller. These election rules were, however, amended several times and thus parliamentary elections took place under very different electoral rules, 'including a block vote system (1992), a party list and candidate list system (1996), and a first-past-the-post system (2000)' (Landman *et al.* 2005: 27).

However, even without technically quantifying the size of the winning coalition for each of Mongolia's elections, it is important to note that the coalition includes part of the electorate, and thus the broader population. Even if only a fraction of votes makes the difference, candidates running in elections have an incentive to please as many voters as possible, since voters are free to choose whom to give their vote to in each election anew. Consequently, the interest of the broader population and public opinion are of importance to election candidates.

As such, one specific feature of the Mongolian population, and hence the Mongolian electorate, with regard to its foreign policy preferences is highly relevant here; namely, a fear among the Mongolian population of China. Many Mongolians fear being over-run by the PRC. On the one hand, the immense demographic pressure in China constitutes a potential threat for a population as small as Mongolia's. Migration from China could easily turn Mongolia's 2.5 million population into a de facto ethnic minority on its own territory. On the other hand, the concerns also have historical roots and stem from the long and complex history under common statehood that has been discussed earlier. Key issues in this regard are the opposing views on history and conflicting constructions of their national identities: 'While Mongolians see themselves as one of Asia's oldest ethnic nations like Han Chinese, Chinese regard Mongolia as a former part of the Middle Kingdom and view Mongolians as their ethnic minority' (Batchimeg 2005b: 54). Moreover, China's Autonomous Region of Inner Mongolia, in which a Mongolian minority of six million people is dominated by a Han Chinese majority, is considered a precedent for Chinese expansionism. In the past, these fears of Chinese expansionism have been substantiated further by the repeated publication of Chinese official maps that showed the territory of Mongolia as a part of the PRC (Campi 2005).

Against this background, some sort of Sino-phobia has evolved among Mongolians with sometimes extremist attacks on Chinese immigrants. Politics has reacted to these emotions by introducing fees for companies employing non-national labour and the newspapers regularly report on roundups of Chinese labour without proper documents. More importantly, however, politicians tried to capitalize on Sino-phobia in several electoral campaigns. Whereas all major political parties have relations with the CCP (Batchimeg 2005a), in Mongolian politics, the 'China card' has frequently been played. For example, in 1998, a state-owned Mongolian newspaper alleged the Chinese ambassador to be involved in the events leading to the resignation of the Enkhsaikhan government, even though these allegations turned out to be unsubstantiated (The Economist

Intelligence Unit 1998b: 49). In 2003, the Minister of Justice and Internal Affairs, Tsendiin Nyamdorj, was accused by the oppositional DP of having connections with the Chinese intelligence service (The Economist Intelligence Unit 2003), and during the presidential elections in 2009, the incumbent president tried to discredit his competitor by accusing him of being of Chinese descent.

The oligarchs

Thus far, the discussion of the selectorate and the winning coalition in Mongolia has focused on the constitutional rules. However, in recent years, observers of Mongolia's democratization process have noticed a trend of 'oligarchization' in Mongolia's political system (Barkmann 2006). As a result, it would be misleading to look at the constitutional setting alone in order to identify the Mongolian winning coalition. To do so would limit the analysis of the winning coalition to the phase of democratic transition and overlook an important trend in the phase of democratic consolidation.

The oligarchization of Mongolia's politics is, in part, a result of the country's rapid transition process from a planned to a market economy. The simultaneous political and economic transformation forms a specific challenge for post-communist transitions. In Mongolia, the institutional setting for the political transformation was introduced relatively quickly with the new constitution. The task of reforming the socialist economy, in contrast, dominated much of the political process during the 1990s. During communist times, the Mongolian economy was nationalized and deeply integrated with the Soviet Union. When the Soviet Union withdrew its financial support, Mongolia's economy plunged into crisis. Faced with serious food shortages (Heaton 1992: 53), Mongolian leaders had to find ways to substitute the subsidies from the Soviet Union.

Mongolia's reformers pursued a neo-liberal shock therapy in order to establish a market system and, in doing so, found support from Western donor agencies that stepped in. But assistance was conditioned on structural economic reforms in line with the then-dominant paradigm of the 'Washington Consensus'. The agreed reform programme was truly radical: initially, it was planned to privatize 40 per cent of SOEs within two to three years with the state retaining control over some key sectors, such as energy, mining, transportation and banking (Heaton 1992). In 1993, the country reached its lowest level of real GDP of US$0.52 billion or US$236 per capita (Demirbag *et al.* 2005). It is widely believed that the transition process could be implemented relatively smoothly, because Mongolia's economy was traditionally based on a large nomadic agricultural sector and Mongolia, therefore, 'did not confront any major problem in terms of large-scale dislocation of redundant industrial workers', who would potentially have protested (Demirbag *et al.* 2005: 308). Nevertheless, economic reforms stimulated urbanization and unemployment sharply increased from 31,000 in February to over 80,000 in September 1991 (Heaton 1992). While there was considerable ownership on the part of Mongolian reformers, Mongolia's transition process was dominated by donor agencies insisting that democratization should go together with transition to a pure market system. Ironically, however, some of the economic policies they enforced effectively undermined democratic principles (Rossabi 2005b: 111).

The recent oligarchization of Mongolia's politics has its early roots in this transition of the economy and, specifically, the privatization process of the 1990s. Initially designed to ensure equality, the privatization process de facto greatly contributed to inequality in the distribution of wealth among the society. In the countryside, the early privatization of livestock in 1991 impoverished nomadic herders who reverted to subsistence farming, while the subsequent increase in the total number of animals dramatically spurred desertification due to over-grazing of the fragile grasslands (The Economist Intelligence Unit 1998a). Moreover, in order to privatize Mongolia's SOEs, the government distributed vouchers to the population. However, this process not only overstretched the ability of many people to fully understand the process, but also underestimated their need for cash in the midst of economic crisis and reduced state services. Many sold their vouchers for ridiculous prices, resulting in the concentration of vouchers in a few hands. At the same time, persisting political power could be exploited to increase economic gains. Throughout the process, under-priced sales of well-functioning state enterprises or state banks and misappropriation and theft of state assets were reported (Rossabi 2005b). Similarly, the 2003 Private Land Act, which credits 0.7 hectares of land to every Mongolian, played into the hands of insiders because of unequal access to information about the quality of land (Rossabi 2005b).

As a result, in the 2000s, the struggle over redistribution in the economic arena translated into a process of oligarchization in the political sphere. A small elite, which had succeeded in transferring much of the country's wealth into a few private pockets, started to monopolize the political scene and increased entrance barriers for newcomers. From 2000 onwards, the increase in the number of businessmen in the political sphere was considerable, many of whom started to invest massively in political parties and to join politics primarily in order to increase their business opportunities or to obtain parliamentary immunity (Barkmann 2006).[2] The 2009 election of Sukhbaataryn Batbold, one of the country's wealthiest businessmen, into the office of the prime minister is a good example of this (Bulag 2010). This oligarchization of politics resulted in exorbitantly expensive electoral campaigns that effectively closed the political contest to newcomers. For example, in the 2004 parliamentary elections, the reported price for standing as an election candidate in a countryside constituency was between US$15,000 and US$23,000 (Tugrik 20 million to Tugrik 30 million), rising to approximately US$115,000 in Ulaanbaatar (Tugrik 150 million) (Batbajar 2006: 388).

Since 1999, a controversial amendment of the constitution has allowed members of parliament to simultaneously serve in the government. This opened the door for the engagement of entrepreneurs in politics beyond mere lobbying. Countless conflicts of interests among such dual office holders arose and corruption was spurred. This is reflected in Transparency International's Corruption Perception Index which ranked Mongolia as 85 out of 180 countries in 2004, deteriorating to 105 in 2006 and to 120 in 2009 (Transparency International

2009). The fact that, due to the majoritarian electoral system, election campaigns in the past were often not driven by programmatic competition, but rather by personalities, also did little to increase the accountability of political office holders. Only in 2011, the Freedom of Information Act was passed in an attempt to increase accountability and transparency.

To summarize, after the breakdown of the Soviet Union, Mongolia has transformed remarkably peacefully and quickly into a parliamentary democracy. In the 20 years of its democratic history, the election results translated several times into leadership turnovers. Therefore, the Mongolian electorate forms part of the true selectorate and effectively participates in the winning coalition. With respect to its relations with China, which will be analysed in the following, the widespread Sino-phobia among the electorate is an important factor in Mongolian politics. Moreover, there are strong vested interests that have succeeded in becoming a permanent member in the coalition, i.e. the Mongolian group of oligarchs that increasingly dominates the political process.

China's interaction with Mongolia

The previous section presented the constituencies of Mongolia's relatively large winning coalition. Against this background, the following sections investigate the nexus between Chinese and Mongolians actors. The section firstly discusses China's engagement with the small vested interests and then turns to China's approaches towards the population who forms the electorate. Because the coalition is inclusive, this section has no subsection dedicated to the disenfranchised.

Charm offensive towards government

With regard to the Mongolian government, the Chinese government, very prudently, tried to show its will to maintain good relations with its Mongolian counterparts. In order to do so, it has repeatedly offered to support the Mongolian government financially. In 2003, Chinese President Hu Jintao offered a US$300,000 soft loan for infrastructure projects (Batchimeg 2005a), but the Mongolian government was undecided about what to do with this offer. In 2003, China donated US$4 million to the Mongolian government to support the construction of the Mongolian Chamber of Commerce and Industry and the development of an industrial park in the free trade zone in Altanbulag (*The UB Post* 2003b). The Chinese also funded five kilometres of Mongolia's Millennium Road. In 2007, a project proposal to use the loan to construct a hydropower project, which had been on the table since the 1990s – and which had already been evaluated as unviable – was finally rejected.[3] It appears that the Mongolian government was deliberately reluctant to accept Chinese strategic investments and state loans during the 1990s and until the 2008 global financial crisis. According to *The China Post*, hit by falling prices for coal, copper and cashmere during the global financial crisis, the Mongolian government asked China for a US$3 billion loan in 2009 (*The China Post* 2009); whether this loan has actually been provided, however, cannot be substantiated. Finally, in 2011, China agreed to provide a US$500 million loan to Mongolia after both countries had signed a 'strategic partnership agreement' (Reuters 2011).

In the framework of government-to-government relations, it is known that the Chinese government also addressed the Mongolian military. China provided more than US$1 million of military assistance in total. It consisted of medical equipment supply and two Chinese language teachers to the Mongolian armed forces (worth US$360,000) in 1997, and the finance provision of accommodation for officers and improved training facilities (worth US$960,000) in 2000 (The Economist Intelligence Unit 1997a, 2000; Liu 2007). The former provision formed part of a border confidence-building agreement signed in 1996 (The Economist Intelligence Unit 1996: 47; 1997a).

At the individual level, the Chinese government seeks to maintain good relations with Mongolian policymakers, whether parliamentarians or members of the cabinet. Therefore, as the chief of the CCP's International Liaison Department reassured one opposition party, it is Chinese policy to cultivate ties to all important Mongolian parties and their high-ranking party officials, regardless of whether they are in government or in opposition (*The UB Post* 2003c).

Win-win relation with oligarchs

As many of the Mongolian politicians are known for being corrupt and for abusing their political position for profit-making, it seems likely that they can easily be manipulated by outside actors. It is very likely that Chinese capital is involved in some of the businesses of the local Mongolian elite. On the one hand, it is suspected that Chinese investors benefited from the privatization in Mongolia and they are said to have acquired shares through Mongolian bidders (The Economist Intelligence Unit 1997a: 41). On the other hand, business collusions between Mongolia's oligarchic elites and investors from China are likely since companies from Japan, China and South Korea are generally more prone to investing in Mongolia in the form of joint ventures than in the form of fully owned subsidiaries (Demirbag *et al.* 2005). In addition, many local officials legally and illegally award mining licences against bribes to Chinese companies or they finance their own mining activities using Chinese entrepreneurs who later buy the product (Sieren 2008; Reeves 2011). In my interviews, many Mongolians expressed their belief that the financial dependence of Mongolian decision-makers on the national level was the entry point for Chinese interests.[4]

Since national politics in Mongolia is dominated by oligarchic businessmen, it is very likely that Mongolian decision-makers are sensitive to pressure from their business partners. According to anecdotal evidence, the party secretary of Mongolia's Civil Will Party made use of an official delegation visit to China to deepen his private business connections. It is rumoured that, much to the embarrassment of the other Mongolian delegation members, he continued to discuss private business interests with the Chinese counterpart immediately after the completion of the official part of the visit, which he led in his function as party secretary. Besides the party, he also also represented the Bodi Group, a holding company with a wide range of interests including banking, real estate, IT and media.[5] He was later elected into parliament for the Democratic Party, and then offically stepped down from the Bodi Group chair. It is also rumoured that political decision-makers frequently receive invitations to spend leisure time in China.

Widespread corruption makes Mongolian decision-makers and officials vulnerable to manipulation. As previously argued, corruption is a home-grown illness in Mongolia. The country's immense richness in terms of natural resources and the competition among foreign investors to gain access to these resources has further exacerbated this problem. However, as will be elaborated, this high level of corruption notwithstanding, Chinese companies face difficulties in realizing their interests in Mongolia's large-scale natural resource deposits by solely targeting private goods at the Mongolian business elites or decision-makers.

Attempts to charm the Mongolian electorate

Whether or not Mongolian policymakers cooperate with Chinese business interests in private, they can hardly take a very pro-Chinese position in public because of the strong Sino-phobic emotions among the Mongolian population. It appears that the Chinese government has begun to understand the incentive system of Mongolian decision-makers and, in particular, the image problem that China faces in Mongolia.

In accordance with this insight, the Chinese government has implemented measures to increase the receptiveness to Chinese interests in Mongolia. More specifically, it tried to address and to show its goodness to the population 'to bolster its image' (Campi 2005). Even though it is difficult to gain a comprehensive picture of China's assistance to Mongolia and, specifically, its aid to the Mongolian government, local newspapers published stories on several Chinese philanthropic activities in Mongolia. In addition to the investment related projects mentioned earlier, for example, the Chinese government provided disaster relief from 1997 to 2002 in order to mitigate winter livestock disasters (US$200,000 in 1997; US$240,000 in 2001). In 2003, the Chinese ambassador donated Tugrik 3 million (approximately US$2,300) to elderly disabled Mongolians (*The UB Post* 2003a) and, in 2007, an aid shipment of 2,000 tonnes of wheat was provided. Moreover, the provision of funds for solar-powered generators, hospitals and the repair of bridges was reported (Rossabi 2005a). The Chinese government also abandoned visa requirements for Mongolian citizens to ease cross-border traffic and concluded a bilateral agreement that allows Mongolians to use Chinese health care facilities for medical treatment (Campi 2005).

The Chinese government has also tried to use education as a specific approach to reach out to the broader population. In 1996, an educational exchange programme was initiated, which, from 2000 onwards, enabled Mongolians to study in China with free loans from China. According to the Chinese Ministry of

Foreign Affairs, between 2002 and 2003 180 Mongolian trainees and students received education in China, while only 15 Chinese trainees went to study in Mongolia (Ministry of Foreign Affairs of the PRC 2010). This educational cooperation has been drastically reinforced during the 2000s. In 2008, a Confucius Institute, the Chinese official language institution, was established at the National University of Mongolia. Tellingly, this was announced in one Mongolian newspaper with the headline 'Confucius Institute Aims to Change Famously Frosty Attitudes' (Tucker 2008). In 2009, an aggressive promotion of Chinese culture in Mongolia with the aim to 'charm Mongolia with its soft power by training large numbers of Mongolian students and teachers of the Chinese language' was reported (Bulag 2010: 102). On a visit to Ulaanbaatar in 2010, Premier Wen Jiabao announced an additional 2,000 government scholarships for Mongolian students during the following five years and invited 300 youths from Mongolia to visit China. He also initiated the establishment of youth exchange mechanisms (Sumiyabazar 2010). Given that Mongolia's total population amounts to less than three million, the extent of this educational programme is rather exceptional and observers have linked these efforts directly to the attempt to 'oil bilateral economic cooperation, especially in the mining sector' (Bulag 2010: 102).

Finally, in order to improve China's image among Mongolians, the Chinese government has specifically addressed the Mongolian educational elites as a link to the broader society. The Chinese Academy of Social Sciences, a leading Chinese think tank connected to the Chinese Ministry of Foreign Affairs, has established a joint Chinese-Mongolian research project to jointly re-write Mongolia's political history between 1911 and 1990. I was told researchers would work hard to arrange history and to reach consensus on disputed issues.[6]

Summary

To conclude this section, three observations should be emphasized. Firstly, the Chinese government makes efforts to maintain good state-to-state and party-to-party relations. It invests in ties with both Mongolian policymakers in their function as members of the parliament or the cabinet and the Mongolian parties, regardless of whether they are in power or in opposition. The Chinese government has also tried to reach out to the Mongolian armed forces. However, the military does not play an independent role in the Mongolian winning coalition and the Chinese donations to the Mongolian armed forces can plausibly be understood as a confidence-building measure to improve the security situation with a neighbour with which China shares a rather long border.

Secondly, many of the Mongolian oligarchs who have entered politics during the 2000s are knowingly corrupt. These politicians represent not only the Mongolian population, but also their private business interests and, therefore, abuse of political positions for profit-seeking is common. However, the extent to which this is a gateway for manipulation from China is difficult to assess.

Finally, the majority of voters formed part of the winning coalition and these domestic incentives had consequences for Chinese-Mongolian relations and the interaction between Chinese and Mongolian actors. On the one hand, Mongolian politicians tried to use public opinion and, specifically, the common anti-Chinese feelings of the population for their own power politics. Political actors repeatedly played the 'China card' to discredit political opponents.

On the other hand, Chinese actors reacted and adapted to Mongolia's political economy. The Chinese government well understood the democratic mechanisms in Mongolian politics and its implications in terms of incentives for Mongolian decision-makers. Accordingly, the Chinese government addressed both the decision-makers and, to a lesser extent, the electorate. Individual decision-makers were addressed directly through state-to-state and party-to-party relations, most likely also involving business collaborations and corruption. The Mongolian public, the electorate, was also directly and indirectly targeted. The Chinese government has specifically addressed the Mongolian population as an important member of the winning coalition with philanthropic programmes to show its goodwill and to improve China's reputation among ordinary Mongolians. These efforts have been related to China's difficulties in securing access to Mongolia's large-scale mining. However, the Mongolian public was also collectively punished by sanctions when its government officially received the Dalai Lama. Both will be discussed in Chapter 7.

Targeting the very root of Mongolian Sino-phobia, the Chinese government even attempted to improve its standing in the Mongolian public with the help of Mongolian historians by changing historical narratives. The intention of all these attempts was to reduce voters' sensitivity and fear of China and Chinese engagement, thereby increasing the space to manoeuvre for Mongolian leaders to respond to Chinese interests.

Finally, with respect to Mongolia's domestic stability, it is difficult to assess whether the increased Chinese interests affected the quality of Mongolia's democratic institutions. Even though Chinese companies were frequently accused of bribing Mongolian politicians, many Mongolians perceived corruption as a home-grown problem. Similarly, the various conspiracy theories around the violent riots in the aftermath of the 2008 elections, the astonishingly slow and reluctant attempts to investigate the incident and the refusal of any political party or figure to take political responsibility, raised additional questions about the political culture in Mongolia.

Notes

1   The three major parties emerging from the democracy movement in 1989 as the new political forces were the Mongolian Democratic Party, the Mongolian National Progress Party and the Mongolian Social Democratic Party. There have been several alliances, coalitions and mergers as well as splits and break offs between them and other minor parties since 1989. Only in 2004 was the DP found to be a major and durable merger, embracing 'the whole spectrum of the democracy movement' (Prohl and Sumati 2008: 28).

2   Private Source, Ulaanbaatar, 25 September 2008.

3   Private Source, Ulaanbaatar, 9 October 2009.
4   Private Source, Ulaanbaatar, 6 October 2008; 14 October 2009.
5   Private Source, Ulaanbaatar, 12 October 2009.
6   Private Source, Beijing, 31 October 2009.

7   Does China realize its interests?

This chapter compares how successful China has been in realizing its foreign objectives in the three case study countries by comparing their compliance with each of the three Chinese interests. After discussing the countries' compliance with the 'one China' policy, with providing access to natural resources to Chinese companies, and with China's geopolitical interests, the chapter draws a comparative conclusion. It finds that compliance is, indeed, connected to coalition size. The two authoritarian small-coalition governments in Burma and Cambodia are more compliant with China's interests than the more inclusive, more democratic government in Mongolia. Recall that while the investigation principally considers the post-Cold War period until the end of 2012, the focus for Burma lies on the period up to the end of 2010. Until then, Burma's domestic reforms had little effect on its domestic politics and, consequently, on its compliance with Chinese interests. However, the finding of Chapter 4 that Burma's leaders have become more responsive to domestic anti-Chinese sentiments and have challenged Chinese projects in the country after 2010, are actually much in line with the overall argument.

After discussing a number of alternative explanations for these findings, the chapter reflects on the scope conditions of the theory and the generalizability of the presented findings. The chapter then proceeds with a comparison of the observed foreign policy behaviour of China across the three cases and provides a detailed reflection on the patterns of China's foreign relations. Finally, the case study investigation concludes with some critical reflections on the theoretical framework.

The 'one China' policy

The comparison starts with the 'one China' policy; thus, as elaborated in Chapter 3, it focuses exclusively on the Taiwan question and Tibet. Recall the three ideal types on the spectrum of compliance: a country at the refusal end of the spectrum outrightly rejects the 'one China' policy by diplomatically recognizing Taiwan. The eager reaction, in contrast, does not even unofficially deal with Taiwan and proactively promotes the Chinese cause at an international level. The middle position, the reluctant reaction, recognizes the PRC, while at the same time pragmatically maintaining unofficial relations with Taiwan.

As to a country's dealings with the Dalai Lama, reactions are interpreted similarly with regard to their location on the spectrum of compliance: refusal corresponds to outright rejection, for example by actively seeking contact with the Dalai Lama – even when representing offical state functions. The eager position, on the other end of the spectrum, rejects contact with the Dalai Lama as a matter of principle, and hence may also include the denial of an entry visa to the country. The reluctant reaction is a pragamatic middle position that tries to depoliticize interaction with the Dalai Lama by emphasizing the unofficial nature of such interaction.

Burma

On both issues concerning the territorial integrity of the PRC, the government of Burma accommodates China's interests, repeatedly reiterates its adherence to the 'one China' policy and indicates eagerness to comply with the 'one China' policy.

The government of Burma has no official diplomatic relations with Taipei and, in 2000, it even closed down the offices of Taiwan's unofficial representation, despite strong business ties and an estimated 100,000 Taiwanese citizens of Burmese origin. The fact that a new trade agreement between the Taiwanese and the Burmese government was signed in 2009 did not cause the junta to rethink this decision, but the Taiwanese presence was said to continue underground in the form of informal trade offices and Chinese temples (Moe 2010b). In late 2012, the Taiwan and Myanmar Economic and Trade Cooperation Association was launched in order to facilitate economic relations; but, at the time of writing no Taiwanese representation had been re-established in Burma (Taipei Economic and Cultural Representative Office 2012; Embassypages.com 2013).

Similarly, the Dalai Lama has never visited the country. Theravada Buddhism is prevalent in Burma and the Burmese government has made use of Buddhism to strengthen its own grip on power and to dominate minorities, especially Islamic groups. Interestingly, the Chinese government facilitated the tours of the Tooth of the Buddha Relic from Beijing to Burma in the 1990s, which were 'enthusiastically welcomed by the masses' and served to increase the legitimacy of the government by demonstrating its religiosity (Tin 2003; Chenyang and Fook 2009). Similarly, the generals supported the Fourth World Buddhist Summit, held in Burma in 2004, as a means of increasing their legitimacy and promoting tourism (AsiaNews.it 2004).

As the form of Buddhism prevalent in Burma differs from Tibetan Buddhism, which the Dalai Lama represents, it is not meaningful that the Dalai Lama did not participate in the Fourth World Buddhist Summit in 2004. Hence, his absence does not necessarily imply that he was not allowed to participate. Even if he had been denied participation, however, it would be difficult to establish that this only happened in consideration of the wish of China: the Dalai Lama had earlier lobbied for the release of pro-democracy activist Aung San Suu Kyi, and thus the generals had their own reasons for not allowing him to visit the country (Naing 2010).

However, to the extent that the Dalai Lama was banned from appearing in Burma's state-controlled media, the government of Burma adhered to a very strict interpretation of the 'one China' policy. For this reason, observers interpreted it as an expression of protest against the Chinese when Burma's state media released an article about the Dalai Lama's visit to Taiwan in 2009. This was the first time in two decades that the Dalai Lama appeared in the state media; and this at a time when ties between oppressed monks in Tibet and Burma had become ever closer through mutual statements of solidarity following the suppression of protests in both countries (Naing 2008). Given the timing of the press release in the aftermath of a military operation against one of the ethnic minorities in the border area to China, the publication was interpreted as a message towards the Chinese expressing disagreement with the Chinese reluctance to stop support to ethnic rebel groups along the Chinese border (Jagan 2009).

To conclude, with regard to the Dalai Lama, it is difficult to assess the degree of the Burmese compliance as the junta's self-interest converged with the Chinese request to marginalize the Dalai Lama. However, it seems fair to say that their dealings with the Dalai Lama appeared to be at least partly driven by political considerations with regard to their relations to the Chinese government. Together with the fact that there was no Taiwanese representation office in Burma, the military junta's adherence to the Chinese 'one China' policy was very strict.

Cambodia

In both areas concerning the territorial integrity of the PRC, Cambodia's government pursues a pro-Chinese approach that goes beyond Chinese expectations and thus eagerly complies with Chinese interests.

Taiwan and Cambodia never had diplomatic relations. In early 1999, the Taiwanese representative office in Phnom Penh was closed by Prime Minister Hun Sen. Since then, he has always expressed his support for the Chinese Taiwan policy; he vocally supported the Chinese anti-secession law in 2005 (Storey 2006) and, in 2007, the Cambodian government condemned Taiwan's bid to join the UN. Domestically, the Cambodian government actively undermined Taiwanese statehood through Cambodian administrative regulations. These prevented Cambodian officials from travelling to Taiwan on their diplomatic passports and required Taiwanese migrants to present official Chinese documents (Mengin 2007). According to a high-ranking Cambodian official, this latter policy was designed to undermine Taiwanese statehood and was not intended as a mere measure against human trafficking of Cambodian women to Taiwanese brothels, which is the way it is perceived by many Cambodians.[1]

Most importantly, Cambodia's dealings with Taiwan have a domestic component and they give a vivid example of how leaders trade policy concessions for external support against domestic opponents. In 1997, an armed conflict evolved in Phnom Penh between two rival factions, the royalists led by Prince Norodom Ranariddh and the former Vietnamese-backed Communist Party under Hun Sen. Both parties had formed a coalition government, even though the first parliamentary elections in 1993 were won by the royalists (Roberts 2002). Against this background, the royalist FUNCINPEC party welcomed investments from Taiwan to improve their financial situation. These links to Taiwan, it was argued later by Hun Sen, had been used to re-arm the royalists in order to challenge the dominance of Hun Sen. He therefore closed down the Taiwanese representation (Peou 2000). By doing so, he aimed at cutting external support to his domestic competitor; at the same time, this allowed him to overcome the historical division that existed between himself and the Chinese because of his Vietnamese connections (Marks 2000). In 1999, he received one of the highest foreign assistance guarantees and interest-free loans given by China at that time (Marks 2000; Cock 2010b).

Hun Sen rejected an attempt to re-open a Taiwanese representation in 2008 with explicit reference to the 'one China' policy. He was quoted as saying: 'Don't dream of reopening Taiwan's representative office in Cambodia while I am in power' (Xinhua 2008b). A Taiwanese representation in Cambodia would have facilitated Taiwanese investments in the country, creating much-needed jobs; it would also have legalized the status of several hundred Cambodian women who had been trafficked to Taiwan (Xinhua 2008b, 2008c). In addition to securing support for the 'one China' policy with Cambodia's leadership, China has also sought to shape public opinion in Cambodia on this issue. In a private talk with a newspaper journalist from one of Cambodia's Chinese-language newspapers, the journalist acknowledged that newspapers were coerced into not reporting on the Taiwan issue in a way that diverged from the Chinese position. The Chinese threatened to mobilize Cambodia's Chinese communities by encouraging them to withdraw their newspaper advertisements in this case.

In sum, China's interest in isolating Taiwan clearly coincided with Hun Sen's interest in weakening the links between his domestic opponents and their Taiwanese financiers during the 1990s. However, today, these domestic opponents are marginalized. Hun Sen's self-interested power considerations cannot, therefore, fully explain his recent rejection of resuming unofficial relations with Taiwan.

Cambodia's dealings with the Dalai Lama are similarly rigorous: despite Buddhism being the state religion, the Dalai Lama has never been allowed to visit Cambodia. Similar to Burma, the form of Buddhism that is dominant in Cambodia is Theravada Buddhism, which differs from the Tibetan Buddhism of which the Dalai Lama is the spiritual leader. Nevertheless, there is convincing empirical evidence that Cambodian authorities have prevented him from visiting the country in order to please China. In the context of the World Buddhism Conference, which took place in Phnom Penh in 2002, Religion Ministry secretary Chhorn Iem reportedly said that the Dalai Lama was still not welcome in Cambodia because of China's strong views on the subject. According to him, the Dalai Lama had not asked for entry to Cambodia as 'the policy was made clear'. But, with reference to the 'one China' policy, he explained: "We could not welcome him here even if he asked because Cambodia must implement the government's policy", Iem said. "Cambodia follows the One China Policy."

Interestingly, the same official also regretted this position and expressed admiration for the Dalai Lama. 'However, he said he could not predict the future, and Cambodia remained hopeful that someday political obstacles would no longer stand in the way of a visit by one of the world's most venerable Buddhists' (World Wide Religious News 2007). Hence, Cambodia's policy of treating the Dalai Lama as persona non grata is clearly motivated by the desire to comply with China's foreign policy interests.

Mongolia

With respect to both the Taiwan question and the Dalai Lama, Mongolian politicians have only been partially compliant with Chinese interests, despite the government's regular assurances that it will adhere to the 'one China' principle.

Mongolia's dealings with Taiwan are 'reluctantly' compliant, although for reasons partly unrelated to the PRC. It is a historic legacy of Taiwan's establishment as a nation dating back to the Chinese civil war that, according to the Taiwanese constitution, Mongolia forms part of the Republic of China, Taiwan. Consequently, the Taiwanese government vetoed Mongolia's accession as a member of the UN in the 1950s and 1960s. Under these circumstances, it would be odd to expect a Mongolian government to recognize Taiwan diplomatically; instead, one would predict that Mongolia would reject any relations with Taiwan. However, this is not the case.

In 2002, Taiwan upgraded Mongolia's status by acknowledging Mongolians to be entitled to visas, instead of entry permits (*The China Post* 2002). In the same year, a Taiwanese trade representative office was established in Ulaanbaatar; a Mongolian representation in Taipei followed in 2003 (Campi 2004). In 2004, bilateral trade between the two countries had risen from close to non-existent to around US$5 million per year. Taiwan has also evolved into a migration destination for Mongolians. With its relations to Taiwan becoming more rather than less formalized during the last decade, Mongolia's compliance with the 'one China' policy with regard to the Taiwan question is reluctant.

This reluctance to comply with China's interests is also evident with respect to the Dalai Lama, but its dealing with the Dalai Lama is much more complicated than the Taiwan question. The Dalai Lama has visited Mongolia eight times since 1979, three times after 2000 when China's rise had become more manifest (Chung 2009; Dalailama.com 2013). In reaction to the Dalai Lama's 2002 visit, when he was received by Mongolian politicians, the Chinese government closed cross-border train traffic for several days under the pretext of technical problems. As this border closure led to an immediate increase in prices in Mongolia, it could be understood as a collective punishment with the clear intention of letting Mongolians feel China's economic leverage over the country. From the perspective of the voter, it could be read as a call to abandon religious and spiritual practices and values in favour of economic well-being.

During his visit in 2006, the Dalai Lama was not received officially by government representatives, but most likely met the president in private (Sumiyabazar

2006). Although there was no state reception, the Chinese government subsequently suspended a high-ranking diplomatic meeting between both nations (Mashbat 2007). Finally, during his most recent visit to Mongolia in 2011, the Dalai Lama met President Tsakhiagiin Elbegdorj, a meeting to which he referred in a letter when he congratulated Elbegdorj on his re-election in 2013 (Dalailama.com 2013).

Mongolia's reluctant position with regard to the Dalai Lama is underlined by the role Buddhism plays in Mongolia's culture and national identity. Buddhism has enjoyed a resurgence after a period of suppression under socialism. Moreover, there are close historical links between Buddhism in Tibet and Buddhism in Mongolia, as both follow a Lamaist tradition. The Dalai Lama is the religious authority for Mongolian Buddhists. For these reasons, China's request to repudiate the Dalai Lama forces Mongolian leaders to choose between a policy pleasing their own winning coalition and selectorate and one that is beneficial to the Chinese leadership, but is opposed by the majority of Mongolians. For this reason, Mongolian leaders were only partly willing to comply with this interest of the Chinese government.

The Dalai Lama issue illustrates how the Chinese government has successfully used its economic leverage to restrict the Mongolian government's policy options. However, it has by no means achieved a complete submission of the Mongolian government and it is also very unlikely to be successful in the future. The Dalai Lama issue will likely remain a stumbling block and, depending on where the next Dalai Lama will reincarnate, it could become even more delicate in the future.[2] Therefore, the Mongolian position on this issue on the compliance spectrum is classified as reluctant.

Summary

The comparison of compliance with the 'one China' policy reveals some divergence between the three different countries with regard to how they handle this Chinese foreign policy objective. The small-coalition governments in Burma and Cambodia are both considered eager compliants; Mongolia's large-coalition government, in contrast, has reacted reluctantly to the Dalai Lama and the Taiwan question.

The Burmese government was the first country to diplomatically recognize the PRC. In 2000, it closed the unofficial Taiwanese representation in Burma, although trade relations between the two countries continue to flourish. With respect to the Dalai Lama, the Burmese junta has completely ignored him and never allowed him to pay a visit to the country. It has even banned him from the state media for reasons of loyalty to the Chinese government. This corresponds to an eagerness to support China's 'one China' policy.

Regarding the Taiwan question, Cambodia vocally supports the PRC as the only legitimate Chinese state. There is no official Taiwanese representation office in Phnom Penh, despite significant foreign investments from Taiwan, but the Cambodian government also seeks to undermine Taiwanese statehood with its domestic regulations concerning the treatment of Taiwanese nationals living in Cambodia. In addition, the government has never allowed the Dalai Lama to visit the country. Both policies correspond to an eager response to Chinese interests.

With respect to the status of Taiwan, Mongolia recognized the PRC as the only Chinese state, but it enjoyed active relations with Taiwan, and unofficial representations have been established in both of the countries in recent years. Against the background of Mongolian Lamaism and a broad sympathy for the Dalai Lama among the population, the Dalai Lama has visited Mongolia several times. His Holiness was even received by the Mongolian government in 2002, which caused serious reactions on the part of the Chinese authorities. The Mongolian government did not, however, oppose a renewed visit in 2006, although it then stressed the apolitical nature of the Dalai Lama's visit. This position corresponded to a reluctant compliance with Chinese interests.

Access to natural resources

The second Chinese foreign interest to be compared is China's access to natural resources in each of the three case-study countries. When comparing how successful Chinese companies have been in achieving access to natural resources, the responses translate in the following way to ideal type positions on the spectrum of compliance: a response at the refusal end of the spectrum rejects the Chinese by either marginalizing or even fending off Chinese attempts to gain access to natural resources. The opposite position at the eager end of the spectrum would treat Chinese interests preferentially, and ease heavy Chinese investments in the resource sector. The reluctant middle position neither discriminates against, nor favours Chinese interests, but treats Chinese investors equally to any others.

Burma

China has been very successful in extracting resources from Burma in exchange for crucial support for the leaders and their winning coalition in Burma. Burma's oil and gas sectors not only illustrate vividly how the exploitation of natural resources in autocracies translates into private revenues that can be redistributed among the members of the winning coalition, they also show how external players try to make use of this mechanism and how mutually beneficial policies are exchanged between the leaders in both small winning coalitions in China and Burma.

Burma's gas fields are the second largest in Southeast Asia. The interest of all its neighbours in exploiting these gas fields is so high that the situation has been described as an 'intense bidding war' between Thailand, India and China (Zhao 2007: ii). Investments in Burma's oil and natural gas sectors from abroad more than tripled from 2006 to 2007. In 2010, it even represented 100 per cent of all officially decleared FDI (Turnell 2011). The struggle over access to Burmese gas is often described as a competition between India and China, even though investors from South Korea, Thailand, Singapore, France, the US and Malaysia are also operating in this sector. The South Korean company Daewoo seems to play a key role.

In this respect, it seems that Chinese companies gained privileged access to the Burmese reserves. Observers contend that the Burmese government has granted China privileges in the exploitation of its oil and gas reserves against the infrastructure investments of Chinese companies, especially in Burma's hydropower sector (Guo 2007; International Crisis Group 2009). They do not, however, provide more detailed evidence of this claim. In 2001, Chinese and Burmese authorities signed a Memorandum of Understanding to encourage scientific research institutions and enterprises in geology and mineral resources and to establish and conduct cooperation to promote investments on exploration, mining and utilization of mineral resources (Liu 2001).

Both Chinese and Indian companies are involved in joint gas exploitation with the Burmese. However, initially, it was a Korean-Indian joint venture that started offshore gas exploration in Burma's Shwe fields in 2001. India was planning to export the extracted gas through a pipeline via Bangladesh to India, but it faced difficulties in reaching an agreement with the Bangladeshi government. Determined to increase its energy security, the Indian government was prepared to construct a much longer, more expensive alternative pipeline (Lall 2006). To the surprise of the Indian government, however, the Burmese junta swiftly decided to sign an export Memorandum of Understanding with PetroChina instead, when it became clear that the Bangladesh pipeline would most likely not be realized. Gas exploited by the Korean-Indian consortium is, therefore, going to be exported to China's city of Kunming via a pipeline, the construction of which started in late 2009 (Zhao 2007; Seekins 2010). After the pipeline has been completed in 2013, China is expected to become Burma's largest gas consumer (International Crisis Group 2010b).

Not only has China prevailed over India as an end-consumer for Burmese gas, but Chinese companies have also succeeded in buying exploration rights to seven blocks, covering an area of over 9.58 million hectares, thereby crowding-out Indian bidders. In 2006, the Korean-Indian consortium announced that they had found a huge gas field (Lall 2006). Although China was not involved in the exploitation of gas in the early stages, it later seemed to be winning exploitation concessions over India. In 2007, for instance, even though it was outbid by an Indian competitor, China was rewarded with a major oil and gas concession (Kleine-Ahlbrandt and Small 2008). Moreover, while China could increase its stakes, the Burmese authorities enforced a contractual provision to reduce the stakes of two Indian shareholders, ONGC Videsh and GAIL – from 20 per cent to 17 per cent, and from 10 per cent to 8 per cent, respectively – in two Shwe blocks in order to increase the shareholdings of the state-owned Myanmar Oil and Gas Enterprise in 2008 (60 per cent of the shares in this field is held by South Korean Daewoo) (The Shwe Gas Movement 2010).

It is striking that the major oil concession that Chinese companies received in 2007 was rewarded to China just three days after China had vetoed a UN resolution on sanctions on Burma (Kleine-Ahlbrandt and Small 2008). This vividly illustrates the logic of political survival: it appears that the Chinese government obtained these desired concessions in the oil and gas sector in exchange for its protection of the Burmese military regime at the international level. It is note-worthy, though, that the Chinese UN veto might not even have been vital to the junta's survival, because Russia vetoed the resolution too.

In addition to these disputed fields, Chinese companies now hold a range of concessions in deep-sea and onshore gas blocks. Until early 2010, Chinese invest-ment accounted for US$1.8 billion, or 11.5 per cent of Burma's total FDI (Burma News International 2010). In 2010, Chinese companies, with more than US$8 billion of investments in Burma's hydropower and oil and gas sectors, further strengthened their grip on the Burmese energy sector.

In a nutshell, it appears that Chinese companies have secured privileged access to Burma's natural resources. Not only, but also because the Chinese government was able to shield the Burmese central government from external intervention, Chinese SOEs could prevail over other international competitors in the gas and oil sector. On the other hand, as elaborated in the previous case study, local Chinese authorities in China's Southern provinces have heavily capitalized on a power vacuum between competing Burmese authorities at the central and provin-cial level in order to gain access to Burma's natural resources. China's investors have thus profited from arrangements made under the incumbent small winning coalition in the country, which evolved in the course of Burma's post-colonial history. The heavy Chinese investments connected to the exploitation of these resources in Burma create a very strong incentive for maintaining the status quo in the distribution of power.

Cambodia

Cambodian NGOs and civil society have frequently criticized the way in which Cambodian elites continue to give away the nation's wealth. During the 1980s, illicit timber and gem trade (mostly with the Thais) financed the resistance against the Vietamese-backed State of Cambodia. However, deforestation has increased since 2000 in comparison to the previous decade (Food and Agriculture Organization of the United Nations 2005). In addition to timber, Cambodia's leaders have found alternative resources for exploitation and they have now captured the country's natural resources in the mining, oil and gas sectors. In 2006, US$403 million of investment in the mining sector was approved by the CDC, a one-stop agency for investments directly under the control of the prime minister (Global Witness 2009b). And Cambodia's total fossil fuel reserves have been estimated as high as 2 billion barrels of oil and 10 trillion cubic feet of natu-ral gas, although these estimates are being contested (Crispin 2007).

The oil and gas sector exemplify the discretionary mechanisms for redistribut-ing the nation's wealth by a small coalition. In this sector, the requirement for public oversight over the distribution of concessions, laid down in the 1991 Petroleum Regulation, has been systematically circumvented ever since the late 1990s. In conflict with existing law, the Cambodian National Petroleum Authority was established by royal decree in 1998. It put the process of distributing oil concessions directly under the control of the prime minister (Cock 2010b; Burgos and Ear 2010). Furthermore, the set-up of the Cambodian National Petroleum Authority proved to be highly dysfunctional due to internal divisions and disrupted flows of information: 'only a handful of individuals at the top of the Cambodian government have any knowledge, or involvement in, the negotiation of contracts signed with petroleum companies' (Global Witness 2009b: 41). Moreover, it is widely acknowledged that the distribution of concessions comes with 'signature bonuses', which are left out of Cambodia's official government revenue statistics (Global Witness 2009b: 49). As a result, the distribution of exploration concessions seems to be at the discretion of the leading coalition with de facto no checks and balances in place (Cock 2010b).

> In March 2002, the CNPA [Cambodian National Petroleum Authority] awarded offshore Block A to a subsidiary of U.S. oil company Chevron and its partners. Since that point, the CNPA appears to have allocated all remaining oil blocks to other petroleum companies of varying degrees of experience. None of this information has come into the public domain directly from the CNPA. Instead it has leaked out in dribs and drabs via oil companies, the media and government power-point presentations that have been posted online by other organisations.
>
> (Global Witness 2009b: 42)

Just as the small ruling elite has maximized its control over whatever assets the country does possess, the CPP has ensured that it has a handle on the resources that flow into the country. All larger foreign investments need the approval of the CDC. Furthermore, Cambodian land law does not allow non-nationals to acquire land and, therefore, stimulates the inclusion of a Cambodian partner. However, because of high corruption and weak rule of law, it seems advisable anyway to engage a domestic partner for investments. Only foreign investors that are ready to accept this investment environment can successfully operate in Cambodia.

The CDC statistics, according to which the volume of investments from mainland China since 2004 exceed the foreign investment from other nations, suggest that the Chinese are more successful than other foreign investors. Of course, due to the intransparency around such deals, it remains difficult to judge whether Chinese companies in fact receive preferential treatment over other investors in Cambodia.

Anecdotal evidence indicates that Chinese companies are involved in all kinds of raw material exploitation for export from Cambodia, whether it is timber or minerals, in the agri-business or energy sector. Many of these companies have violated Cambodian law. Various examples of dubious Chinese joint ventures in the resource sector suggest the tight collaboration between foreign investors and the members of the Cambodian winning coalition. For instance, the Chinese state news agency, Xinhua, reported that Pheapimex, mentioned in Chapter 5, was one of two Cambodian companies in a joint venture with the Chinese SOE China

National Machinery & Equipment Import & Export Corporation, which started collaboration in an iron ore mine in 2005. Hun Sen was cited as having given his full support. According to the NGO Global Witness, the mine was guarded by military personnel and belonged to the commander-in-chief of the RCAF and chief joint staff. The mine was later transferred to a South Korean mining company (Global Witness 2009b). In 2007, it was announced that four Chinese state-owned steelmakers were setting up a joint venture to explore and develop other iron ore mines in Cambodia (Kurtenbach 2007). One joint venture received publicity because the unnamed Chinese company, in collaboration with the commander of the RCAF infantry forces and the head of Cambodia's military development zones, was accused of holding concession rights in a controversial chromium mine that conflicted with Cambodian environmental law because of its location in the national reserve of Phnom Samkos Wildlife Sanctuary (Global Witness 2009b: 27). Another unnamed Chinese-owned company together with Malaysian and Korean companies was reported to be involved in sand shipping from Cambodia to Singapore for use in land reclamation. The overall operation was allegedly controlled by a well-known CPP Senator and tycoon (Global Witness 2009b: 31).

According to Chinese import statistics, exports of plywood and sawn wood from Cambodia to China totalled US$50 million between 2003 and 2007 alone. It is not clear whether Chinese companies are only the buyers of these woods or whether they were also involved in logging. Since this trade does not appear in Cambodian export statistics, for the period from 2003 to 2006 alone it translated as an estimated loss of tax revenue for the state of Cambodia of US$4.5 million (Global Witness 2007).

Lastly, in the oil sector, a number of Chinese companies succeeded in obtaining concessions for at least three out of six exploration blocks. Two blocks were entirely in Chinese hands: according to a report by Chinese news agency, Xinhua, Chinese National Offshore Oil Corp signed a contract for off-shore oil and gas exploration of Block F in 2007 (Xinhua Economic News 2007; Cock 2010b). Another block, Block C, is owned 100 per cent by a company named Polytec Asset Holdings Limited, a company incorporated in the Caymans and headquartered in Hong Kong. With its core business in property, ice, frozen products, finance and investment, it has no expertise in oil and gas exploration. The company's executive director, who also owns 59.5 per cent of the company's shares, is one of Hong Kong's richest men. As a member of the Chinese People's Political Consultative Conference, he is linked to the CCP, or, at least, he is a target of the CCP's co-optation efforts and thus most likely a member of the Chinese winning coalition (Global Witness 2009b). The third block with Chinese involvement, Block D, is held by an oil software services firm from Singapore, together with a mysterious Cambodian-registered company. This second firm is 'part-owned by another unknown company, a Chinese investment company and a Chinese state-owned crude oil import company' (Global Witness 2009b: 47).

In conclusion, the empirical evidence suggests that Chinese companies have been quite successful when it comes to the exploitation of Cambodian raw materials – even though they are by no means the only ones to exploit Cambodia's natural resources. However, the strong involvement in the oil sector, where Chinese companies have stakes in three out of six exploration blocks, together with the fact that some beneficiaries lack the necessary experience in the field, suggests that the decision on the part of the Cambodian government was based on criteria other than the suitability of these companies. It could well be that Chinese companies have gained preferential access to these resources. For this reason, I consider the Cambodian government as responding eagerly to the Chinese quest of gaining access to Cambodia's natural resources.

Mongolia

Mongolia's soil contains several of the world's largest deposits of minerals, such as coal, zinc, gold and copper. Neighbouring China is the largest market for such resources. Considering this complementarity, China has had major difficulties reaching its objective of acquiring access to natural resources in Mongolia. The analysis of Chinese involvement in the exploitation of Mongolian resources shows a seemingly contradictory picture. On the one hand, Chinese investors experienced much resistance to being included in the development of a few, albeit huge, resource deposits for which concessions have been allocated in recent years. On the other hand, many smaller sites are exploited directly or indirectly by Chinese investors with more or less legally valid concessions (Reeves 2011). Overall, however, this is consistent with selectorate theory, as it shows that the existence of democratic institutions and a large winning coalition limit the extent to which Mongolia's natural resources can be exploited by elites. At least with regard to the large resource deposits, the interest of the wider public must be taken into account. However, the weakness of the Mongolian state also allows Mongolian decision-makers to benefit from a trade in exploitation licences in cases that are less in the public eye.

Due to its landlocked position, Mongolia's economy is dominated by its two neighbours. Mongolia's only access to the north pacific is through the Chinese port of Tianjin, which has been leased from the PRC since 1991. Reaching Tianjin, however, requires transportation through more than 1,000 kilometres of foreign territory. While trade with Russia decreased from 80 per cent to approximately 25 per cent from 1990 to 2001, China's trade with Mongolia increased steadily (Campi 2004). Even though Russian and Chinese exports to Mongolia each accounted for roughly 30 per cent of total Mongolian imports in 2010, Mongolia's trade is characterized by strong imbalances that create dependencies. For example, 80 per cent of Mongolia's energy needs are met by Russian imports. At the same time, in 2010, 85 per cent of Mongolia's total exports, or US$1.4 billion, most of them metals and ores, went to China (Ministry of Economic Development 2013; Reeves 2013).

Mongolia's economy does not only depend on its two neighbours for its trade; China is also the biggest foreign investor in Mongolia, even though numbers on Chinese investments in Mongolia are controversial. In 1998, over US$24 million, or 64 per cent of the investment was reported to be supplied by Chinese firms (The Economist Intelligence Unit 1999: 55). This number apparently fell during the early 2000s, but thereafter it increased again. By 2010, Chinese investments had risen to 51 per cent of Mongolia's US$1.76 billion in FDI (Reeves 2013). The dominance of China in Mongolia's economy becomes apparent when contrasted with Mongolia's second and third largest sources of FDI, Canada and the Netherlands, which provide 6 per cent and 8 per cent, respectively (Reeves 2013). In order to prevent further dependence on Chinese investments, the Mongolian parliament revised its 1994 National Security Concept in 2011 and included a clause that limits FDI from any one state to Mongolia to a third (Reeves 2013).

Given the strong inroads that Chinese capital has made into the Mongolian economy, astonishingly little is known about these Chinese investments. In the mid 2000s, the majority of these investments was described to be small in scale, technologically poor and concentrated in the retail and gastronomic sectors (Batchimeg 2005b). The textile sector also attracted Chinese investments until 2005 because of export quotas to the US market (The Economist Intelligence Unit 2005a). In 2000, the construction of a Mongolian-Chinese industrial zinc venture was reported as the first large Mongolian-Chinese mining venture (The Economist Intelligence Unit 2000). A second major Chinese investment project, Heilonjiang Huafu Industrial's US$200 million oil refinery, followed in 2005 (The Economist Intelligence Unit 2005b). The number of Chinese-owned metal-lurgical plants in Ulaanbaatar increased from eight in mid-2006 to 40 by the end of 2006 (Batmonkh 2007).

If Chinese investment in Mongolia remains opaque, there seems to be consensus on the view that Mongolia's liberal economic reforms have promoted Chinese investments and interests in Mongolia. Radical liberalization during the 1990s deprived the Mongolian government of the means to protect domestic processing industries against competition from China where access to capital to buy inputs, such as raw cashmere for example, was generally better (The Economist Intelligence Unit 1996). 'The shock therapy proposed by these [international donor] agencies has actually facilitated Chinese leverage over the Mongolian economy' (Rossabi 2005a). Moreover, after the transition to market economy, Chinese exploitation of smaller mining sites has been spurred by officials at the provincial level who frequently use legal loopholes to award mining licences to Chinese investors (Reeves 2011).

Even though China de facto has gained considerable leverage over the Mongolian economy, the Chinese interest has been frustrated with regard to Mongolia's huge mining sites. Mongolia has a dozen major and many small-scale resource deposits. Because of their immense size, some of these deposits are expected to give the exploiting company some leverage over world market prices. Oyu Tolgoi, for example, is one of the world's largest copper (36 million tons) and gold (45.2 million ounces) mines and is located only about 80 kilometres from the border to China in South Gobi province. It was the first of Mongolia's enormous resource deposits to be developed. Tavan Tolgoi, another mining site, is the largest unexploited coke coal deposit in the world. Considering their proximity to the Chinese border, Chinese investors have faced considerable difficulties in gaining access to these sites.

The Mongolian government does not have the financial and technological capacity to exploit these natural resources and therefore needs international investors. A number of mining companies from Canada, Australia, the US, China and Russia are interested in these deposits. It is noteworthy that in order to develop these two sites, the construction of major transportation routes for export are needed. These are of strategic relevance in their own right as the length, route and gauge of the railway are expected to determine the competitiveness of Mongolian exports, the economic development of the country as a whole and the potential leverage of its neighbours over the Mongolian economy. Currently, there is only one railway line running through Mongolia from north to south, connecting Moscow with Beijing. This line has a Russian gauge, which is not compatible with the Chinese gauge.[3]

Among the government's considerations on how to develop these enormous mining sites, fears of overdependence on the Chinese market have been raised. During the 1990s, the Mongolian government 'deliberately' restricted Chinese investments in state industries including the mineral sector (Campi 2004). In 2003, Chinese President Hu Jintao openly stated the Chinese interest in investing in Mongolia's mining sector and offered a soft loan to improve infrastructure (Batchimeg 2005a), but the Mongolian government resisted pressure to quickly develop the area (Campi 2004).

The first investment agreement on the exploitation of Oyu Tolgoi with the Canadian mining company Ivanhoe took more than six years to set up; but, in 2009, despite numerous allegations of bribery, the agreement finally reached international standards. It is widely believed in Mongolian civil society that the whole process of reaching the Oyu Tolgoi agreement was delayed because of corruption and greed. Hiding behind the discussion on the state's role in exploration operations, members of parliament and the government were suspected of trying to increase their private gains in the investment deal. At the same time, it was argued that members of parliament were subject to manipulation and corruption from investors as everybody wanted 'to have something for making decision on behalf [of] their home country' (Baabar 2009).

While personal greed was very likely a motivation on the part of some of the Mongolian officials to delay the whole process, other observers directly linked the messy state of decision-making in Mongolia to the interests of its two giant neighbours. It was reasoned that protests against the initial and subsequent deals with Ivanhoe had been organized along with 'systematic steps' to scare off Western investors (Tsenddoo 2010). Accordingly, both China and Russia would gain most if Mongolia's resources were not exploited by Western companies. Chinese energy giants, such as Chinalco and Zijin Mining, had certainly been interested in the Oyu Tolgoi project in 2002, but their government-supported bids fell apart when faced with political opposition in Mongolia (Narangoa 2012a). Indeed, Western investors seemed to become less attracted to investing in Mongolia. In the context of Mongolian considerations to amend the mining law, and faced with several 'blackmail' protests, the North American Mongolian Business Council, alarmed, submitted a letter to the Chairmen of the Mongolian Security Council pointing to the lack of security and rule of law for investments in the mining sector. In July 2010, Mongolia was rated the world's least attractive jurisdiction for mineral exploration and development by the Fraser Survey (Shinebayar 2010). However, given the enormous economic interests at stake on all sides, it is difficult to substantiate whether Russian or Chinese actors truly tried to influence the process or whether Western investors simply tried to play the 'China card' to make Mongolia's decision-makers speed up the process.

In any event, decisions taken with regard to Tavan Tolgoi were equally frustrating for China. Tavan Tolgoi is located only approximately 180 kilometres from the Chinese border in South Gobi province and the Chinese government has proposed investing in a second trans-Siberian line with narrow gauge, as used in China. In 2010, it also promised a US$300 million loan for infrastructure at the border where both gauges meet (Mendee 2010). However, later that year, the Mongolian parliament, with an eye on opening up alternative markets in South Korea and Japan for Mongolia's coke coal, instead approved plans to build 5,000 kilometres of new railways to connect the existing railway network with Russian gauge to the Russian ports of Vanino and Vostochnyi (Mongolian Mining Journal 2009; The Economist Intelligence Unit 2010). Consequently, the time-consuming and costly procedure of changing carriages at the border to China will be maintained and coal exports continue to rely on truck transports. Moreover, China's inclusion in the exploitation of this coal deposit experienced several serious setbacks. Even though Shenhua Group, a Chinese coal company, initially won 40 per cent of the Tavan Tolgoi tender, this decision was later revised (Narangoa 2012a) and, in 2012, China's Chalco was blocked from acquiring a stake in the Tavan Tolgoi mine by parliamentary legislation limiting state-owned companies from investing in Mongolia's strategic mineral deposits (Reeves 2013).

Given the deliberate attempts to prevent Chinese investments in Mongolia, it appears that the Mongolian strategy to develop its natural resource deposits is, at best, one of reluctant compliance with China. In its strategic thinking, the Mongolian government is hesitant when it comes to allocating major mining concessions to Chinese companies. Indeed, for the sake of the national interest, it prefers a position at the refusal end of the compliance spectrum. This becomes most apparent when fears of overdependence on the Chinese market and the limited willingness of Chinese investors to process these resources in Mongolia are raised. It even led the Mongolian government to reject Chinese offers to improve transportation networks to the mining areas, even though infrastructure is badly needed in the country. However, Mongolia finds itself de facto located in a reluctant position, rather than at the refusal end of the spectrum. The strategic attempt to protect Mongolia's economy from further domination by China is at odds with the country's landlocked position and its weak capacity to implement the central government's policies and the widespread practice of collaboration with Chinese investors at the local level. Mongolians cannot ignore the fact that the country's geographic position limits their room for strategic maneouvre, while porous borders, corrupt customs services and bribery of local officials are a reality.

However, one caveat is in place here. While it seems obvious that the Mongolian reaction to China's interest is one of reluctance, it is less evident whether this necessarily stems from Mongolia's large winning coalition, or whether, instead, this is driven by other factors, such as the influence of other major powers, Mongolia's historical alliances during the Cold War, or the specifically anti-Chinese attitude among the population.

Some observers have argued that Mongolia's reluctance to the inclusion of China in the exploitation of its natural resources is primarily a consequence of strong Sino-phobia among the population, rather than its more inclusive political structure (Li 2011). Indeed, the widespread mistrust of China among the population certainly leads to a particularly critical attitude towards investments from China and makes it very difficult for Mongolia's leaders to present and defend decisions in favour of Chinese investors – even if they are, in fact, beneficial to the country. Moreover, in part, the assessment of the effect of Sino-phobia also hinges on the observer's belief as to what the best strategy is for turning Mongolia's resources into development for the whole country, which is a very complex question in itself. However, it can be argued, as Mendee points out in his blog, that Mongolia's recent decisions in the mining sector also reflect a response to a demand for more development-oriented policies, rather than mere Sino-phobia:

> Before making quick conclusions on either anti-Chinese attitudes or resource nationalism, there are other rationales forcing Mongolian politicians to make a unanimous decision to limit the investment of the foreign state-owned enterprises in key economic projects. Since 1990, Mongolian citizens have always been able to challenge the government's key political and economic decisions if it is against their will, livelihood, and future. This time, Mongolian people did not oppose the parliamentary decision of restricting Chinese investors because they want responsible and sustainable mining. [...] Like any other nations, reliant on the extractive industries, Mongolians also want to make more value out of their natural resources because they are not renewable. The establishment of short rail links with Chinese processing factories will benefit only a few mining companies, accelerate extraction process, and increase the Chinese reliance on low-cost coal from Mongolia.
>
> (Mendee 2012)

In addition, and closely connected to Mongolia's Sino-phobia, one could also object that Mongolia's reluctant reaction vis-à-vis the Chinese is a function of its Cold War alliance with the Soviet Union and a reflection of the prevalent interests of another major power in the country, i.e. Russia. It is, therefore, appropriate to take a closer look at Russia's role in Mongolia. While Russia's leverage over Mongolia declined dramatically during the first decade after the dissolution of the Soviet Union, the Russian government started to actively pursue its economic interests in Mongolia in the 2000s and re-emerged as a player in Mongolia. Russia retains some direct influence over the Mongolian economy via two Russian-Mongolian joint ventures that date back to pre-1989 times; namely, Erdenet, Mongolia's major copper mine in which Russia has a 49 per cent stake (Blagov 2005), and the Ulaanbaatar Railway, a 50-50 joint venture. Since the Ulaanbaatar Railway is Mongolia's main means of transportation, handling around 80 per cent of domestic and 100 per cent of export-import shipments, Russia's stakes mean that it retains some strategic leverage (Ooluun 2009b).

In recent years, the Russian government has explicitly used this leverage in order to protect its strategic interests in Mongolia's mining sector, thereby, putting the Mongolian government under considerable pressure. In 2009, for example, the Russian government used its 50 per cent share in Ulaanbaatar Railway to force the Mongolian government to cancel a US$188 million modernization programme for the Mongolian railway by the US Millennium Challenge Corporation (Sumiyabazar 2009). Instead, it promised to invest in Mongolia's transportation system, but on the condition that it receive shares in Mongolia's exploitation activities in Oyu Tolgoi and Tavan Tolgoi, or 'at least 25% of the profits', respectively (Yakunin as cited in *The UB Post* 2009a). Given the bankruptcy of the Russian Railway, Mongolians understand the nature of Russian interests as a blend of national security and large-scale private business, which are promoted by the Russian government 'by backing the interest of [Russia's] oligarchs and strengthening their support by means of raising its influence in Mongolian politics' (Ooluun 2009a).

It becomes clear that Russia still has some leverage over Mongolian politics, but is this the reason for Mongolia's reluctant compliance with Chinese interests? One can argue that while the discussion about *some* investors in Mongolia is very vivid, Russian investments are sometimes less questioned. For example, in a conversation, one staff member of a Mongolian strategic think tank considered it 'a very clever move' by the president to focus public attention on the Oyu Tolgoi agreement, while secretly negotiating with Russia over Mongolia's Madrai uranium fields.[4]

However, to the extent that the discussion on foreign investments in recent years has been triggered by civil society groups, NGOs and the population, it would be misleading to reduce Mongolia's reluctance to comply with Chinese interests to Russia's influence. Civil society actors are generally concerned with the environmental and developmental impact of resource extraction in Mongolia. Therefore, Mongolia's reluctance should instead be understood, at least in part, as government responsiveness to its domestic constituency, the voters. Despite the obvious corruption problem in Mongolian politics, and despite the fact that Mongolia's elites have frequently tried to benefit personally from investment deals, the Mongolian government has taken up and reacted to these public concerns. 'The irresponsible, careless mining of both foreign and domestic companies has caused public outrage, with calls to strengthen the mining regulations and make the license-issuance business transparent' (Mendee 2012). The resulting policies, such as Mongolia's commitment to the Extractive Industry

Transparency Initiative, the suspension and review of mining licences, or the issuing of shares to the Mongolian public, aim at preventing domestic corruption, at improving environmental standards, at spreading the profits to the whole population and at generally constraining illicit influence of external actors. These concerns are valid for all investors alike. 'The latest efforts to investigate corruption in the mining regulatory institutions, to suspend the issuance of mining licenses to foreign investors, and to increase Mongolian shares in strategic mines are a few visible responses taken [made] by Mongolian politicians for [to] the public outcry' (Mendee 2012).

Summary

With regard to China's economic interest in gaining access to natural resources, the small-coalition regimes in Burma and Cambodia have responded eagerly. Mongolia's large-coalition government has refused to comply with this interest. China has been very successful in accessing Burmese oil and gas reserves, especially when compared with India's attempts to increase its leverage over the reserves. Even though Chinese companies were not initially involved in the exploration, they gained considerable concessions later. Furthermore, much of the explored gas will be exported to China and not to India, although the Burmese generals had initially been in negotiation with India. Most recently, while Chinese companies gained new concessions, the shares of Indian stakeholders were forcibly reduced by the Burmese government. This reaction corresponds to that of an eager compliant.

The Cambodian government has welcomed Chinese state and private investments in the country. Several of the most prominent domestic tycoons, who are heavily engaged in Cambodian politics, established joint ventures with Chinese companies. In the newly developed oil sector, Chinese SOEs acquired several exploitation concessions. Thus, the Cambodian government complies eagerly with the Chinese quest for access to natural resources.

The Chinese government has faced deliberate opposition from Mongolian policymakers with regard to Mongolia's huge natural resource deposits. In a heated public debate on the exploitation of Mongolia's top mineral deposits, fears of Chinese companies extracting the minerals without developing the country were raised. Moreover, in the past, the government rejected offers of Chinese infrastructure investments in Mongolia's mineral-rich regions, denying the Chinese access to Mongolian natural resources. Hence, the Mongolian government refused to comply with Chinese interests.

Geopolitical interests

Finally, I turn to the comparison of compliance with China's geopolitical interests in Asia. As explained in Chapter 3, these interests refer, equally, to China's attempts to mitigate or pre-empt containment by the US, to the regional security architecture and to the strategic importance of China's regional environment for

China. Again, it is important to first establish how a country's possible response to these interests is interpreted in terms of degree of compliance. The notions of balancing against and bandwagoning with China are useful concepts for projecting a country's strategic response to this type of Chinese interest on the spectrum of compliance. Accordingly, a balancing strategy corresponds to refusal, whereas bandwagoning corresponds to eagerness. Hedging, then, is a neither-nor reaction, putting a country in the middle of the spectrum at a reluctant position.

Burma

At the core of China's strategic interests in Southeast Asia as a whole, and Burma in particular, is the desire to keep the US out of Southeast Asia. At the same time, the Chinese government seeks to increase its own influence vis-à-vis other regional players, particularly India, in order to secure strategic access to the Indian Ocean (Chenyang and Fook 2009; Ganesan 2011). The Chinese government has successfully achieved this objective and is considered to occupy a privileged position (Zhao 2007: ii). However, in contrast to the conventional perception of Burma as a client state of China, the relationship between the Chinese government and the Burmese junta is troubled by mutual distrust. More specifically, even before the domestic political reforms, the Burmese government tried to diversify its foreign relations (Storey 2007, 2009). It should become clear in the following why the Burmese foreign policy strategy was one that tried to hedge, but effectively ended up bandwagoning with China.

On the one hand, China has been quite successful in the implementation of its strategic goals. With respect to strategic access to the Indian Ocean, Chinese companies have developed the ports in Hainggyi, Coco, Sittwe, Zadetkyi Kyun, Myeik and Kyaukphyu where they assisted in the construction of radars, communication and refuelling facilities. They were also involved in a series of airfield construction projects in north and north-western Burma (Selth 2003: 4). These Chinese activities in Burma reached such an extent that Indian observers claimed that the Burmese government had allowed the Chinese to establish several intelligence stations in order to oversee India's naval activity (Selth 2003). The Burmese authorities, for their part, have consistently denied 'any Chinese military presence in Burma or establishing a strategic alliance in China's favour' (Tin 2003: 208), despite their strong reliance on the Chinese supply of military equipment and weapons. These Indian allegations eventually proved unfounded (International Crisis Group 2009).

This does not change the fact that the Chinese government sought not only to use Burma's strategic location to improve Chinese access to the Indian Ocean from a geo-strategic perspective, but also as a transit country to facilitate trade relations with the rest of the world. About 80 per cent of Chinese oil imports is shipped from the Middle East and Africa through the Indian Ocean and through the Strait of Malacca, a chokepoint that is controlled by US naval forces. This vulnerability of China is frequently referred to as the 'Malacca dilemma'. The Chinese government is worried that a blockade of the Strait of Malacca due to conflict over Taiwan, for example, would have devastating consequences for the Chinese economy. This vulnerability could be mitigated by acquiring direct access to the Indian Ocean and the Gulf of Bengal through harbours in neighbouring countries. Direct access would improve the security of major sea lanes for Chinese oil tankers and, in the long run, even help to avoid the passage through the Malacca Strait entirely if oil was further transported to China by pipelines (Chenyang and Fook 2009).

In the past, the Burmese government has been sceptical about the Chinese intentions to extend the Burmese infrastructure (Tin 2003; Clapp 2007b). However, in the mid 2000s, 'China has finally succeeded in wearing down this reluctance, probably with the lure of very large financial returns' (Clapp 2007a: 12). Finally, in 2009, construction began on a more than US$1 billion twin pipeline for oil and gas through Burma, connecting the Burmese port of Kyaukphyu with the Chinese provincial capital Kunming. At the same time, there were persistent confrontations in Sino-Burmese relations pushing the government of Burma to search for alternative partners. The generals, even though they were able to strengthen their power due to Chinese military assistance, disliked and distrusted the Chinese government because of its interventionist policies in the past. Thus, even though China had achieved major strategic objectives, the bilateral relationship was not without contradictions. In particular, persistent distrust and insecurity over Chinese willingness to back the junta vis-à-vis the ethnic ceasefire groups led the military government to diversify its foreign relations.

Given these disagreements, the Burmese central government attempted to balance China's influence by diversifying its external ties. It is noteworthy that there had been great interest in engaging the junta on the part of other Asian states. In addition to economic interests, a major concern of all these states was the perception that isolation would drive the military junta further into the arms of China (Selth 2003). Apart from a number of regional players, such as Thailand, Singapore, Indonesia, Malaysia, Vietnam, Japan and South Korea as well as the ASEAN as a whole, it is India in particular that has also lent itself as a counterweight to overdependence on China. The Indian government is relying on the Burmese government to tackle its own separatist insurgencies and is competing with China over influence in the Indian Ocean and access to natural resources. Against this background, the Indian government shifted its approach towards Burma from criticism over human rights issues during the 1980s to pragmatic engagement, including military assistance (Zhao 2007). India's ambassador Bahtia tried hard to convince the Burmese junta that it would not interfere in its domestic affairs: 'I wish to reassure my Myanmar friends that while India is proud to be a democracy, we are not in the business of exporting it' (Ambassador Bhatia cited in Matthews 2006: 216).

Moreover, the Burmese junta began to proactively diversify its external relations with other weapon suppliers, such as North Korea, Iran, Israel, Ukraine and Russia. In 2001, Russia agreed to supply the junta with jet fighters and, in 2007, to provide assistance with an air defence missile system. 'Reportedly, the Russian MIG military aircraft company has maintained a representative office in

Myanmar since October 2006 and helped upgrade the country's main military airstrip' (International Crisis Group 2009: 29). Along with China, Russia vetoed the UN Security Council resolution against the Burmese military government in 2007.

The junta was also keen to improve its ties with the US, which were far from normal throughout the last two decades. Since 1990, no US ambassador had been dispatched to Burma; instead, there was continued representation by chargés d'affaires ad interim. The US unilaterally imposed sanctions on investments in Burma in 1997. These were gradually extended to imports from Burma and to restrictions on financial transactions and visa bans for members of the junta. It was the US, together with Britain, that tabled the UN resolution to impose UN sanctions on Burma in 2007.

Against the calculation that improved relations between Burma and the US would be beneficial to China, by averting US aggression or international inter- vention in Burma, the Chinese government brokered talks between representatives of the two nations to facilitate incremental improvements of bilat- eral relations under the Obama administration. It also backed the efforts of the UN special envoy Ibrahim Gambari to promote national reconciliation between the generals and the democratic opposition in Burma (Lee *et al.* 2009; Holliday 2009; Steinberg 2010). But, suspicious of the Chinese, the military junta inter- preted the Chinese mediation as an attempt to use Burma as a bargaining chip in Sino-US relations (International Crisis Group 2009). All this has drastically changed with Burma's political liberalization. In the early 2010s, the US eased its sanctions on Burma and Burma received visits from both Secretary of State Clinton and President Obama.

To sum up, even though not much is known about the Burmese junta's strate- gic calculations, it appears that, until the domestic reforms of 2010, the junta was not such a vassal of China as was usually assumed. In fact, severe disagreements between the Chinese and the Burmese leaderships persisted. Against this back- ground, the generals pursued a strategy of hedging and tried to diversify their external relations to ease dependence on China. India, in particular, tried to improve its relations with the junta. In reality, however, the Indian government was unable to offer the diplomatic protection that China could provide with its veto power in the UN Security Council. The junta's relations with both India and Russia, however, never reached levels comparable to those with China.

Given all this, for the period until 2010, the Burmese government is catego- rized as a de facto eager compliant with China's geo-strategic interests. Clearly, the generals wanted to hedge against China more actively; but, given the interna- tional pressure on the regime, there was not much space for manoeuvring. The junta was left with no real alternative than to bandwagon with China.

Cambodia

Geopolitically, the Chinese government considers Cambodia part of the Chinese 'soft underbelly', reflecting its strategic importance to the Chinese government.

This importance has long been connected to the competition between Vietnam and China over influence in Southeast Asia. Even though nowadays conflicts no longer arise along ideological lines, new cleavages between Vietnam and China emerge with respect to the South Chinese Sea. On the one hand, there are territorial conflicts between China and Vietnam over resource-rich islands that have recently been elevated to the status of a 'core interest' for China's territorial integrity, along with Tibet, Taiwan and Xinjiang (*South China Morning Post* 2010). On the other hand, the significance of the South China Sea for the Chinese government also lies in its strategic importance for Chinese energy security. The strategic objective here is to secure access to the Indian Ocean in the light of US hegemony over strategic shipping lanes. While China has been very successful in realizing this strategic goal, little is known about the Cambodian strategic foreign policy perspective. The fact that Cambodia does not articulate any security concerns with China's rise and frequenty highlights solid ties and shared values with China, characterizes Cambodia's bandwagoning with China (Chung 2009).

Similar to Burma, Cambodia plays an important role in improving China's energy security, because it can offer access to the Gulf of Thailand. In 2006, Jiangsu Taihu International, a Chinese firm, in a joint venture with a Cambodian partner, set up a new 178-hectare Special Economic Zone near Sihanoukville, the only city in Cambodia with an international deepwater port. According to observers, Chinese companies have upgraded this port (Storey 2006). When the project was discussed for the first time in 1999, the Chinese side was represented by Wang Jun, chairman of the China International Trade and Investment Corporation, and of Polytechnologies, the largest corporate entity owned by the PLA (Marks 2000). At that time, the establishment of a shipbuilding and repair facility was also discussed (Chanda 2002).

Given this involvement by PLA agents and against the background of the Chinese 'Malacca dilemma' (as mentioned earlier), security analysts have pointed towards the potential military use of ports like Sihanoukville by the Chinese (Burgos and Ear 2010). The Chinese government has successfully acquired access to a chain of deep water ports not only in Cambodia, but also in other countries in the region.[5] These ports, dubbed the 'string of pearls', are primarily for commercial use, but their dual-use character has been stressed and they may be used as 'maritime surveillance and listening posts or as supply and pre-positioning sites for naval deployments' in the future (Job and Williams 2009: 24). Certainly, the harbour at Sihanoukville would be helpful for both securing shipping lanes and pressuring Vietnam if it is used by visiting Chinese naval forces (Storey 2006). 'Situated in the center of mainland Southeast Asia, the Cambodian port of Sihanoukville would provide an excellent base for projecting maritime power into the Gulf of Thailand and the Straits of Malacca' (Marks 2000).

But China was not only successful at realizing its geo-strategic interests on Cambodian territory. It was also successful in using Cambodia to defend its security interest vis-à-vis the ASEAN group as a whole (Cock 2010a). This became most apparent when, for the first time ever, the Cambodian chair of the 45th annual ASEAN Ministerial Meeting in 2012 failed to produce a joint communiqué on the discussion on the territorial disputes in the South China Sea (Paal 2013). Earlier, the Philippines had raised complaints about China's actions to seize control of the disputed Scarborough Shoal.

With regard to regional security, it seems the Chinese have succeeded in winning the loyalty of Cambodia's government and its armed forces. Under circumstances in which the possibilities of siding with the US were slim, the Cambodian government sought to consolidate old ties with China and maximize assistance and protection from Beijing (Chung 2009). Whereas the American government suspended all direct bilateral aid to the Cambodian government following the armed conflict in 1997, the Chinese government has constantly shown its support with the provision of arms and – with numerous visits by high-ranking militaries to Cambodia – its willingness to act as a close military partner. Until 2007, the US was the only major donor that did not engage in government-to-government aid to Cambodia, but operated only through Cambodian or foreign NGOs and local governments (Lum 2007). When the sanctions were lifted, the American government not only re-established flows of economic assistance to the Hun Sen government, but also its military aid. In 2007, the US navy visited the port of Sihanoukville twice; these were the first visits since 1975. Yet, relations between the US and the Cambodian government remain conflictual, especially with respect to human rights concerns. In 2010, even though joint US-Cambodian military exercises were held (Heder 2011), the US suspended the provision of military trucks to the Cambodian government, because the latter had deported 20 Uighur refugees to China. The shortfall was swiftly filled by the Chinese government which even increased the supply (The Associated Press 2010a).

Against this background, I consider the Cambodian government's behaviour to be bandwagoning, which corresponds to a position at the eager end of the compliance spectrum.

Mongolia

Sino-Mongolian relations illustrate vividly the key issues in China's neighbourhood policy. The topics that are relevant for Sino-Mongolian relations generally follow the overarching themes of Chinese regional foreign policy. In 2003, Hu Jintao named economic matters, security and the support for Mongolia's policy against having foreign troops deployed within its borders as the three focal points of Sino-Mongolian relations (Wang 2009).

Mongolia is a vast country; it is underdeveloped in terms of infrastructure and transportation networks; it has long borderlines and few inhabitants; and it has proclaimed itself to be a nuclear weapon-free zone. Thus, if Mongolia ranks as a security issue on the Chinese foreign policy agenda it is not because of its potential military threat. From the perspective of neighbouring China, the security concern refers to Mongolia allying with any other major power. This could imply the potential deployment of military forces on Mongolian territory, which would then result in a direct threat to China's national security (Wang 2009: 21).

The Mongolian government pursues an explicitly stated strategy of balancing. Mongolia's relations with its neighbours have always been a vector of the relationship between both sides. Integration into the Soviet camp was strongly motivated by the search for protection and the need not to be crushed by China (Batchimeg 2005b: 51). Later, deeply integrated into the Soviet camp, Mongolia had no choice other than to follow the Soviet attitudes towards China during the Cold War. During the Sino-Soviet honeymoon period in the 1950s, Sino-Mongolian relations were cooperative and trade and assistance flourished. Following the Sino-Soviet split, Sino-Mongolian relations lay fallow for two decades; Soviet troops were stationed in Mongolia and the country's economy relied exclusively on Soviet assistance (Campi 2004, Batchimeg 2005b). When the Soviet Union collapsed in 1989, Russian influence diminished significantly. Mongolia's subsequent orientation towards the West, and especially towards the former East and Central European Soviet satellites, was strongly motivated by the fear of renewed Chinese dominance. In the post-Cold War period, Mongolia continued to balance the influence of its giant neighbours with the engagement of other great powers. While Mongolia's role as a buffer between China and Russia decreased in current terms, it was worrisome for the Chinese government that the US evolved as a counterpart in the first decade of the twenty-first century (Wachman 2009).

In the early 1990s, the Mongolian government adopted the 'third neighbour' policy. It sought non-involvement and neutrality with respect to potential disputes between its two neighbours and was designed to counterbalance both China and Russia by maintaining good relations with other powerful countries. However, since 2000, this policy has shifted to one that aims at balancing China, albeit indirectly, through engagement with the US and other strategic partners, be they Japan, South Korea, India or Germany (Reeves 2012).

Reeves characterizes Mongolia's foreign policy behaviour towards China since 2000 as one of a 'complex balance of influence':

> The manifestation of Mongolia's post-2000 balance of influence behaviour is its bilateral military engagement with the US, its re-establishment of military relations with Russia, its military engagement with other strategic states and institutions in Asia, and its continued relations with Beijing so as to indirectly balance China.
>
> (Reeves 2012: 591)

This policy became most effective in the aftermath of 9/11, when Afghanistan and the central Asian region received more attention from the US. The Mongolian government took this opportunity to develop closer ties with the US; it joined the war on terrorism and sent troops to Iraq and Afghanistan. As early as 1994, the Mongolian military forces held joint training sessions with the US army. The Mongolian armed forces also received equipment, funding and training facilities from the US. In 2001, a joint humanitarian rescue exercise was carried out, but from 2003 onwards the previously small-scale rescue missions carried out by civil defence troops were expanded to annual large-scale manoeuvres in Mongolia. These exercises were expanded again in 2006 into multinational coordinated warfare training sessions including regular army troops from the seven nations of Mongolia, the US, Bangladesh, India, Thailand, Tonga and Fiji (Wang 2009). In 2004, the Bush administration announced that Mongolia would receive a US$1 billion grant within the framework of the Millennium Challenge Account. A joint statement by the two presidents was issued declaring 'a new era of cooperation and comprehensive partnership between two democratic countries based on shared values and common strategic interests' (Khirghis 2005; Byambasuren 2006: 23). In the course of 2005, Mongolia's strategic position further increased when the US was pushed out of Central Asia by members of the Shanghai Cooperation Organization (SCO), and some US military bases in Uzbekistan and Kyrgyzstan were closed. In 2005, for the first time ever, an American president paid a visit to Ulaanbaatar. Thus, after 9/11, the 'third neighbour policy' became more successful in its aim to enhance the security situation of the country.

Mongolia's rapprochement with the West has not passed unnoticed by the Chinese government, which is trying to counterbalance US leverage over the Mongolian government. For example, after Mongolia had enjoyed its first visit by an American president in 2005, the Mongolian president was subsequently invited to pay a visit to Beijing. In order to balance US-Mongolian relations, a Chinese-Mongolian joint statement was released declaring that both countries would not ally or sign any treaty or agreement with a third country that may adversely affect the interest of each other (Wang 2006).

Consultations on security and defence between China and Mongolia began in 2004 (Wang 2009). In 2009, a first joint military exercise with Mongolia, Singapore, Gabon, Russia and China was held (*The UB Post* 2009b; Bulag 2010). Multilaterally, the Chinese government attempted to integrate Mongolia into the SCO to balance Mongolia's coalition with the US by offering observer status (Campi 2005).

Different Mongolian governments have pursued the 'third neighbourhood policy' as a strategy to improve Mongolia's security situation. Mongolia clearly pursued a strategy of balancing Chinese and Russian influence by choosing the US as a strategic partner. The orientation towards America and the European Union – including the choice of a democratic political system – after the collapse of the Soviet Union was a deliberate strategy to move closer under the security umbrella of the US. Also, the support of the US was seen 'as a guarantor of Mongolian democracy' (Bulag 2010: 102). Subsequently, Mongolian governments tried to increase attention from US leaders for their country.

However, due to its landlocked geographical position, Mongolia's abilities to bend too strongly to one or the other side are limited: all traffic must pass through Russia or China. This puts physical limits to Mongolian self-determinism, because China or Russia can potentially refuse to open up airspace or seaports to Mongolia. (This actually happened in August 2008 when Chinese authorities refused to allow foreign military aircraft to fly over its territory during the Beijing Olympic games [Bulag 2009].) Under such circumstances, multinational joint exercises with other countries could not take place because arrival of personnel and equipment would be disrupted (Wang 2009).

This limited policy space is also reflected in Mongolia's diplomacy. After receiving the US president, the Mongolian president had to pay a visit to China, and Beijing could impose a declaration of non-alignment on the Mongolian government. Furthermore, the economic dependence of Mongolia on the PRC gives the Chinese great leverage to sanction Mongolia's snuggling with any third neighbour. For example, Chinese fear of US influence in Mongolia emerged as a reason to avoid building a new gas pipeline from west Siberia to China through Mongolian territory in 2001 (Batchimeg 2005b: 56). The Mongolian government had hoped to gain from better infrastructure, transportation networks and opportunities to increase its state revenues through transit fees (Blagov 2005; Rossabi 2005b). Instead, the pipeline was built along the Japan-bound Taishet-Nakhodka route and Mongolia was left out.

Against this background, Mongolia's compliance with China's geo-strategic interests is classified as reluctant. It becomes clear that the Mongolian government preferred to balance China more actively, but it has only limited possibilities to do so. It ends up hedging. However, given its small manoeuvring space, its geographic location – sandwiched between Russia and China – and the great economic leverage of China over Mongolia, the Mongolian balancing act is quite impressive.

Summary

The variation in compliance between the three different countries that can be observed with regard to the 'one China' policy and with regard to the provision of access to natural resources, is also visible with regard to China's geopolitical interests: Burma's and Cambodia's governments have responded much more eagerly to China's geopolitical interests than Mongolia.

Not much is known about the junta's strategic calculations. Empirical evidence, however, suggests that China has been relatively successful in realizing its geo-strategic objectives. This is because, although the Burmese government tries to reduce its reliance on China, in reality, until very recently, it has not found an alternative partner of equal weight that would allow the junta to hedge against China more actively. The empirical evidence suggests that the Burmese government, at least until 2010, falls into the category of eagerness.

Against the background of a strategic competition between China and the US in Asia, the Cambodian government, despite its official policy of neutrality, bends heavily towards China. It has allowed China to invest in commercial infrastructure, which, ultimately, could turn out to be of crucial military importance in the event of a conflict between China and other players in the region. Moreover, during the last 15 years, the Cambodian government has enjoyed heavy military support from China, while simultaneously experiencing sanctions from the US during most of this period.

Different governments in Mongolia have pursued the 'third neighbour' policy, which is aimed at balancing the influence of China and Russia. As a result, the

Mongolian government showed a reluctant position on the spectrum of compliance with China.

What the comparison tells us. Conclusion and discussion of findings

Was the Chinese government more successful in realizing its interests in small-coalition than in large-coalition systems? In an attempt to find an answer to this question, this chapter discusses the results of the structured comparison of how three countries with different sizes of winning coalition – Burma, Cambodia, and Mongolia – comply with three different Chinese foreign policy interests: the country's territorial integrity, the access to natural resources and China's geopolitical objectives.

Table 7.1 provides a summary of the degree of compliance by these countries. Each country's degree of compliance is classified based on its behaviour. As can be seen in Table 7.1, the comparison suggests that compliance is linked to coalition size as, regardless of issue areas, the degree to which China could obtain policy concessions from other governments varied with the size of their winning coalitions. The governments of both small-coalition systems, Burma and Cambodia, were highly compliant with China's interests. As China was able to realize its strategic objectives in Burma quite successfully, Burma was classified as an eager compliant. Similarly, in Cambodia, the Chinese government pursued its interests during the last two decades with great success. The extent to which Cambodia's leadership under Hun Sen responded to China's foreign interests in all three issue areas clearly exceeded a reluctant position. In my general assessment of Cambodia's compliance with Chinese objectives, I therefore classified the Cambodian government as an eager compliant. In Mongolia, the country with

Table 7.1 Compliance by issue area and country

Country	Size of nominal/ true selectorate/ winning coalition	'One China' policy (relation to Taiwan/ treatment of Dalai Lama)	Resource access (treatment of Chinese investment)	Geopolitics (strategy towards China)
Burma	none/small/small	eager (no relations/ persona non grata)	eager (preferential)	eager (hedging)
Cambodia	large/small/small	eager (no relations/ persona non grata)	eager (preferential)	eager (hedging/ bandwagoning)
Mongolia	large/large/large	reluctant (unofficial relations/ welcoming)	reluctant (equal)	reluctant (balancing/ hedging)

Source: Adapted from Bader (2013), see www.tandfonline.com.

the larger coalition, the government complied only reluctantly or even refused to respond to China's interests at all. In general, the Chinese government faced serious Mongolian opposition and scepticism to Chinese interests. Mongolia's compliance with the interests of the Chinese government was average at best.

In sum, in all issue areas, China could very successfully realize its interests in the small-coalition countries, while it faced difficulties pursuing its objectives in the large-coalition country. Thus, overall, the compliance patterns illustrated in Table 7.1 appear to be in line with my theoretical expectation: they support the expectation that China is more successful in realizing its interests in countries with small winning coalitions as expressed in hypothesis 1.

A critical observer could object that the classification of countries in Table 7.1 does not always fully reflect the policy preferences of governments in Burma, Cambodia and Mongolia. The previous case studies revealed that, sometimes, the degree to which a government agreed and the willingness with which it complied with China's interests diverged from its actual compliance. More specifically, both the Burmese and the Mongolian governments appear to be more reluctant than their positioning on the spectrum would suggest, while only the classification of Cambodia as eagerly compliant truly matched its attitude towards China. In particular, the case of Burma, which despite its very small winning coalition is often portrayed as neither China's puppet, nor its pawn (Storey 2007), appears startling and is, to some extent, not entirely in line with the theoretical expectation. The fact that policy outcomes did not always fully match with policy preferences, and the mismatch between winning-coalition size and perceived policy preference in the case of Burma raises questions as to whether compliance was truly driven by coalition size as the theoretical argument would suggest.

In other words, the question is, what is it that drove the observed compliance patterns? What role did coalition size play, and to what extent were other factors responsible for this outcome? Theory would suggest that a leader's considerations on how to deal with external interests depend greatly on his own logic of political survival, and on whether what he receives in exchange for policy concessions is beneficial for his own survival. In some instances, a temporal correlation between successive bilateral interactions allowed me to establish that policy exchange indeed took place. For example, the provision of concessions to Chinese companies to exploit gas in Burma just days after the Chinese government had vetoed the UN Security Council resolution on Burma's human rights violations, or China's donation of military vehicles to the Cambodian government after the extradition of Chinese Uighur refugees, come to mind. In both cases, the exchange was strongly driven by and highly beneficial to, the narrow interests of the leaders in power. In other instances, however, it appeared more difficult to establish a direct causal link or it remained unclear how a leader's policy choice with regard to specific Chinese foreign interests related to the size of his winning coalition.

Alternative explanations

The discussion of compliance by each of the three countries has revealed that a number of alternative and additional factors appear to interact with coalition size in producing the observed outcome. For example, compliance can be driven by factors such as a country's cultural similarity with China or its susceptibility to China's soft power; by external constraints on a government's policy options resulting from exposure to other major powers' interests or their integration in, or isolation from, the international community. More precisely, one may wonder to what extent international isolation enhanced compliance in the case of Burma; to what extent cultural similarity or China's soft power pushed compliance in Cambodia, and whether competing major power interests and popular Sinophobia prevented compliance in Mongolia.

As discussed in the case studies, I am not able to completely refute all of these alternative explanations, as some of these factors certainly seem to affect compliance in some of the cases. However, I argue that these alternative explanations complement, rather than challenge, the overall argument that small-coalition size increases exploitability. The comparison of the cases suggests that none of these explanations is able to explain the outcome of compliance patterns on their own.

Consider the issue of soft power. Soft power, as posited by Joseph Nye, refers to the ability to get others to do what one wants 'through attraction rather than coercion or payment'; thus, it is 'the ability to shape the preferences of others' without using carrots and sticks (Nye 2008: 94, 95). Such attractiveness is largely based on a country's culture, political values and foreign policies, provided that these are attractive to others and are perceived as legitimate and having moral authority (Nye 2008: 96). Accordingly, when China's soft power is high, the likelihood increases that Chinese interests are considered. The question is, then, to what extent is compliance produced because of this attractiveness of China in the three countries, rather than by coalition size (and the related exchange of goods and policies)?

Proponents of a soft power argument could argue that the degree of China's success in realizing its interests is merely driven by a country's cultural similarity with China and the degree to which China's political system appeals to its leaders. Intuitively, such an explanation is appealing as it corresponds well to compliance patterns in Cambodia and Mongolia and their remarkable difference with regard to the perceptions of China in public opinion in these countries. From this perspective, compliance patterns in Cambodia and Mongolia can be considered over-determined because the popular collective memory of these countries' history with China, popular affinity with Chinese culture, the convergence of authoritarian leadership style between Cambodia and China and the resulting Chinese soft power (or the lack thereof) would equally predict the observed compliance patterns. (Chinese involvement during the Khmer Rouge regime is not widely known among ordinary Cambodians.)

However, for several reasons, soft power alone is not an entirely satisfying explanation. First, it should be noted that, despite its neat fit in Cambodia and

Mongolia, the soft power argument is considerably weaker with regard to Burma, where it runs counter to the observed pattern of high compliance despite limited Chinese popularity among the population. Hence, soft power is expected to reinforce a government's responsiveness to external interests, but soft power is not a necessary cause of compliance.

Second, soft power seems to complement, rather than counter, the importance of coalition size and political regime type, as coalition size is decisive for whether or not policymakers are sensitive to popular perceptions. When policymakers need to justify their decisions domestically, this is always easier when public opinion is favourable rather than malign. Soft power can, therefore, help policymakers to justify domestically the policy concessions they make to external players. But, the logic of political survival converges with Nye's view that public opinion is more relevant in non-authoritarian contexts than in small-coalition regimes where policy decisions usually do not require justification (Nye 2008: 99).

Empirically, this latter argument is widely supported by the three case studies. Comparison indicates that the Chinese soft power strategy is shaped by how the Chinese government perceives the role of the broader populations and their potential influence on decision-makers. In Burma, where the population was least able to influence policies, it did not receive specific attention from China. From 'China's perspective, public opinion in Myanmar did not constitute a critical challenge to China's interest as long as the government backed Chinese projects' (Sun 2012: 90). This is reflected in the fact that, before Burma's political opening up, there was very little documented Chinese philanthropic development assistance to Burma, and China's leadership was widely insensitive to the growing anti-China sentiment in Burma during the 2010s (Sun 2012). In Mongolia, the only country in which the electorate forms part of the winning coalition, the Chinese government appeared keen to influence public opinion and to be seen as caring for the population's well-being. While the Chinese government assisted Mongolia in handling food crises and donated to vulnerable population groups in Mongolia's society (*The UB Post* 2003b; Rossabi 2005a; Campi 2005), observers have frequently connected the Chinese government's investment in scholarships for Mongolian students to China's inability to pursue its material interests in Mongolia (Tucker 2008; Sumiyabazar 2010; Bulag 2010). As to the case of Cambodia, the CDC's detailed database on China's assistance to Cambodia suggests that the Chinese perception of, and approach to, the Cambodian population also reflects the fact that, despite nominally forming part of the selectorate, Cambodia's population has no real say in choosing the government. The support of Chinese communities and schools in Cambodia, despite the fact that Cambodia's population has little influence on the government's decision-making, is not necessarily a contradiction here. To the extent that the facilities and activities of these associations are primarily sustained by local ethnic Chinese communities, it is relatively costless for the Chinese government to use these already existing networks as a vehicle to shape public opinion in Cambodia. Taking advantage of existing ethnic Chinese communities, which maintain local facilities with their donations, may, therefore, not require much of an investment.

Finally, independently of whether or not the involved actors find China's culture and cultural values attractive, to the extent that the analysis finds compliance to be connected to material incentives, it is problematic to attribute compliance with Chinese interests to China's soft power. Even in the case of Cambodia, where China's soft power is perceived to be the highest, China uses material benefits or sanctions to push for its interests. For example, Sino-Khmer elites profit materially from facilitating Chinese interests in Cambodia. At the same time, non-compliance has, in some instances, been found to be connected to coercion, for example, when Cambodian newspapers are pressured by China if they report negatively on the Taiwan question.

In addition to soft power, another possible explanation for compliance patterns that needs further consideration is a country's integration into, or isolation from, the international community and the absence or presence of alternative major power interests in a country. In Chapter 6, the presence of Russian interests in Mongolia was discussed in detail. Russian interests in Mongolia certainly constrain the Mongolian governments' leeway to respond to Chinese interests. However, as argued earlier, this cannot explain why Mongolian governments have opted for policies that attempt to increase transparency in policymaking, thereby decreasing influence from both China *and* Russia.

Here, it remains to be discussed whether Burma's extraordinary compliance is a product of its international isolation and the absence of other external interests, rather than Burma's small-coalition size. It seems impossible to dismiss the fact that Burma's isolation has pushed it towards compliance. Yet, it seems that Burma's isolation has furthered Chinese interests, mostly in economic terms, while it was less useful for, or even an impediment to, other interests that are more diplomatic.

To begin with, Burma's international isolation cannot be considered independently from its political system. Rather than rejecting Burma's small coalition as an explanation for exploitation, the case of Burma suggests that isolation reinforced the logic of exploitation to the extreme. As discussed in Chapter 4, repression and violence was the initial cause of Burma's international isolation. In this situation, China offered assistance to support the Burmese junta domestically and internationally. In return, it received increased compliance by Burma's leaders. This becomes especially apparent in the gradually increasing Chinese influence over the Burmese economy during the 2000s and it is, ultimately, exemplified in the award of oil and gas concessions to China, despite higher bids by competitors. Indeed, alert over China's rising influence in Burma has, arguably, motivated other Asian states to (re)-engage the junta, and several observers consider over-reliance on China and the desire to balance China's economic presence in the country as an important motivation for the junta's steps to reform (Selth 2003; Bünte 2008; International Crisis Group 2009; Zin 2012).

However, the reforms in Burma's domestic politics, and the subsequent abolishment of international sanctions, offer some insight into the role of international isolation. Investigating the Sino-Burmese relationship on the basis of interviews with Chinese experts on Burma, Sun (2012) convincingly argues that, from the Chinese perspective, the Burmese reform steps were considered to be widely conducive to China's interests. On the one hand, the junta's transition to civilian leadership was expected to increase the Burmese government's domestic and international legitimacy, at least in the eyes of other Asian governments, and especially in the context of ASEAN. This gradual re-integration into the international community was expected to enhance Burma's role as 'a solid, powerful diplomatic supporter of China's national interests and policy preferences in the region' (Sun 2012: 82). After years of shielding Burma internationally, 'the time has come for Myanmar to 'reciprocate'' (Sun 2012: 82). On the other hand, China's experts did not expect Burma's domestic transition to be far reaching enough to satisfy Western standards of democratization and so they anticipated Western dissatisfaction with Burma's reforms and the continuation of Western economic sanctions. With Western foreign investment kept out of the country, China's experts expected that the Burmese government's subsequent attempt to boost its domestic legitimacy by stimulating economic development would open up tremendous opportunities for Chinese businesses. It is clear that the Chinese severely underestimated the democratic momentum in Burma by interpreting the Burmese reforms as a tactic to strengthen the military's legitimacy 'with no clear intention to give up power' (Sun 2012: 90). This is, however, not of importance here. The point is that whereas Burma's international isolation was beneficial for Chinese business interests by limiting international competition, for China's broader diplomatic interests, international isolation was a liability rather than an asset. Countries without international acceptance are unlikely to be influencial in international or multilateral fora and, as such, they are of limited instrumental use to represent or push for a desired position.

In the final assessment, it appears that the examined cases offer valuable insights into the political economy of autocratic cooperation and the observed outcomes are, on the whole, in line with the theoretical expectations. Having said this, it needs to be acknowledged that the most-similar system case study design, initially intended to 'control' for alternative explanations, turned out to provide a weaker instrument than hoped for in terms of refuting some of these alternative factors. Consequently, various factors are suspected as also having influence on the observed compliance patterns.

Scope conditions

If the theoretical assumption that China is more successful in realizing its interests in countries with small winning coalitions is confirmed by the case study investigation, one may wonder to what extent this finding can be generalized to other countries. Or, put differently, is the investigated sample of countries representative enough to draw conclusions about their exploitability for a wider set of countries and, if so, which ones? Despite the specific characteristics of the investigated cases, it seems reasonable that the theoretical framework, which expects the exploitation of autocratic small-coalition regimes, is not limited to the investigated sample, but should also hold for other poor (and resource-rich) countries in other world regions.

Considering geography, as argued in Chapter 3, there are many reasons to expect that regional proximity increases the incentives for target states to comply with external interests. Yet, there is no plausible reason to assume that distance as such would compromise the validity of the exploitation argument. Thus, there is no a priori reason to expect that compliance, as achieved by the means of policy exchange with an external power, would not work in other world regions – even though geographic proximity may privilege one external actor over others. Indeed, many readers will inevitably think of China's engagement on the African or Latin American continents. Similarly, one would expect that none of the more substantively 'Asian' characteristics of the cases is essential for the argument to work. These factors may facilitate compliance with specific external interests (a point that is discussed in the next section); but, the overall argument that small-winning-coalition size facilitates external exploitation should be equally valid for countries with other religions than Buddhism, cultures that are more distant to the Chinese and without historical Chinese influence.

The scope conditions of the argument are more difficult to define when other characteristics of the investigated cases are considered. To what extent, for example, is the argument bound to cases with low national income and high resource richness? Thinking of resource-rich, high-income countries such as Saudi Arabia, Norway or Australia, one would still expect that small-coalition governments have more discretion in the allocation of resource rents than large ones. In principle, then, exploitation through policy exchange could still plausibly happen in rich small-coalition countries. However, as governments in rich countries are less dependent on external rents and foreign investments for resource extraction, one would expect richer countries to be less vulnerable to external exploitation, all else being equal. Thus, the exploitation argument may be more applicable to medium or low income countries.

Moreover, this investigation concentrated on countries with abundant natural raw materials in the expectation that these would arouse the interest of the resource-hungry Chinese economy. Theoretically, resource abundance is not a necessary condition per se for the argument to work, as exploitation can involve both economic and political concessions. Nevertheless, one can argue that if exploitation involves economic concessions, a government's willingness to make such concessions may be dependent on the overall structure of that country's economy and on the degree to which the economic sectors in question complement or compete with that of the external power. In the investigated cases, the countries' economies with a low degree of industrialization happened to be highly complementary to the Chinese. Other economies, however, will find themselves in a much more competitive situation with China. When concessions affect competing industries, for example by reducing import tariffs, they are likely to harm domestic interest groups that may form part of the domestic winning coalition. Because leaders do not want to hurt the members of their winning coalition, governments should, all else being equal, be more inclined to make concessions when the economic strucuture is complementary to that of the external power.

To sum up, while the cases on which the investigation of the theoretical framework has been based share some very specific features, it can plausibly be argued that the mechanism of exploitation of small-coalition countries by outside powers should be globally applicable to rather poor (resource-rich) countries.

Observations on China's foreign policy behaviour

What can we learn from the comparative case studies about China's foreign behaviour more generally? The three cases and their comparison reveal a number of interesting observations about China's external behaviour. A comparison of how the Chinese government interacts with different actors in the three countries, and how the Chinese government treats the coalition partners and the disenfranchised in large- and in small-coalition systems is insightful. It helps to better understand how targeting of key constituencies in a leader's winning coalition connects to a leader's compliance as well as understanding how such targeting responds to perceived changes in the composition of winning coalitions.

Firstly, it is worthwhile considering how the Chinese government addressed the decision-makers; that is, the governments in the three differently sized coalition systems. Much in line with China's official foreign policy guidelines, i.e. the five principles of peaceful co-existence, which include the principle of non-interference (Wen 2004), the Chinese government established good state-to-state relations with all incumbent governments regardless of the size of their winning coalition. The main characteristic of China's foreign behaviour in this regard is one of principle. However, at the same time, China accepted whoever prevailed in domestic conflicts over power and turned a blind eye to any question of legitimacy. It can, therefore, also be described as extremely pragmatic, if not opportunistic.

In all three cases, the Chinese government consistently stuck to this principled pragmatism. In Burma, the Chinese government welcomed the oppositional NLD into power after their landslide victory in the 1990 elections; later, however, after the military SPDC had restored its authority, the Chinese continued to accommodate the military junta (Ruisheng 2010). With regard to the ceasefire groups along the Chinese border, the Chinese government held on to its principles by officially not maintaining direct contact with these groups while at the same time, pragmatically delegating this task to lower level provincial governments (International Crisis Group 2009). To the extent that this practice only changed when Beijing realized that it was unable to align the behaviour of provincial agents with its own interests, this exception proves the rule.

China's approach towards Cambodia is also very coherent in this regard. The Chinese government did not comment on the 1997 coup in Phnom Penh, but declared it an internal affair. When it became clear that Hun Sen had de facto won the power struggle and would dominate the political scene for some time to come, the Chinese leadership pragmatically shifted its loyalties from the former anti-Vietnamese coalition to its former rival, Hun Sen (Storey 2006; Marks 2000).

Finally, in Mongolia, China's non-interference principle resulted in the acceptance of all government turnovers brought about by Mongolia's elections. In a nutshell, with regard to its dealings with governments elsewhere in the world, my case studies confirm the principled pragmatism of China's foreign policy, which is rhetorically underlined by the principle of non-interference.

In all three case studies, a focus of Chinese attention on coalition members as the primary targets of China's external engagement can be observed. To a certain degree, this is a logical consequence of its focus on government-to-government relations. Interestingly, two collective actors, business elites and a country's military appear to be particularly important targets of Chinese engagement.

Business elites seem to be specifically addressed in Cambodia and Mongolia where they form part of the coalition. However, it is difficult to assess how far business tycoons in Burma were addressed independently, as they are most often army-bred. As became most obvious in the Cambodian case, business elites with close connections to the government were targeted not only for economic, but also for political objectives. They were native business partners for investment projects in the country (Global Witness 2009b), but also served to channel specific political Chinese interests to the government (Lintner 2002; Jeldres 2003).

In all three countries, the armed forces were among the recipients of Chinese assistance. In Burma, they were provided with equipment worth more than US$1.2 billion (Tin 2003; Guo 2007; International Crisis Group 2009). In Cambodia, they repeatedly received several US$ millions in assistance (Rith and Cochrane 2005; Storey 2006; Burgos and Ear 2010). The military in both Burma and Cambodia was among the most important of the coalition members. But even in Mongolia, where the military is not an independent coalition member, China spent at least US$1 million on the Mongolian armed forces (Rossabi 2005b; Liu 2007). However, not only was the amount of military assistance that the Chinese government provided to Mongolia dwarfed by the amounts provided to Cambodia's or Burma's armed forces; some of these investments, most illustratively the payment for Chinese language teachers, also formed part of a border confidence-building accord signed between China, Mongolia and its Central Asian and Russian neighbours (The Economist Intelligence Unit 1997b).

As a consequence of China's principled pragmatism, in which the Chinese can officially only interact with incumbent governments, the Chinese government sought to establish contacts to all potentially powerful political actors. Comparison of the three cases reveals that once the Chinese government perceived that alternative parties or individuals could potentially replace or challenge an existing government, it sought to reach out to them. In such cases, the Chinese attempted to establish contacts with potential challengers regardless of whether or not they belonged to the winning coalition.

From how an actor is treated one can, to a certain extent, read the Chinese assessment of his political potential. For example, in Burma, the Chinese government increased contacts with the opposition groups only *after* it perceived it necessary to increase the current government's legitimacy. The Chinese government thus attempted to make the Burmese opposition more willing to accept a power-sharing arrangement with the existing government, rather than challenging its rule (International Crisis Group 2009). Similarly, the Cambodian opposition parties were reportedly approached by the Chinese government *only* at times when they had the potential to become a coalition partner in the government; they were ignored during other periods (Kurlantzick 2007). In contrast, in Mongolia, where elections can easily lead to new government formations, the Chinese government, through the CCP's International Department, maintains persistent party-to-party relations with *all* major Mongolian political parties and regularly emphasizes that it will continue to work with all major parties equally (Batchimeg 2005a; International Department CCP 2013a, 2013b). The case studies suggest that the Chinese strategy of approaching alternative actors is quite coherent across cases. It appears to primarily focus on establishing and maintaining contacts with the aim of co-opting crucial leading individuals. By courting individuals, and without necessarily providing material or financial support to their political parties or organizations, the Chinese seemed to attempt to influence leading individuals and to manipulate their perceptions of China, thus increasing their responsiveness to China's objectives.

In conclusion, on the whole, the comparison of interaction patterns between the Chinese government and different actors in the case study countries reveals that the Chinese government primarily addressed those actors that were perceived to be important for a government's compliance with Chinese external interest. The Chinese military aid to Mongolia or the support to Cambodia's ethnic Chinese associations, which were not necessarily independent or influencial actors (Mongolia's military), appear to be anomalous in this regard. Upon closer inspection, this Chinese engagement appears, however, in line with the argument and can be explained by Chinese self-interest. Overall, the results of the comparison are in line with the expectation that the interaction between China and domestic leaders adapted to the logic of political survival in the recipient state.

Another interesting insight concerns China's preferences with regard to political stability elsewhere. The finding that coalition size varies with the degree of compliance suggests that there are, indeed, incentives for external actors to cultivate or prop-up small-coalition systems elsewhere in the world. However, as argued above, and in line with its foreign policy rhetoric, the Chinese government has pragmatically accepted the change in leadership elsewhere. In the past, China has not necessarily created the highly exclusive political structures that facilitate economic exploitation of developing countries – even though it may, in some cases, have contributed to unequal income distribution or facilitated the rise of particular elites, as has been argued in the case of Cambodia (Mengin 2007). However, with China's economic rise, this may well change in the future. The increasing amount of Chinese investments allocated to other autocracies over the last decade has created vested interests for Chinese business elites in the stability of these countries. Thus, the incentives for Chinese foreign policymakers to maintain prevalent autocratic political structures under the disguise of political stability have dramatically changed and are likely to de facto translate into a strong Chinese preference for autocracies in the future.

Having said that, it would be misleading to equate China's wish for political stability with a preference for the status quo per se. The case of Burma, which clearly illustrates the Chinese recognition that some political reforms were required, is instructive in this regard. It seems that the Chinese government draws heavily on its own experience when it perceives economic development and well-being to be a cornerstone of political, and hence autocratic, stability.

For quite some time, the Chinese government has been deeply frustrated with the performance of the Burmese regime, which frequently provoked international critique and thereby embarrassed the Chinese leaders who were widely perceived as Burma's autocratic patron (Kleine-Ahlbrandt and Small 2008). It was an impediment to the development of close relations and for the pursuit of China's interests in Burma that the SPDC, obsessed with its own security, was very suspicious of China's intentions (Storey 2007). For this reason, and in anticipation that this would increase the SPDC's legitimacy, the Chinese government encouraged economic reforms and better governance, and lobbied for some gradual political reforms in Burma. On the other hand, the Chinese call to work on national reconciliation and political reforms aimed at establishing a political regime that would be more inclusive and would be able to co-opt the excluded opposition forces into a strong centralized government (International Crisis Group 2009; Sun 2012). China was thus in favour of Burma's seven-point roadmap to democracy, as it expected that the process would increase the legitimacy of the SPDC's leadership, help to destigmatize the SPDC and thus alleviate the SPDC's international isolation, while, at the same time, strengthening the regime's grip on power.

Comparing the dissatisfaction that Chinese leaders formulated with Burma during the 2000s with the ease with which they could operate in Cambodia, it appears that China's leaders favour political stability while recognizing that political legitimacy and a leadership's feeling of security in power crucially contribute to this. In contrast to the worrisome relationship with the Burmese regime, in its liaison with the Cambodian regime, the Chinese government achieved all its objectives without much irritation. Cambodia's government was extremely willing to embrace China's interests, while having close ties to the Cambodian government had no costs for China's international reputation. Even though the Cambodian government was criticized from time to time for its low compliance with Western aid conditionality, unlike in the case of Burma, this critique did not implicitly or explicitly fall back on the Chinese government. In brief, Cambodia's electoral window dressing and its integration into the international community made it a much more comfortable and beneficial partner to maintain autocratic cooperation with.

Reflections on the theoretical framework

Finally, the case study investigation concludes with a brief reflection on the theoretical framework. In general, the theoretical framework based on the selectorate theory appears to offer a powerful analytical tool to combine and assess the domestic logic of survival and the interaction between authoritarian elites across countries. Much of its power stems from its simplicity and its high level of abstraction. This notwithstanding, the application of the theoretical framework in this study also reveals some of its limitations and weaknesses.

As far as the case study investigation is concerned, the overall fit between theory and empirics seems to be relatively good – even if one acknowledges that some additional, previously discussed factors may also have contribtued to the observed outcome. The case studies illustrated how the different domestic political systems can be conceptualized in terms of winning coalitions and selectorates. They exemplified the interaction between elites in China and the three countries and tried to identify the targets of such interaction. In this way, they illustrated how leaders in small winning coalitions can monopolize gains achieved by cooperation with external players and showed how these gains are, in turn, redistributed amongst domestic supporters and so perpetuate a given power distribution.

However, two empirical observations are not easily explained and hint at limitations or the need for refinements of the broader theoretical framework. First, it appears that the protection of rogue states, in addition to offering opportunities for exploitation, can also induce reputational costs for their patrons. On the one hand, Cambodia's compliance – and the fact that China's leaders themselves anticipated Burma's domestic reforms to be conducive to Chinese interests – suggest that regimes, with a large nominal, but a small true selectorate and winning coalition rather than closed regimes with small selectorates and a small winning coalition, appear to be most compliant with external interests. Hence, so-called competitive authoritarian systems (Schedler 2006; Levitsky and Way 2010), in which incumbents succeed in maintaining control over the political process and economic resources, while the political arena is seemingly competitive and pluralistic, appear to offer most opportunities for external exploitation. Considering only the national level, this is neatly in line with selectorate theory, which assumes that such a constellation stabilizes a leader's domestic position in power, thereby increasing the leader's discretionary leeway with regard to his domestic distribution (Bueno de Mesquita *et al.* 2003).

On the other hand, however, such competitive regimes may not only be easier to exploit, but also induce fewer reputational costs for the patron. The Chinese leadership endorsed political reforms in Burma not only in anticipation that this would increase the junta's domestic legitimacy, but also in the expectation that the country would regain some international respect (at least at the regional level). Authoritarian regimes that are more in line with international norms evoke less international criticism, which may fall back on the patron and induce reputational costs. (In the specific case of Burma, such criticism referred to the violation of *Western* democratic rather than universal international norms.) This strongly suggests that the theoretical framework needs to consider not only the benefits that accrue for major powers from cultivating authoritarianism abroad, but also needs to incorporate an analysis of the costs that such autocratic patronage may induce for the patrons.

A second observation that needs reflection is that, depending on the composition of the winning coalition, the domestic costs of compliance with the very same external interest can vary considerably for different leaders. This observation points to an important weakness in the theoretical framework. With its emphasis on the winning coalition, the selectorate theory is helpful to identify those groups that are relevant to a leader, but it cannot necessarily tell us what exactly their preferences and interests are (see Gallagher and Hanson [2013] for a similar argument). Therefore, it can be difficult to explain merely on the basis of the size of a winning coalition the salience of an issue in domestic politics and the choice for a specific policy option. For example, it was argued earlier that a country's economic structure and the specific economic interests of the coalition members should be decisive with regard to the question how exactly leaders react to external economic interests.

If one assumes that the preferences of the winning coalition members may be shaped not only by material interests, but also by ideas, beliefs or identities, this problem becomes even more apparent. Consider the Dalai Lama question. Even though research has found that frustrating China on the Dalai Lama issue is connected to material sanctions (Fuchs and Klann 2013), this cannot fully explain why similarly democratic countries differ in their willingness to bear these costs. Due to the country's religious affiliation with Tibetan Buddhism, Mongolian leaders will probably always find it more difficult to reject a visit by the Dalai Lama – even in comparisons to other democracies.

A similar difficulty arises with regard to explaining Burma's domestic reforms. As argued in Chapter 4, political reforms in Burma are only in line with the selectorate theory as long as they are interpreted as an attempt to move towards, and institutionalize a different form of authoritarian rule with a broader selectorate. Many factors that are believed to have been important, such as economic pressure and the need to achieve the lifting of sanctions, are compatible with the broader predictions of selectorate theory. However, considering that reforms have been pushed beyond expectations, they are more difficult to reconcile with the selectorate theory. The selectorate theory disregards some of the most compelling causes of the political reforms, namely the ideational divisions between members of the junta and the generational change in the country's leadership.

Hence, since winning coalitions can include very different domestic groups, the theoretical framework fails to provide satisfactory answers with regard to the question of why and when leaders consider some policy options to be more costly than others given the size of their winning coalition. Relying only on the *size* of the winning coalition, it remains unclear why, sometimes, the same policy concessions are associated with different domestic costs (or benefits) in different countries, despite similar regime types. In order to explain concrete policy outcomes, one would need a framework that extends beyond the identification of winning coalition size. Instead, a fully specified model would need to acknowledge the variety of interests that different coalition members may have, and to specify how such different interests are aggregated. It is thus a task for further research to examine whether and how the selectorate theory can be combined with existing approaches to explain policymaking without losing the theory's parsimony.

Notes

1 Private Source, Phnom Penh, 17 November 2009. However, organized crime rooted in Taiwan apparently also played a prominent role in illegal migration from China via Cambodia to the US and Canada (Lintner 2002: 220).

2 The Dalai Lama has indicated that the fifteenth Dalai Lama should reincarnate in a democratic country. A Dalai Lama from Mongolia would complicate China's difficulties with its domestic minorities because, as a Mongolian, he would most likely enjoy great support from the Mongolian minorities in China's Autonomous Region of Inner Mongolia and increase their identification with both Buddhism and Mongolia. This would extend the Chinese authorities' concerns of separatism from Tibet to Inner Mongolia, which has recently been a relatively quiet region. One Mongolian analyst reasons that even though the Chinese government would have greater oversight over a Dalai Lama in Mongolia than in India, because it has more means of influence over Mongolia than India, one can expect that Chinese authorities will try to avoid an independent nomination of the Dalai Lama at all by appointing a different person. This is possible, because there are conflicting interpretations of the recognition process. In 1996, in contradiction to the announcement of the Dalai Lama, Chinese authorities announced a 6-year-old boy as the figure of succession of the Panchen Lama, whose previous figure had deceased earlier. Shortly thereafter, the Panchen Lama recognized by the Dalai Lama disappeared (Mashbat 2007). Such a scenario would most likely pose a great challenge for Mongolian policymakers in terms of manoeuvring between the Mongolians' request for religious freedom and the Chinese government's interests.

3 Conference on 'Strategy for Railway Infrastructure Development of Mongolia', Ulaanbaatar, 14 October 2009.

4 Private Source, Ulaanbaatar, 6 October 2009.

5 For example, the Sittwe Port, Ramree Island and Coco Island in Burma, Chittagong in Bangladesh, Hambantota in Sri Lanka, on the Maldives, and Gwadar in Pakistan.

Part III
Autocratic cooperation?
Patterns and consequences

8   Does China target other autocrats?

This chapter investigates whether China specifically targets autocratic small-coalition systems in its foreign relations. In order to assess this question, which reflects hypothesis 2, this chapter presents a statistical analysis. It is designed to examine whether the Chinese government targets some countries, but not others.

The remainder of this chapter is structured in the following way: I start off with measurement issues. Most importantly, the first section presents data on China's economic cooperation with foreign countries and discusses why this data can be used as a proxy for targeting. Furthermore, I introduce measurements for the size of winning coalition and regime type. Then, section two assesses the role of winning-coalition size and regime type in determining the allocation of Chinese economic cooperation. I analyse whether winning-coalition size or regime type influence whether the Chinese government targets a country with economic cooperation projects. Section three discusses my results in the broader context of the research project.

How to measure Chinese targeting

Economic cooperation

As elaborated in Chapter 2, there are plausible reasons for expecting that governments try to buy-off other governments in order to make them more lenient to their external interests. In line with this argumentation, hypothesis 2 predicts that the Chinese government specifically targets autocratic small-coalition systems in its foreign relations. As a proxy for such attempts to buy-off others, studies that have investigated similar questions have used foreign assistance and flows of development aid (Bueno de Mesquita and Smith 2007, 2009).

In the case of China, finding a good indicator is more complex. First, there is no data on aid transfers available; and second, it is an explicit Chinese policy to link foreign investment, trade and aid (Brautigam 2009). The Chinese government does not publish disaggregated aid disbursements that would allow us to investigate annual Chinese development assistance to individual recipient countries.[1] However, the Chinese understanding of what development aid entails is also not comparable to the common definition of official development assistance by the Development Assistance Committee (DAC) of the Organisation for Economic Cooperation and Development (OECD). The Chinese aid statistics, in contrast to the OECD statistics, not only include subsidies on interests, but also military aid (Brautigam 2009).

Moreover, China's financial and development assistance explicitly aims at promoting benefits for both the recipients' *and* the Chinese economies. In 1995, the Chinese aid architecture was fundamentally restructured to better serve the goal of China's domestic modernization. This was further complemented by the Chinese 'go out' policy. This policy was launched in 2001 and aimed at enhancing the global competitiveness of state-owned enterprises by stimulating China's state-owned companies to invest overseas. In addition to a wide range of preferential treatments in the domestic context, such as tax breaks and cheap land and capital, the Chinese government strengthened its back-up of its corporations on the international stage.

As a result, Chinese assistance has a strong focus on export promotion and securing access to natural resources (Davies *et al.* 2008). This becomes evident from the fact that much of China's economic assistance comes in the form of concessional lending. The criteria for loans generally are plentiful resources, a large market and favourable economic prospects (Hubbard 2007: 7). Loans are tied to procurement from Chinese firms and the money is directly allocated by the Chinese government through its state banks to Chinese contractors that carry out investment projects abroad. The recipient countries are invoiced for the loan, but hardly see any cash money.

Given this conscious strategy to link foreign investment, trade and aid, I make use of data that is published by the National Bureau of Statistics of China (2010) on the annual turnover of all projects carried out by Chinese companies abroad. China's economic cooperation includes:

(1) overseas civil engineering construction projects financed by foreign investors;
(2) overseas projects financed by the Chinese government through its foreign aid programs;
(3) construction projects of Chinese diplomatic missions, trade offices and other institutions stationed abroad;
(4) construction projects in China financed by foreign investment;[2]
(5) sub-contracted projects to be taken by Chinese contractors through a joint umbrella project with foreign contractor(s);[3]
(6) housing development projects. (National Bureau of Statistics of China 2010)

This melting pot of trade, aid and state and commercial FDI figures is used as a proxy for China's engagement abroad. It has been argued that Chinese economic cooperation data is most likely correlated with financial engagement, given that Chinese financial and development assistance is tied (Berthélemy 2011). With regard to my purpose, it is clearly not a perfect measure as it can include purely private investments. However, given that Chinese state support can be assumed for larger foreign investment projects, and lacking a more reliable proxy (such as purely financial transfers from China), this bias is acceptable. Thus, although there is some noise in the data, I use *Economic Cooperation* to measure Chinese targeting.

Data on Chinese economic cooperation is available from 1998 onwards. Figure 8.1 illustrates how the total amount of Chinese economic cooperation has increased over time for OECD and non-OECD countries. As can be seen, the lines for OECD and non-OECD countries are relatively parallel until the early 2000s, when economic cooperation to non-OECD countries began to increase dramatically. The steep increase in economic cooperation projects from 2003 onwards reflects China's 2001 'go out' policy, which specifically encouraged Chinese engagement in the developing world.

In 1998, China's economic cooperation projects, per country, averaged around US$56 million; one decade later, in 2008, this amount was almost six times higher and reached almost US$335 million per country. Thus, the distribution of economic cooperation among countries varied considerably: averaged over the whole period, the biggest recipients, Singapore and Sudan, received projects worth more than US$1 billion annually. Paraguay, received, on average, the smallest amount with a volume of around US$35,880.

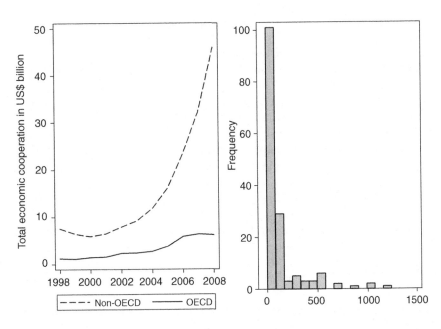

Figure 8.1 Total amount of Chinese economic cooperation (in constant US$ billion) by year and average Chinese economic cooperation by country

Size of the winning coalition or regime type

According to my hypotheses, I expect China's economic cooperation to a country to be determined by its regime type, whereby autocratic countries or small-winning-coalition countries are expected to be more likely to receive economic cooperation. Determining a country's winning-coalition size or its regime type is a complicated and controversial undertaking. Therefore, I have built on two existing approaches: Bueno de Mesquita *et al.*'s (2003) measurement of winning-coalition size, and a measurement of democracy versus autocracy based on the Polity IV dataset.

I measure the size of a winning coalition in the same way as Bueno de Mesquita *et al.* (2003) by using their variables W (size of winning coalition) and S (size of selectorate). Basically, a winning coalition W is considered to be large if the recruitment of the executive is open and competitive and the chief executive is selected by elections, as opposed to heredity or rigged, unopposed elections. Additionally, military regimes in particular are considered dependent on a highly exclusive group (Bueno de Mesquita *et al.* 2003: 134f; Bueno de Mesquita and Smith 2010: 940).[4] The variable is standardized to range from 0 to 1, whereby higher values indicate a larger winning coalition.

To measure S, Bueno de Mesquita and Smith (2010) refer to the selection process of the legislative as an indicator of the inclusiveness of the selectorate. The size of the selectorate S is coded 0, if no legislature exists according to Bank's *LEGSELEC* variable; 1, if selection is non-elective, i.e. it is heredity or ascribed; and 2, if the legislature is elected. Again, this variable is standardized to range from 0 to 1 by dividing it by two. Larger values indicate a larger selectorate (Bueno de Mesquita and Smith 2010: 940). The disadvantage of this data set is that it only covers the years up to 2006.

In addition, I use a measure for democracy versus autocracy. In order to do so, I create a dummy based on Polity IV's *polity2* variable (Marshall and Jaggers 2013). This variable is coded 1, when *polity2* exceeds six, and 0 otherwise. I chose a binary measure instead of a polychotomous classification of regime type, because the most common classifications (Freedom House and Polity) are distributed bimodally with many cases in the low and high ends. This bimodal distribution explains the high correlation between dichotomous and polychotomous cases, but it is also most likely the force behind the empirical patterns in studies concerned with political regimes. Once the cases at the extreme ends are deleted, the correlation drops significantly. The critique here is that there is no agreement on the conceptual specificity of the cases in the middle categories and no substantial interpretation of what a move from one category to the other empirically means (Cheibub *et al.* 2010). For this reason, I chose a dichotomous measure of regime type instead of a polychomous measure.

Both measures for winning-coalition size and regime type, W and *Democracy*, are expected to have a negative effect on the allocation of economic cooperation, as autocratic small-coalition systems are hypothesized to be more likely to be targeted. As to the volume of economic cooperation projects, the theory suggests that autocrats are disadvantaged in comparison with their democratic fellows. Consequently, size of winning coalition *W* and *Democracy* are expected to have a positive effect on the volume of economic cooperation.

Other determinants of economic cooperation

A number of other factors are likely to impact on the allocation and volume of Chinese economic cooperation projects. As mentioned before, China's allocation criteria for extending concessional loans explicitly include a country's resource endowments, the size of its market and its economic prospects (Hubbard 2007: 7). Moreover, adherence to the 'one China' policy is the cornerstone on which the government of the PRC has built its relations with other states in the past and this is the only explicitly named political conditionality of Chinese foreign aid. It is plausible that this principle also affects other aspects of China's foreign relations, such as the more commercially oriented aspects that are equally captured in the data on China's economic cooperation. In the following, I briefly describe how I operationalized these factors. Table 8.1 presents descriptive statistics for all variables.

Economic prospects

A country's economic prospects are accounted for in two ways. First, I include a country's GDP per capita (Heston *et al.* 2011). This variable is logged and lagged by one year.[5] However, with regard to this variable, the direction of the effect is not obvious. The effect could be negative, when developing countries – as opposed to developed economies – receive more attention as they promise dynamic markets and higher future returns. However, when Chinese companies

Table 8.1 Descriptive statistics

Variable	Obs.	Mean	Std Dev.	Min.	Max.
Economic Cooperation Dummy	1,708	0.908	0.288	0	1
Economic Cooperation (>2.5/<2.5mio)	1,708	0.751	0.432	0	1
W_{t-1}	1,486	0.663	0.267	0	1
S_{t-1}	1,524	0.946	0.201	0	1
$Democracy_{t-1}$	1,706	0.531	0.499	0	1
Oil reserves$_{t-1}$ (ln)	1,673	−6.211	6.830	−13.815	5.586
Oil Dummy$_{t-1}$	1,693	0.262	0.439	0	1
Minerals$_{t-1}$	1,707	0.131	0.208	0	1
Taiwan	1,708	0.107	0.309	0	1
Population$_{t-1}$ (ln)	1,671	16.061	1.491	12.909	20.840
GDP/c$_{t-1}$ (ln)	1,671	8.421	1.347	4.764	11.723
Growth$_{t-1}$	1,671	3.439	7.820	−40.011	122.237
FDI$_{t-1}$ (ln)	1,550	19.910	3.006	−13.815	26.495

seek to invest in highly developed countries in order to buy brands or acquire technical skills, the effect of *GDP/c* could also be positive.

Second, I control for economic prospects by including GDP growth rates instead of GDP levels. *Growth* is calculated on the basis of GDP and lagged by one year. As more dynamic markets are assumed to be more attractive targets, I expect *Growth* to have a positive effect on allocation decisions, and on the volume of *Economic Cooperation*.

Size of market

In order to control for market size, the model contains size in terms of population (Heston *et al.* 2011). Variable *Population* is logged and lagged by one year. Population size is expected to have a positive effect on the likelihood for and volume of economic cooperation.

Resource endowment

Measuring resource abundance is not a straightforward undertaking. I concentrate on two very simple alternative measurements of natural resource endowments, oil reserves and an index of mineral wealth. Firstly, I took proven crude oil reserves in billion barrels (US Energy Information Administration 2010). Because oil reserves are distributed unevenly around the world, with a few countries having very large resources and many others with nothing, I created a dummy indicating whether a country's oil reserves belong to the worlds' biggest deposits. The dummy was coded 1 for countries with oil reserves that exceed 0.6 billion barrels (corresponding to the sample's 75th percentile), and 0 otherwise.

In addition, I constructed an index of five strategic minerals. These minerals are iron ore, chromium, cobalt, copper and manganese (US Geology Survey 2008). To avoid the problem of aggregation, I created dummy variables for each mineral, coding it 1, if a country was involved in the production of the respective mineral, and coding it 0 otherwise. Then I constructed an index adding up how many of the five minerals a country possesses and normalizing the index to range from 0 to 1 by dividing by five.

Because a couple of years might pass between the exploration and development and the actual exploitation of natural reserve deposits – particularly in the case of subsoil deposits – it would be desirable to use data on actual mineral deposits, rather than on the production of these minerals. However, for many resources no satisfying data exists – in terms of existing resource deposits, rather than extraction – on the basis of which the abundance of different types of resources can be aggregated. Production data are both more accurate and more accessible, even though using production data implies the risk that Chinese attention, in the form of economic cooperation to resource-rich countries with the prospect of exploiting resource deposits in the future, might not yet be highly correlated with extraction data.[6]

As the Chinese economy is in need of all these different natural resources, it is assumed that resource endowment should increase both the likelihood that a country is targeted with economic cooperation projects, and the volume of economic cooperation. Thus, *Oil* and *Minerals* should positively affect the allocation and volume of economic cooperation projects.

Taiwan

Taiwan is a binary variable that is coded 1 for each year during the period of investigation in which a country officially recognized Taiwan, and 0 otherwise.[7] Diplomatic relations with Taiwan are expected to be detrimental to the allocation of economic cooperation, thus the effect is expected to be negative.

However, from descriptive statistics it becomes clear that non-compliance with the 'one China' principle and the recognition of Taiwan does not strictly lead to the withdrawal of economic cooperation projects or non-disbursement in the first place. Most of the 183 observations in the sample that did have diplomatic relations with Taiwan still received some economic cooperation from China. Only in 47 cases was no economic cooperation delivered, while the rest continued to receive economic cooperation. However, compared to the overall sample, countries with diplomatic relations to Taiwan received considerably lower amounts. Only a handful of countries, most notably Senegal, Chad and Panama, continued to receive substantial amounts of economic cooperation despite recognizing Taiwan, whereas the average amount among this group of countries lay at around US$8 million, and the median was far below US$1 million (US$10 million corresponds roughly to the 80th percentile). The fact that for the vast majority of cases very low amounts, rather than no economic cooperation, is reported seems to indicate that ongoing economic cooperation in these cases is mostly driven by noise in the data; *Economic Cooperation* is not strictly limited to state projects, but also contains projects funded by third parties.

Are autocrats targeted?

This section presents the results of my investigation of whether my theoretical predictions are correct. It was expected that the Chinese government specifically targets autocracies with economic cooperation (hypothesis 2). The examination of what determines Chinese cooperation covers the period between 1998 and 2008. The sample contains 155 countries and, in total, 1,670 observations.[8] The unit of observation is the country-year.

In order to investigate the question of whether small-coalition autocratic countries are primary targets, that is, whether they are more likely to receive economic cooperation than democracies, a series of probit regressions are run. This estimation procedure is designed to examine why the Chinese government delivers economic cooperation to some countries, but not to others. This estimation procedure requires a binary dependent variable. Therefore, a dummy variable based on *Economic Cooperation* was created. The dummy takes on only two values: 1, when economic cooperation takes place in a given year, and 0 otherwise. Accordingly, negative regression results indicate that a given variable *decreases* the likelihood that a country receives economic cooperation, whereas positive coefficients indictate the opposite; that is, a variable should *increase* the chance of being targeted with economic cooperation. All of the following models were estimated with robust standard errors clustered by country. The results of my first series of probit regressions on whether or not a country is targeted with Chinese economic cooperation are presented in Table 8.2.

Size of the winning coalition W and selectorate S are the variables of primary interest in Model 1. In Model 1, they are both negative, but not statistically significant. In line with my expectations, the sign of the coefficient indicates that large-coalition systems are less likely to be targeted with economic cooperation.

Table 8.2 Probit regression of whether China provides economic cooperation

	Economic cooperation			
	(1) *Yes/No*	*(2)* *Yes/No*	*(3)* *>2.5/<2.5mio*	*(4)* *>2.5/<2.5mio*
W_{t-1}	−0.102 (0.328)		−0.393 (0.287)	
S_{t-1}	−0.428 (0.612)		0.338 (0.340)	
Democracy$_{t-1}$		−0.315** (0.159)		−0.346*** (0.134)
Oil$_{t-1}$	0.122 (0.163)	0.095 (0.162)	0.289** (0.133)	0.242* (0.124)
Taiwan	−0.458** (0.191)	−0.516*** (0.183)	−0.776*** (0.209)	−0.746*** (0.202)
Growth$_{t-1}$	−0.009 (0.007)	−0.011* (0.007)	−0.004 (0.005)	−0.005 (0.005)
Population$_{t-1}$ (ln)	0.144** (0.058)	0.132** (0.053)	0.197*** (0.046)	0.192*** (0.040)
GDP/c$_{t-1}$ (ln)	−0.061 (0.061)	−0.016 (0.056)	−0.117** (0.053)	−0.065 (0.049)
Lagged dependent variable	2.159*** (0.205)	2.098*** (0.211)	1.945*** (0.157)	1.964*** (0.150)
Constant	−1.350 (1.203)	−1.737* (1.029)	−1.821** (0.882)	−1.881** (0.747)
Observations	1294	1503	1442	1656
Countries	151	154	151	154
Log pseudolikelihood	−221	−247	−455	−500
Chi-squared	290	272	499	586
Pseudo-R-squared	0.3980	0.4016	0.4442	0.4560
Year dummies	Yes	Yes	Yes	Yes

Note: Standard errors in parentheses, clustered by country. * p<0.1, ** p<0.05, *** p<0.01

However, being insignificant, winning coalition size W does not seem to be a selection criterion when the Chinese government decides to allocate economic cooperation projects. Things look different when W is replaced with a binary measure for democracy versus autocracy. In Model 2, the coefficient on *Democracy* is negative and significant. This suggests that autocracies are, indeed, specifically targeted with economic cooperation projects.

However, given the composition of *Economic Cooperation*, it might be misleading to interpret only zero values of economic cooperation as non-targeting. Given the variety of activities that are captured in this variable, one should expect the value of economic cooperation as it is reported to be slightly inflated. Recall that the data also comprises projects financed by third parties or the construction of Chinese diplomatic facilities abroad. Both of these activities could result in a situation where activities that are reported in the economic cooperation data take place; that is, non-zero values of economic cooperation are reported, even when the Chinese government has decided not to allocate projects of economic cooperation to a specific country. On the other hand, one can plausibly assume that, in certain situations, the Chinese government perceives the complete withdrawal from or non-disbursement of cooperation projects to be counterproductive to the achievement of its external objectives. Sustaining some economic cooperation on a very low level, so as to 'save face' could, therefore, be a strategic alternative.

Progressing on from this, I recode the dependent variable *Economic Cooperation* so as to allow the disbursal of very low amounts of economic cooperation without treating it as intended targeting. I assume that the amount of economic cooperation is likely to be relatively small when the Chinese government is not willing to cooperate with a country, but rather wants to 'save face' or when the reported activities are driven by third party funding or reflect purely private commercial investments. Therefore, I chose a threshold that is small both in absolute terms and relative to the distribution of the sample. Accordingly, the dependent variable is now coded 0 when the absolute amount of Chinese economic cooperation that a country receives in a given year falls below US$2.5 million. This threshold is considerably lower than the mean (US$122 million) or median (US$21 million) amount of received economic cooperation in the sample, and it corresponds to the 25th precentile of the sample (against the 9th percentile when only 'true zeros' are interpreted as non-targeting). In sum, the chosen threshold is very conservative.

With regard to W, S, and *Democracy*, the results of Models 3 and 4 with the modified dependent variable replicate my earlier findings. Even when the threshold of what constitutes concious targeting is increased, the coefficient on W and S remain insignificant, while *Democracy* is negative and significant. As will be discussed in more detail below, the fact that *Democracy* is significant while W is not, is likely driven by multicollinearity between these two variables and *GDP/c*. Models 3 and 4 include the lagged dependent variable and year dummies to control for changing allocation patterns over time. Even though the results are not shown, the reported findings for W and *Democracy* are, however, robust to the exclusion of the lagged dependent variable and the year dummies (or both).

In line with my prediction that autocracies are more likely to become partners for cooperation, the Chinese government seems to specifically select autocracies to distribute economic cooperation. My findings supports hypothesis 2 that autocratic small-coalition systems are targeted by the Chinese government.

Considering Models 3 and 4 as my main models, I refer to these models when discussing the results for the control variables. My analysis finds that resource endowment is only partly decisive in terms of whether or not China targets a given country. As can be seen in Models 3 and 4, the coefficient on *Oil* is positive and statistically significant. This result is in line with the criteria for China's concessional lending to developing countries (Hubbard 2007). However, I find no evidence that mineral endowments determine whether a country is targeted with projects of economic cooperation. When *Minerals* is used to measure resource endowment (models not shown), regardless of model specification, the results are never significant. Thus, whether resource endowment turns a country into a specific target for economic cooperation seems to depend on the type of resources that a country has to offer.

The *Taiwan* dummy is always negative and highly significant. Even though the recognition of Taiwan does not automatically lead to the complete cessation of economic cooperation projects, as discussed earlier, countries with diplomatic relations to Taiwan are clearly less likely to receive Chinese economic cooperation.

The coefficient on *Population* is positive and significant in Models 3 and 4, which indicates that big countries are more likely to be targeted with economic cooperation. This result makes sense in economic terms and seems to be in line with the allocation principles for concessional loans, which refer to the size of a country's market. When economic cooperation projects constitute infrastructure development, bigger countries are more likely to be the recipients of such projects – with land mass being positively correlated with population size. On the other hand, when economic cooperation projects flank investments that seek to gain market access, bigger consumer markets are more attractive destinations of such investments.

In contrast to this, I do not find that dynamically growing markets specficially attract economic cooperation. In Models 3 and 4, the coefficient on *Growth* does not impact on whether a country is targeted with economic cooperation. This even holds when *Growth* replaces, rather then complements, *GDP/c*; that is, when the model contains only *Growth*, but not *GDP/c* (results not shown).

In Models 3 and 4 the coefficient on *GDP/c* is negative, indicating that poor countries have a higher likelihood of receiving Chinese economic cooperation. The negative relationship between a country's wealth and the likelihood of being targeted is consistent with earlier findings (Berthélemy 2011; Dreher and Fuchs forthcoming) and underlines the fact – as illustrated in Figure 8.1 – that the majority of China's outward projects captured in the economic cooperation data focuses on projects in developing markets. Theoretically, one reason for targeting poor countries could be the Chinese expectation that once economic cooperation is given, governments with few own resources are easier to convince to accept a policy deal. A government with higher domestic resources at its disposal should have a better bargaining position and, therefore, be able to demand more in return for compliance with Chinese interests.

However, wealth is not a robust determinant of whether economic cooperation is given. Only in Model 3 is *GDP/c* statistically significant. The fact that *GDP/c* is significant and *W* is not in Model 3, while the results are reversed for Model 4, point to multicollinearity issues. It is thus troublesome that regime type, wealth and *Population* are all correlated with each other, whereby the corrrelation between *GDP/c* and *W* is stronger than that between *GDP/c* and *Democracy*. Such multi-collinearity can typically lead to unstable or insignificant results when the effect of one coefficient is absorbed by another. For this reason, I run two robustness checks. First, I replace *GDP/c* and *Population* with a country's net *FDI* inflows (World Bank 2010), a variable that is correlated with both *Population* and *GDP/c* (and *W* and *Democracy*, but to a lesser degree). The variable is logged and lagged by one year. As can be seen in Models 5 and 6 of Table 8.3, this variable has a positive coefficient. In Model 5, *W* too becomes statistically significant, while the inclusion of *FDI* does not affect the results of any of the other variables in the model.

Second, in order to ease the problem of potential multicollinearity, I limit the sample to the developing world by excluding all OECD member countries. Without this set of rich democracies, the correlation between *W* and *GDP/c* decreases dramatically and moderately for *Democracy* and *GDP/c*, respectively. Interestingly, when only developing countries are compared, as can be seen in Models 7 and 8 in Table 8.3, *W* does not seem to play a decisive role, whereas the finding that democracies are less targeted is robust when regime type is measured with *Democracy*.

Conclusion and discussion of findings

This chapter attempted to assess whether the Chinese government targets small-coalition autocracies over large-coalition democracies (hypothesis 2). In order to do so, I introduced a measurement for such targeting, i.e. China's economic cooperation projects. This variable is provided by the National Statistics Bureau of China (2010) and captures the annual turnover of all projects carried out by Chinese companies abroad. Making use of this data, I statistically analysed whether autocratic and small-coalition systems are more likely to be the recipients of such projects.

To summarize the result of my analysis, I find some evidence supporting the expectation of hypothesis 2. When winning-coalition size is measured with a binary measure for regime type, my findings robustly show that autocracies are more likely to be targeted. However, my findings are senstitive to measurement issues. When winning-coalition size is measured in terms of *W* – an indicator initially introduced by Bueno de Mesquita *et al.* (2003) in order to capture winning-coalition size – my findings are less robust, with *W* sometimes being decisive for becoming a recipient and sometimes not. I attribute these different findings and the instability of results when using *W* to the fact that *W* is highly correlated with some economic indicators, notably *GDP/c*, which also affects allocation decisions.

Table 8.3 Robustness. Probit regression of whether China provides economic cooperation

	Economic cooperation			
	(5) >2.5/<2.5mio	(6) >2.5/<2.5mio	(7) >2.5/<2.5mio	(8) >2.5/<2.5mio
W_{t-1}	−0.709*** (0.264)		−0.441 (0.307)	
S_{t-1}	0.435 (0.313)		0.363 (0.338)	
Democracy$_{t-1}$		−0.456*** (0.125)		−0.316** (0.130)
Oil$_{t-1}$	0.263** (0.118)	0.266** (0.112)	0.250 (0.153)	0.211 (0.149)
Taiwan	−0.695*** (0.200)	−0.638*** (0.187)	−0.768*** (0.203)	−0.735*** (0.194)
Growth$_{t-1}$	−0.008 (0.008)	−0.011 (0.007)	−0.003 (0.005)	−0.004 (0.005)
Population$_{t-1}$ (ln)			0.160*** (0.049)	0.158*** (0.041)
GDP/c$_{t-1}$ (ln)			−0.140** (0.066)	−0.088 (0.065)
Lagged dependent variable	2.056*** (0.159)	2.060*** (0.151)	2.120*** (0.170)	2.115*** (0.163)
FDI$_{t-1}$ (ln)	0.018 (0.018)	0.037** (0.017)		
Constant	0.149 (0.405)	−0.747** (0.371)	−1.059 (1.023)	−1.187 (0.895)
Observations	1331	1526	1172	1360
Countries	144	148	124	127
Log pseudolikelihood	−451	−492	−345	−388
Chi-squared	451	560	415	526
Pseudo-R-squared	0.4120	0.4298	0.4793	0.4862
Year dummies	Yes	Yes	Yes	Yes

Note: Standard errors in parentheses, clustered by country. * p<0.1, ** p<0.05, *** p<0.01

A second robust finding is that the decision about whether a government receives Chinese economic cooperation is taken on the basis of whether it adheres to China's key foreign policy interest, the 'one China' policy. When countries diplomatically recognize Taiwan, they are less likely to receive economic cooperation projects from China. Third, the expectation that targeting is driven by a country's resource endowment is supported only partly: it can be shown only for those countries with the world's highest oil reserves. Moreover, the effect vanishes when only developing countries are compared and it cannot be shown for resources other than oil. More dynamic and richer markets do not seem to make countries more prone to being targeted by China. However, bigger markets, that is, more populous countries, are more likely to receive economic cooperation.

Notes

1   There is a database on completed aid projects that is based on newspaper reports, but this data does not contain aid volumes (Hawkins *et al.* 2010).
2   This refers to projects that are carried out a) in China; b) by a Chinese company; but c) financed by a third country; and d) that have publicly been procured. In addition to the fact that this combination of requirements is probably not often met, information distributed by China's Ministry of Commerce hints at the fact that the bulk of China's economic cooperation truly refers to projects carried out abroad. Moreover, the Chinese administrative regulations for international projects also refer exclusively to projects abroad, which also indicates that projects constructed in China are rather rare. (Private Source, Bonn, 22 May 2011.)
3   The fact that China has been increasingly successful in recent years in winning tenders for internationally financed construction projects (by the World Bank, for example) and the fact that these projects are included in this data is a challenge. However, Foster et al. (2009) estimated that in 2002–05 only around 10 per cent of Chinese economic cooperation projects in Africa were not financed by Chinese sources, and the bulk of projects was funded by Chinese money.
4   The size of the winning coalition W is a composite index based on four equally weighed variables *REGTYPE* (Banks 2007), *XRCOMP*, *XROPEN* and *PARCOMP* from the Polity IV data (Marshall and Jaggers 2013). More specifically, one point is added to the index 'for each of the following conditions: if Banks' regime type variable is non-military, if XRCOMP is greater than or equal to 2 (meaning the chief executive is not chosen by heredity or in rigged, unopposed elections), if XROPEN is greater than 2, and if PARCOMP equals 5 (indicating the presence of a competitive party system)' (Bueno de Mesquita and Smith 2010: 940). I take these two variables from a replication data set of Bueno de Mesquita and Smith (2010), which is posted on Bruce Bueno de Mesquita's homepage. See http://politics.as.nyu.edu/object/ brucebuenodemesquita.
5   There are two countries for which I use different data: Myanmar and Turkmenistan. Because of missing data in the Penn World Table, I use the TED data set for Myanmar (The Conference Board Total Economy Database 2011). For Turkmenistan, the Penn World Table contains wrong values, which is why I use data from the World Bank's World Development Indicators (2010).
6   I refrain from using the value of primary commodity exports (or specific commodities) as a share of national income or total exports (Sachs and Warner 1999, 2001; Isham *et al.* 2005) or the UNCTAD's export concentration index, because they do not directly measure resource wealth, but intensity. The share of primary commodities in GDP may be driven by other factors such as policy or the degree to which a country processes its mineral resources instead of merely exporting them (Norman 2009; Bond and Malik 2009).
7   Basic information was taken from Wikipedia, Yahuda (1996), and a number of country specific sources, and then verified with the Taiwanese Ministry of Foreign Affairs in email correspondence.
8   The sample only contains independent countries with more than one million inhabitants and excludes countries under foreign occupation, in transition, or without effective government. This definition of the sample is based on Geddes *et al.* (forthcoming) and is used for all regression analyses in Chapters 8 and 9.

9 Do China's foreign relations lead to autocratic survival?

In this chapter, the impact of China's rise on leadership duration in democratic large-coalition- and autocratic small-coalition countries is assessed. As detailed in Chapter 2, theoretically, it is expected that increased interaction with China supports autocratic survival (hypothesis 3). By the means of a survival analysis, this expectation is quantitatively tested for the post-Cold War period. In the following, I briefly discuss what is understood by autocratic survival and how this concept can be measured, as well as what kind of linkages to China will be considered. I then sketch out the estimation procedure used. My results are presented in section three along with a number of robustness tests. The chapter concludes with a discussion of the findings.

How to measure China's impact

Autocratic survival

Autocratic survival is here operationalized at the level of individual leaders. Thus, autocratic failure refers to the removal of a leader from office while survival refers to a leader's capability to remain in office from one year to the next (Przeworski *et al.* 2000; Bueno de Mesquita *et al.* 2003; Goemans *et al.* 2009; Cheibub *et al.* 2010). This actor-centred conceptualization, focused on the failure or survival of individual leaders and their governments, generally fits well with the theoretical assumption that interaction between inside and outside actors is leader-specific, rather than regime or country-specfic. As argued in Chapter 2, individual leaders are assumed to have great impact on a country's foreign policy orientation; thus, they are instrumental to whether or not a country complies with external interests (Hermann 1990). China's own leadership turnover from Mao Zedong to Deng Xiaoping and the connected shift in foreign policy preferences exemplifies how fundamentally leadership change *within* the same autocratic regime can affect policy preferences. This implies that external powers should be responsive to the compliance of individual leaders. With an eye on realizing their foreign policy objectives, they will reward those leaders that are compliant and sanction those that are not. Granted, external protection of a leader from removal through domestic forces or international intervention usually also finds reflection in the leader's survival in office.

I measure autocratic stability in terms of the survival of leaders in office. The dependent variable, *Leadership Duration*, is measured based on leadership turnover of individual leaders (Goemans *et al.* 2009). Leadership duration ends whenever a leader is removed from office in the subsequent year (coded 1 for failure and 0 otherwise). It is, thus, irrelevant how a leader loses power, i.e. whether he resigns, is voted out of office, has reached his term limits or is overthrown by a coup. (The only exception to this is leaders who die a natural death while in office. These leadership failures are considered to be censored.) Leadership duration simply measures how long a leader stays in power, and hence most directly assesses the ability of individuals to strengthen their grip on power.

Size of the winning coalition or regime type

Selectorate theory stipulates that leadership duration is determined to a considerable extent by the size of a country's winning coalition and its selectorate. According to Bueno de Mesquita *et al.* (2003), leaders in autocratic small-winning-coalition systems are expected to have the best survival prospects (Bueno de Mesquita *et al.* 2003: 289). They find it easiest to create loyalty among their followers by binding their followers' welfare to their own survival in office. For democratic leaders with large winning coalitions and large selectorates, in contrast, it is most difficult to survive in office (Bueno de Mesquita *et al.* 2003: 286). This expectation can easily be tested by including variables for the winning coalition W and the selectorate S, as introduced in Chapter 8.

In line with the spirit of the selectorate theory, I include an interaction term between Chinese influence and W in order to account for the theoretical expectation that the benefits created by interaction with external players are more beneficial to unconstrained leaders; that is, leaders with smaller winning coalitions.

However, as mentioned earlier, a major disadvantage of this measurement is its limited availability, covering only the first period of investigation until 2006. For survival analysis, which crucially depends on observation over time, this is a major concern. For this reason, I again run alternative estimations in which W and S are replaced by *Democracy*, a dummy based on Polity IV (see Chapter 8 for the creation of this dummy).

As autocrats, compared to democrats, are generally expected to remain in office longer, variable W and *Democracy* are expected to be positively signed in the models without the interaction term with the linkage variables. (For the models with the interaction term, the sign of W and *Democracy* is not meaningful as it cannot be interpreted independently.) Table 9.1 shows how leadership failure, indeed, systematically varies with differently sized W and between democracies and autocracies. The Appendix contains a complete list of the sample composition, the leadership duration of individual leaders, the size of their winning coalitions W and selectorates S, and their regime type classification.

In total, the sample contains 2,038 observations, consisting of 453 leaders in 133 countries. As in Chapter 8, the sample only contains independent countries with more than one million inhabitants and excludes countries under foreign

Table 9.1 Leadership failure by size of winning coalition and regime type

	Size of winning coalition						Democracy dummy		
	0	*0.25*	*0.5*	*0.75*	*1*	*Total*	*Autocracy*	*Democracy*	*Total*
No failure	42	276	253	564	303	1,438	888	820	1708
Failure	6	10	11	163	90	280	77	253	330
Total	48	286	264	727	393	1,718	946	1073	2038

occupation, in transition or without effective government (Geddes *et al.* forthcoming). During the period of investigation from 1993 to 2008, 330 leadership failures occurred, while 111 leaders remained in office as of 2008. Hence, while 75 per cent of all leaders were ousted from office during the period of investigation, on the level of observation units – the leader-year – this failure rate corresponds to only 16.2 per cent of the observations.

Linkage to and support from China

Having presented how to measure the dependent variable autocratic survival, I will now discuss how to measure the mechanisms through which China's influence can possibly be transmitted. Here, my analysis is informed by my theoretical argument and the previous case studies.

Both case studies on Burma and Cambodia illustrated China's unwillingness to criticize others on the grounds of human rights violations against their population or the use of repression against political opponents. Moreover, China's use of its veto in the UN Security Council in the case of Burma even demonstrated an extreme measure to hold up the principle of non-interference in international relations, which effectively resulted in the protection of the Burmese junta against external pressure. However, rather than vetoing UN resolutions, China's diplomats often try to prevent such punitive actions from being tabled in the UN in the first place. Thus, China's veto power in the UN Security Council is an effective, but rather rarely used instrument to protect autocratic leaders in power.

Moreover, the case studies also revealed that China's foreign policy practice contains a supportive component that typically manifests itself in high diplomatic interaction and economic and military aid. This component is similar to what Levitsky and Way (2005) described as bilateral linkages.

It seems plausible to follow Levitsky and Way's assumption that the intensity of these linkages matters, implying that the effect of China would most likely be observed in countries for which linkages to China are important relative to linkages to other countries. All indicators for bilateral linkages are, therefore, measured in relative terms or are contrasted with a leader's linkages to other important external players, notably the US. As has become apparent in the case studies, sometimes the Chinese government justifies these manifold linkages with the principle of non-interference. For example, when it defends diplomatic visits of otherwise isolated leaders, or aid and investment deals despite unstable and therefore commercially unattractive business environments, or the transfer of arms to repressive regimes that would otherwise have difficulties in buying weapons. These justifications can be read as an indication that China's relative importance for a country's leader is particularly high, because of international isolation or criticism. Despite China's increasing relevance as an economic partner for many developing countries, and despite a number of internationally isolated countries with substantial linkages to China, notably North Korea, Sudan and Iran, scenarios in which China is the most important player are, however, the exception rather than the rule.

I consider three different forms of linkages (diplomatic, military and economic) and operationalize them using four different variables: diplomacy, military support, economic cooperation and exports.

Diplomacy

'Prestige diplomacy' makes a substantial contribution to China's foreign policy. Therefore, a measure of the intensity of China's diplomatic efforts is used. *Diplomacy* measures how often a country's leader directly interacts with the Chinese prime minister or president, as China's highest representatives, without considering meetings in the context of multilateral summits. This variable was compiled from the 'China aktuell' monthly data supplement (Liu 1993–2008), which, based on several Chinese newspapers, lists all Chinese agreements with foreign countries. Referring to accomplished agreements, rather than diplomatic meetings as such, this source might slightly under report those high-level visits that did not result in any agreements. However, given that bilateral agreements are strategically announced during high-level visits, even when signed long beforehand, this bias should be small. Bilateral agreements as such would be a compelling indicator, but the data source does not allow for a differentiation between different types of agreements and their varying legal implications.

Military support

I measure military support as the amount of *Arms Transfers* from China, expressed as the share of a country's total arms transfers (natural logarithm) (Stockholm International Peace Research Institute 2008).[1]

Figure 9.1 delivers a rough overview of how Chinese arms transfers have developed during the last two decades. The left graph in Figure 9.1 displays the annual total of Chinese arms sales as a share of global arms transfers. As can be seen, in 1998, Chinese arms sales, which, in value, accounted for about 6 per cent, decreased in 1993 to a share of less than 1 per cent of global arms trade. During the early 2000s, Chinese transfers recovered somewhat, rising to 4 per cent of global arms trade, only to drop again after 2003. The several peaks in this graph hint at the fact that China's arms transfers are shaped by a few large arms deals. A look at the right graph in Figure 9.1 supports this suspicion. This graph shows

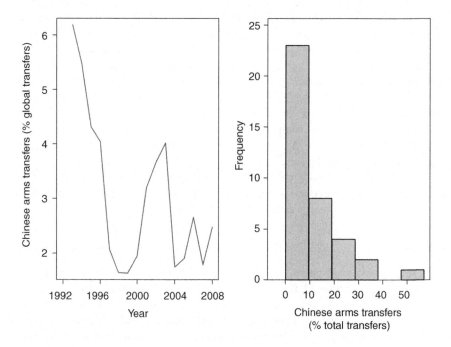

Figure 9.1 Annual total of Chinese arms sales as a share of global arms transfers and
average Chinese arms transfers as percentage of recipient's total arms
transfers

Note: Countries with no arms transfers from China omitted from right graph

the distribution of Chinese arms sales in relation to the recipient's total arms
transfers, averaged by country over time. For the sake of clarity, the graph omits
countries for which average arms transfers from China, as a percentage of total
arms transfers, are zero. A large majority of countries does not buy any arms from
China. China's reported arms sales focus on approximately 35 countries and for
only seven is China a crucial arms supplier providing more than 15 per cent of
total arms acquisitions. Whereas China has been a crucial arms supplier during
the last two decades for a small number of countries, notably, Burma, Iran and
Pakistan (57 per cent, 37 per cent, and 36 per cent of total arm acquisitions,
respectively) as well as Mauritania, Bangladesh, Zambia and Sri Lanka (28 per
cent, 27 per cent, 22 per cent and 20 per cent, respectively), its importance in
global arms trade is rather limited.

Economic cooperation

Economic Cooperation, as introduced in Chapter 8, captures the resources China
invests in another country. Here, it is measured as a share of the recipient's GDP

(natural logarithm). Different from the other linkage variables, data coverage on China's economic cooperation is limited to the period 1998 to 2008.

The left graph in Figure 9.2 shows how the total amount of economic cooperation from China has increased during the post-Cold War period. In 1998, total Chinese economic cooperation amounted to less than US$10 billion. Since 2000, it has steadily increased to US$50 billion. However, as shown in the right graph of Figure 9.2, averaged by country, Chinese economic cooperation accounted for less than 0.5 per cent of GDP in the vast majority of recipient countries. The few countries in which the amount of economic cooperation accounted for more than 1 per cent of GDP on average are Zimbabwe (3.4 per cent), Mongolia (2.2 per cent), Laos (1.5 per cent), Sudan (1.5 per cent), Congo (1.4 per cent), Turkmenistan (1.4 per cent), Mali (1.4 per cent), Liberia (1.4 per cent), Mauritania (1.3 per cent), and Mauritius (1.1 per cent).

If the inclusion of economic cooperation projects funded by third parties constitutes a problem in my analysis, it should bias the estimations downwards, because the effect of Chinese economic cooperation is then produced by even less truly Chinese engagement.

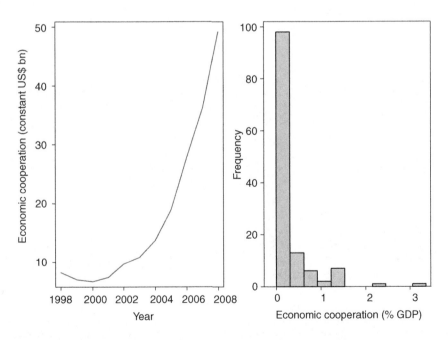

Figure 9.2 Total amount of Chinese economic cooperation (in constant US$ billion) by year and average Chinese economic cooperation as percentage of the recipient's GDP

Exports

Exports to China is a proxy for the resources that China extracts from a country and for the resource rents generated by trade relations with China. Exports to China are expressed as a share of a country's total trade; the variable is logged and lagged by one year (International Monetary Fund 2010). A more direct measure for such rent generation, which would allow us to link resource extraction to China, is, unfortunately, not available for many countries, as most data on raw material exports do not account for the destination of these exports. However, given that China ranks among the biggest markets for many of those commodities, which are usually suspected of generating rents – such as iron ore, manganese, lead, chromium, copper and oil – using *Exports to China* helps to avoid the problem of aggregation.

The top left graph in Figure 9.3 displays how average exports to China expressed as a share of total trade have risen throughout the last two decades from less than 1 per cent to 3 per cent of total trade on average. Similar to the picture that could be observed with regard to arms transfers and economic cooperation,

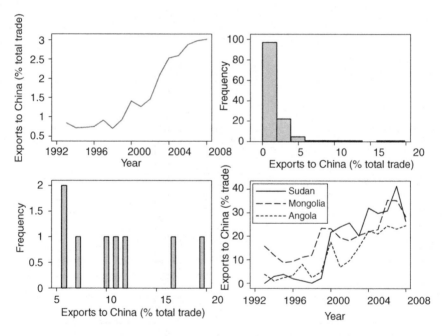

Figure 9.3 Average exports to China as percentage of trading partner's total trade by year (top right); average exports to China as percentage of total trade by trade partner (top left); average exports to China as percentage of total trade by trade partner for countries with high trade dependence on China (bottom left); exports to China as percentage of total trade by year for most dependent trade partners (bottom right)

the importance of China for individual countries varies widely (top right graph). Again, averaged over time, the great majority of countries has very low export dependence on China, reaching no more than 2 per cent of total trade. Taking a closer look at the right tail of this distribution, the bottom left graph shows that for only a handful of countries, export dependence over the whole period of time is higher than 5 per cent on average. These countries are Mongolia (19 per cent), Sudan (16 per cent), Angola (11 per cent), Oman (11 per cent), Congo (10 per cent), South Korea (7 per cent), Gabon (6 per cent) and Kazakhstan (5 per cent). However, as the bottom right graph of Figure 9.3 shows, aggregation over time masks the fact that each of these countries has experienced a dramatic increase in trade dependence on China over time, with levels of trade dependence as high as 40 per cent.

According to the theoretical argument, these linkage variables should have a stabilizing impact on leadership duration, and especially so in unconstrained autocracies. As argued in Chapter 2, the theoretical expectation is that the effect of China's bilateral interaction is conditional on the type of political regime in another country. For this reason, the model contains interactions terms of all China related variables with the measure of regime type W and *Democracy*.

Other determinants of autocratic survival

The literature has identified a number of alternative explanations for leadership duration. In order to control for these potential explanations, I incorporate several control variables.

Economic growth

According to the selectorate theory, the steady distribution of resources among coalition members is of utmost importance for a leader's survival in office. This relationship has also empirically been shown by earlier research, which indicated that the likelihood of surviving economic crises differs among different regime types (Przeworski and Limongi 1997). Economic growth must thus be considered as a determinant for leadership survival. Economic *Growth*, measured as GDP growth lagged by one year accounts for this.

Neighbourhood effects

Proponents of diffusion theory have stressed the spatial dependence of autocratic breakdown and democratization. Popular upheaval and regime change in one country may encourage protests in neighbouring countries, and so create spillover and domino effects (Gleditsch and Ward 2006; Brinks and Coppedge 2006; Levitsky and Way 2005; Leeson and Dean 2009). While regime change does not necessarily need to involve leadership turnover, it often does. I account for this spatial correlation by including a variable (*Failure in Neighbours*) that measures the percentage of a country's close neighbours that experience leadership change in a given year. Close neighbourhood is here defined as direct neighbourhood with land or river borders or separation by a maximum of 24 miles of water. In order to identify a country's close neighbours, I used the direct contiguity data (Correlates of War Project 2007).

Trade openness

Earlier research has found that a country's integration into the world economy, and specifically its openness to international trade, has a stabilizing effect on leadership duration (Chiozza and Goemans 2003). For this reason, I control for a country's trade openness by including a country's total trade as percentage of GDP.

Many more factors that impact on leadership duration have been discussed in the past. For reasons of parsimony, I am keeping my models as simple as possible. However, many additional factors are considered in the robustness tests at the end of this chapter. Table 9.2 provides summary statistics of all variables included in the following analysis.

Table 9.2 Summary statistics

Variable	Obs.	Mean	Std Dev.	Min.	Max.
Democracy	2,038	0.526	0.499	0	1
W	1,718	0.664	0.271	0	1
S	1,761	0.942	0.213	0	1
Diplomacy$_{t-1}$	2,038	0.197	0.442	0	2
Arms from China$_{t-1}$ (% total, ln)	2,010	−12.483	4.564	−13.815	4.710
Econ. Cooperation$_{t-1}$ (% GDP, ln)	1,297	−4.288	3.820	−13.815	1.833
Exports to China$_{t-1}$ (% total trade, ln)	2,038	−2.054	3.909	−13.815	3.721
Growth$_{t-1}$	2,038	2.638	7.209	−45.398	88.723
Population (ln)	2,038	16.380	1.292	13.828	20.854
Trade Openness$_{t-1}$	2,038	37.246	52.830	1.395	919.242
Failure in Neighbours (%)	2,038	0.154	0.222	0	1
No. of Failures in Neighbours	2,038	0.075	0.289	0	3
GDP/c$_{t-1}$ (ln)	2,038	8.350	1.361	4.764	10.895
Population Density$_{t-1}$	2,031	143.341	522.733	1.452	6,583.35
Urban Growth$_{t-1}$	2,028	2.340	2.054	−3.675	20.005
Oil rents/c$_{t-1}$ (ln)	1,943	−5.682	6.824	−13.815	5.586
ODA$_{t-1}$ (% GDP)	2,038	1.466	3.031	−0.460	45.932
Oil Reserves$_{t-1}$ (ln)	1,943	−5.682	6.824	−13.815	5.586
Agricultural Exports$_{t-1}$ (% of merchandise exports)	1,646	6.223	11.760	.000	93.823
Trade$_{t-1}$ (% of Chinese total trade)	2,038	0.638	2.609	0	27.57
Exports to US$_{t-1}$ (% total trade, ln)	2,022	0.576	2.711	−13.815	4.220
Personal	2,038	0.175	0.380	0	1
Monarchy	2,038	0.049	0.216	0	1
Military	2,038	0.036	0.187	0	1
Party	2,038	0.178	0.383	0	1

How to assess China's impact

Having taken a brief look at the data, the estimation procedure for the survival analysis is briefly introduced in this section. The data is time-discrete with leader-years as the unit of observation. Such type of data is known as event history data, where the analyst is interested in examining the time until an event or 'failure' occurs. In event or survival analysis, an observation is considered to 'survive' or to be 'at risk' until the event occurs or the observation fails, respectively. The data is left and right censored; that is, some leaders have been at risk even before the analysis started (left censoring), and some leaders remain in power when the analysis ends (right censoring). Hence, the survival time cannot exactly be known, because the event is not observed before the period of observation ends. In order to assess what determines leadership duration, the analysis models and estimates the so-called hazard rate. The hazard rate is the probability that an event occurs at a given point in time, given that it has not yet occurred (Box-Steffensmeier and Jones 1997).

Previous research found that a leader's prospects of survival from one year to the next crucially depends on time. For example, freshly installed leaders are generally more prone to being overthrown and thus have a shorter survival expectation (Bueno de Mesquita *et al.* 2003). However, autocrats are particularly vulnerable in their early years in power. Over the years, they can identify the relevant members of their winning coalitions and can establish efficient mechanisms to reward these members. When the welfare of these members is tied to the survival of the regime, an autocrat has successfully strengthened his position in power. Since all this takes time, the leader's risk of being overthrown decreases over time.

This implies that the estimation method for assessing China's effect on leadership survival needs to be sensitive to time dependencies. I used a Cox proportional hazard model with time dependent covariates to model the hazard rate. This model assumes a hazard rate in the form: $h(t) = h_0(t)e^{\beta_1 x_i + \beta_2 x_2(t)}$.

Because the Cox model does not specify the form of time-dependency, and thus allows modelling time dependence of an unknown form, it is the workhorse model in survival analysis. The only assumption it makes is that the effects of the covariates on the hazard ratio are proportional during the tenure of a leader. In case this assumption does not hold, Box-Steffensmeier and Jones (1997) suggest including an interaction term of these time-variant variables with the logarithm of time. For each of the following models, I tested whether this assumption held and included the additional interaction terms when necessary. The results of the analysis are presented in the form of estimated coefficients, rather than hazard rates. Negative coefficients indicate that a variable has the effect of decreasing the hazard rate, and thus increasing the survival duration.

What the analysis tells us

This chapter presents the results of diverse regression analyses exploring the effect of linkage with China on leadership survival in small- and large-winning-coalition systems and among different types of autocracies with systematic differences in the size and nature of their winning coalitions. I find robust evidence that export dependence on China supports the duration of leaders in office. High export dependence on China is beneficial to the survival of autocrats in power, but less so for democrats, even though the empirical support seems to be stronger for the first than for the second finding. Moreover, my findings suggest that diplomatic interaction has no influence on a leader's duration in office. With regard to the other China-related variables, my findings are somewhat mixed. There is some evidence that economic cooperation helps autocrats to remain in power and that arms transfers have a destabilizing effect. However, both effects are not robust across different model specifications.

In the following, I present the results of my regressions on *Leadership Duration* for each of the linkage variables. All regressions either include W and S or the *Democracy* dummy in order to control for the size of the winning coalition and the selectorate and regime type, respectively. All models with W and S include an interaction term between coalition size W and the natural logarithm of time, because W was found to have a non-proportional effect on the hazard rate. Similarly, the democracy dummy was found to have a non-proportional effect on the hazard rate. Therefore all models with this dummy include an interaction term with the logarithm of time. All models were estimated with robust standard errors clustered by countries, because even though leaders are the unit of observation, the observations of successive leaders in one country are more similar than observations across different countries. As mentioned above, negative coefficients indicate that a variable's effect decreases the hazard rate and thus increases a leader's survival duration.

The positive and significant coefficients on W in almost all models, and the interaction of W with time, indicate that large-coalition leaders are, indeed, more vulnerable to losing office, and that this effect increases over time. The significant and negative coefficient on S, in contrast, means that leaders with large selectorates have a lower risk of losing office. These findings are in line with my expectations and with earlier research (Bueno de Mesquita *et al.* 2003). In the models with W and S, none of the control variables – *Growth, Trade Openness, Population* and *Failure in Neighbours* – yield statistically significant coefficients.

Table 9.3 presents the models that assess the effect of diplomatic interaction on *Leadership Duration*. In a first step, this variable is introduced without its interaction term. While the direction of the coefficient on *Diplomacy* in Model 1 points in the expected negative direction, it is not statistically significant. When the interaction term between *Diplomacy* and W is introduced in Model 2, neither *Diplomacy* nor its interaction term yields statistically significant results. This negative finding is replicated in Models 3 and 4 where W and S are replaced with *Democracy*. Thus, there is no evidence that diplomatic interaction has any impact on the duration of leaders in office.

Table 9.4 shows the results for Chinese arms transfers. As can be seen in Model 1, arms transfers from China do not seem to have a statistically significant impact on leadership duration. Additionally, introducing the interaction term of *Arms Transfers* with W in Model 2, not only leads the coefficient on *Arms*

Table 9.3 Cox regression on diplomacy with China and leadership duration

	(1)	(2)	(3)	(4)
Diplomacy$_{t-1}$	−0.042	0.058	0.004	0.026
	(0.118)	(0.348)	(0.105)	(0.239)
Diplomacy$_{t-1}$*W		−0.127		
		(0.431)		
Diplomacy$_{t-1}$ *Democracy				−0.029
				(0.273)
W	0.987	1.009*		
	(0.621)	(0.612)		
W*ln(t)	0.993***	0.996***		
	(0.360)	(0.361)		
S	−1.215***	−1.214***		
	(0.363)	(0.362)		
Democracy			−0.007	−0.002
			(0.281)	(0.271)
Democracy*ln(t)			0.734***	0.735***
			(0.166)	(0.168)
Growth$_{t-1}$	−0.005	−0.005	−0.014*	−0.014*
	(0.008)	(0.008)	(0.008)	(0.008)
Population (ln)	−0.010	−0.010	−0.018	−0.018
	(0.057)	(0.057)	(0.053)	(0.053)
Trade Openness$_{t-1}$	−0.004	−0.004	−0.001	−0.001
	(0.004)	(0.004)	(0.002)	(0.002)
Failure in Neighbours (%)	0.183	0.182	0.235	0.235
	(0.186)	(0.186)	(0.159)	(0.159)
Observations	1717	1717	2038	2038
Countries	132	132	133	133
Log likelihood	−1343	−1343	−1625	−1625
Chi-squared	84	84	90	90

Note: Robust standard errors clustered by country. * p<0.1, ** p<0.05, *** p<0.01

Transfers to change from positive to negative, but also produces a significant, but positive coefficient on the interaction term. This indicates that the transfer of arms is actually destabilizing, when the recipient does not rely on an extremely small winning coalition (*W*=0). However, given the simultaneous change in the coefficient on *W*, which becomes unusually big in comparison to Model 1 (and to all other models in the other tables), I am not very confident in the results of Model 2. Together with a sharp increase in the variance inflation indicator, it is an indication that multicollinearity, which is inevitably introduced to the model with the interaction term, affects the regression results. Indeed, Models 4 and 5 do not find evidence that arms sales have any impact on leadership survival. The coefficient of *Arms Transfers* is positive, but insignificant, and so is the coefficient on the interaction term.

Table 9.4 Cox regression on arms transfers from China and leadership duration

	(1)	(2)	(3)	(4)
Arms from China$_{t-1}$ (% total, ln)	0.010 (0.017)	−0.111 (0.071)	0.016 (0.014)	0.009 (0.018)
Arms$_{t-1}$*W		0.185* (0.094)		
Arms$_{t-1}$ *Democracy				0.013 (0.024)
W	0.995 (0.634)	3.606** (1.537)		
W*ln(t)	1.021*** (0.368)	0.933** (0.376)		
S	−1.188*** (0.368)	−1.422*** (0.302)		
Democracy			0.022 (0.289)	0.171 (0.343)
Democracy*ln(t)			0.756*** (0.168)	0.756*** (0.168)
Growth$_{t-1}$	−0.008 (0.008)	−0.006 (0.008)	−0.015* (0.008)	−0.015* (0.008)
Population (ln)	−0.014 (0.058)	−0.011 (0.058)	−0.021 (0.053)	−0.022 (0.053)
Trade Openness$_{t-1}$	−0.003 (0.004)	−0.003 (0.003)	−0.001 (0.002)	−0.001 (0.002)
Failure in Neighbours (%)	0.170 (0.190)	0.195 (0.190)	0.183 (0.151)	0.189 (0.152)
Observations	1695	1695	2010	2010
Countries	130	130	131	131
Log likelihood	−1319	−1316	−1593	−1593
Chi-squared	86	96	98	100

Note: Robust standard errors clustered by country. * p<0.1, ** p<0.05, *** p<0.01

Table 9.5 assesses the impact of *Economic Cooperation* from China. As the coverage of this variable spans a shorter time period, the sample considerably decreases in comparison to the previous regressions. In none of the models in Table 9.5 does *Economic Cooperation* or the interaction with *W* and *Democracy*, respectively, yield statistically significant coefficients. China's economic cooperation thus has no impact on leadership survival.

None of the variables capturing the intensity of China's external relations with others that have been investigated thus far, have been found to impact on leadership duration elsewhere. Let us finally investigate a country's *Exports to China*. As can be seen in Table 9.6, this variable does have a negative and statistically significant coefficient, indicating that increased export dependence on China has a stabilizing effect on the duration of leaders in power. However, when the

Table 9.5 Cox regression on economic cooperation from China and leadership duration

	(1)	*(2)*	*(3)*	*(4)*
Cooperation$_{t-1}$ (% GDP, ln)	−0.013 (0.018)	−0.089 (0.056)	−0.011 (0.018)	0.016 (0.037)
Cooperation$_{t-1}$*W		0.099 (0.066)		
Cooperation$_{t-1}$ *Democracy				−0.035 (0.042)
W	0.127 (0.636)	0.508 (0.655)		
W*ln(t)	1.462*** (0.454)	1.529*** (0.463)		
S	−1.530*** (0.324)	−1.576*** (0.327)		
Democracy			−0.190 (0.281)	−0.306 (0.319)
Democracy*ln(t)			0.759*** (0.177)	0.758*** (0.176)
Growth$_{t-1}$	−0.016 (0.015)	−0.015 (0.015)	−0.026* (0.013)	−0.026* (0.013)
Population (ln)	−0.077 (0.062)	−0.076 (0.061)	−0.065 (0.059)	−0.063 (0.059)
Trade Openness$_{t-1}$	−0.001 (0.003)	−0.001 (0.002)	−0.000 (0.001)	−0.000 (0.001)
Failure in Neighbours (%)	−0.103 (0.228)	−0.098 (0.228)	0.045 (0.200)	0.037 (0.202)
Observations	1001	1001	1297	1297
Countries	132	132	133	133
Log likelihood	−643	−642	−877	−877
Chi-squared	81	80	51	51

Note: Robust standard errors clustered by country. * p<0.1, ** p<0.05, *** p<0.01

interaction term of export dependence and coalition size *W* is introduced in Model 2, this effect disappears. Model 3 reproduces the results of Model 1, finding that export dependence on China generally has a negative and significant impact on the hazard rate. In contrast to Model 2, Model 4 suggests that this effect is robust when the interaction term is introduced and that it is, indeed, different for democratic and non-democratic countries. While the effect is negative for non-democracies (democracy dummy = 0), the effect is positive for democracies (democracy dummy = 1). It is not straightforward to interpret the magnitude of an effect in a duration model, specifically when interactions are involved. Therefore, I will now investigate this latter effect in more detail and provide a more substantive interpretation of its magnitude.

The estimated coefficients express a variable's effect on the hazard rate of

Table 9.6 Cox regression on exports from China and leadership duration

	(1)	(2)	(3)	(4)
Exports to China$_{t-1}$	−0.041***	−0.040	−0.037***	−0.070***
	(0.014)	(0.036)	(0.013)	(0.019)
Exports$_{t-1}$*W		−0.001		
		(0.050)		
Exports$_{t-1}$ *Democracy				0.050**
				(0.023)
W	1.245**	1.241*		
	(0.617)	(0.678)		
W*ln(t)	0.908**	0.909**		
	(0.361)	(0.370)		
S	−1.294***	−1.295***		
	(0.339)	(0.338)		
Democracy			0.076	0.322
			(0.266)	(0.318)
Democracy*ln(t)			0.694***	0.642***
			(0.161)	(0.168)
Growth$_{t-1}$	−0.004	−0.004	−0.011	−0.009
	(0.008)	(0.008)	(0.008)	(0.007)
Population (ln)	0.030	0.031	0.021	0.015
	(0.060)	(0.060)	(0.053)	(0.053)
Trade Openness$_{t-1}$	−0.003	−0.003	−0.000	−0.001
	(0.003)	(0.003)	(0.001)	(0.001)
Failure in Neighbours (%)	0.149	0.149	0.194	0.186
	(0.187)	(0.187)	(0.161)	(0.160)
Observations	1717	1717	2038	2038
Countries	132	132	133	133
Log Likelihood	−1339	−1339	−1622	−1620
Chi-squared	92	94	109	103

Note: Robust standard errors clustered by country. * $p<0.1$, ** $p<0.05$, *** $p<0.01$

failure. The hazard rate, however, is also dependent on time. It is, therefore, most meaningful to illustrate graphically how the hazard rate changes over time and dependent on the level of a country's export dependence when all other variables are fixed at their mean values.

Figure 9.4 illustrates the survival functions for leaders in democracies and autocracies. The probability of survival is displayed on the Y-axis; the X-axis depicts the time a leader has been in power. The solid lines express the survival function of a leader with low export dependence on China; the dashed lines express the survival function of a leader with relatively high export dependence. Low export dependence is here defined in quantities relative to the distribution of the variable *Exports to China* in the sample as one standard deviation below the sample mean. Accordingly, high export dependence corresponds to one standard

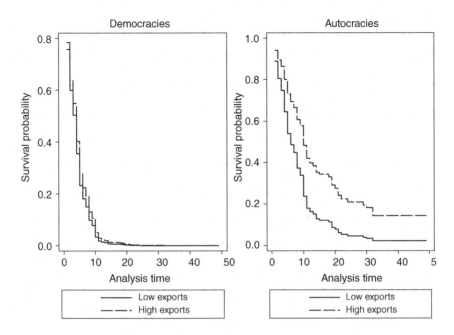

Figure 9.4 Effect of exports to China for the survival of democratic and autocratic
leaders

deviation above the sample mean. These values correspond to ln(0.0026) and
ln(6.3544). As can be seen in Figure 9.4, for democratic leaders, the solid and the
dashed lines are very close together, implying that the survival function for democratic leaders is fairly similar, regardless of the degree of export dependence on
China. For autocratic leaders, in contrast, both lines diverge remarkably from
each other and the dashed line lies above the solid line. The degree of export
dependence thus affects the survival probability for autocrats whereby high
export dependence is connected to a higher survival probability.

When assessing the impact of interaction terms, it is crucial to investigate
whether the effect holds for the whole range of values of the two constitutive
terms, or for only some areas of it (Braumoeller 2004; Brambor *et al.* 2006). It is
possible, for example, that the effect of *Exports to China* on leadership duration
differs with different degrees of *Exports to China*, or even that it is decisive at
specific levels only. Unfortunately, the graphical illustration above does not tell
us how different degrees of export dependence affect leadership duration, and
whether export dependence significantly affects leadership duration at all levels.
In order to better understand how different degrees of export dependence impact
on leadership duration, I estimate the marginal effects of export dependence on
democratic and autocratic leaders for different degrees of export dependence.

Again, all other variables were held constant at their sample mean values. Table 9.7 shows a leader's survival probability when different degrees of *Exports to China* are assumed. Again, these different degrees correspond to values that occur in the sample: zero, is the sample minimum; ln(0.002), which corresponds to one standard deviation below the sample mean; ln(6.354), which corresponds to one standard deviation above the sample mean; and ln(41.325), the sample maximum. Then, the percentage change in survival probabilities, which result from each change in degree of *Exports to China,* are calculated.

Table 9.7 reveals that the effect of export dependence is considerably stronger for autocrats than for democrats. For a democratic leader with no *Exports to China*, the hazard rate is 3.65. It falls to 3.16 when the country's *Exports to China* decrease from zero to 0.002 per cent of a country's overall trade. This corresponds to a decrease in the hazard rate of roughly 13 per cent. For an autocrat, in contrast, the same increase in *Exports to China* results in a decrease of his hazard rate by almost 39 per cent, from 5.04 to 3.08. When *Exports to China* are further increased from one standard deviation below the mean to one standard deviation above the mean, this results in another 14 per cent decrease of the hazard rate for democrats and another 42 per cent decrease of the hazard rate for autocrats. Second, Table 9.7 also reveals that the effect is significant for all degrees of export dependence. Export dependence prolongs leadership survival, regardless of the level of export dependence, i.e. even when the level of export dependence is low.

Before discussing a number of robustness tests, let me summarize the findings of my investigation. Assessing the impact of different forms of bilateral support and linkages, I find, on the one hand, that neither diplomatic interaction, nor arms trade, nor Chinese economic coopertion have an effect on leadership duration. On the other hand, my findings suggest that export dependence increases the survival duration of leaders, regardless of their winning-coalition size; but,this effect is stronger for autocrats than democrats.

Table 9.7 Marginal effects

Export to China (in % of total trade)	Predicted hazard	Standard error	Change of hazard
Democracy			
Minimum (0)	3.650	(3.275)	
Mean-1 SD (ln 0.002)	3.165	(2.778)	−13%
Mean+1 SD (ln 6.354)	2.701	(2.345)	−14.6%
Maximum (ln 41.32)	2.601	(2.257)	−3.7%
Autocracy			
Minimum (0)	5.042	(4.704)	
Mean-1 SD (ln 0.002)	3.083	(2.757)	−38.8%
Mean+1 SD (ln 6.354)	1.785	(1.561)	−42.1%
Maximum (ln 41.32)	1.566	(1.369)	−12.2%

Robustness

Finally, I carried out a number of robustness tests in order to ensure that the relation between export dependence and leadership duration is not driven by the model specification, the set of variables that are included, the sample composition or the estimation procedure.

My first robustness check is inspired by recent research on autocratic durability, which suggests that autocratic regimes vary widely in their ability to moderate internal interactions between rulers, elites and citizens and in their ability to institutionalize the transfer of power to successive leadership generations (Gandhi and Przeworski 2006; Hadenius 2007).[2] Accordingly, regime types provide a powerful explanation for autocratic survival. The regression including W and S can, to an extent, account for such variation, but when W is substituted by the *Democracy* dummy all autocracies are lumped together. More precisely, one could object that the presented analysis is insensitive to negotiated leadership turnover. Even though institutionalized turnovers are less common in autocracies than other modes of exit (Ezrow and Frantz 2011), some autocracies have developed considerable routine with respect to leadership transition and have, therefore, dramatically increased the frequency of leadership turnovers.

As we are particularly interested in the survival of autocracies, I replicate the analysis with a sample that contains only autocracies and with a control for different autocratic regime types. In order to do so, I rely on the regime type categorization provided by Geddes *et al.* (forthcoming). This dataset distinguishes between ten different types of authoritarianism. For my purpose, distinguishing between the main types seems to be sufficient, so the ten categories are collapsed into four: military, personal, monarchic and dominant-party autocracies. A dummy for each of the four categories was constructed. Monarchy is the omitted category in the regressions. In this regression, the variable on leadership failure in the region is more restrictive and assumes that ony leadership transition in neighbouring autocracies are of relevance. *Failure in Neighbours* counts only the number of leadership transitions in autocratic close neighbours.

Table 9.8 shows the results of a regression with four regime type dummies and export dependence on China. In order to correct for non-proportional effects, this model contains interactions between the logarithm of time and the regime type dummies. All of these interactions are highly significant. In addition, a country's growth rate plays a significant role in prolonging autocratic leadership. The coefficient on export dependence is negative and significant. In a nutshell, Table 9.8 strongly confirms the stabilizing effect of export dependence on China for autocratic leaders.

I concentrate further robustness tests on Models 1 and 4 in Table 9.6. Some of the additional models are shown in Table 9.9 (for Model 1) and in Table 9.10 (for Model 3). All models in these tables contain all the independent variables of the initial models in Table 9.6, even though the control variables are not shown and discussed below. Models not shown in these tables are available upon request.

Table 9.8 Robustness. Exports to China and leadership duration

	(1)
Exports to China$_{t-1}$	−0.112***
	(0.027)
Military*ln(t)	1.695**
	(0.660)
Party*ln(t)	1.349**
	(0.665)
Personal*ln(t)	1.007
	(0.647)
Party	−1.662*
	(0.856)
Personal	−1.327*
	(0.723)
Military	−1.593*
	(0.833)
Observations	895
Countries	77
Log Likelihood	−213
Chi-squared	69

Note: Robust standard errors clustered by country. Additional control variables included, but not
    shown. * p<0.1, ** p<0.05, *** p<0.01

To begin with, I introduce various additional control variables to the model
that have been found influential for leadership duration in order to ensure that no
relevant variables are omitted. I begin with a series of socioeconomic variables.
The first additional variable that I introduce is a country's wealth, measured as
GDP per capita (natural logarithm), lagged by one year (Heston *et al.* 2011).
Second, I add the lagged growth rate of urbanization and a lagged measure for
population density (taken from the World Bank [2010]). All these variables have
been connected to social mobilization and collective action in the past and, as
such, they have been discussed as determinants for political stability (Huntington
1968; Lipton 1977; Herbst 2000). Neither of these variables has a significant
effect on leadership duration, nor does their inclusion affect the coefficients on
export dependence or on its interaction term with the democracy dummy (results
are not shown, but are available upon request).

Moreover, the impact of resource abundance and the availability of non-tax
revenues on political stability has been widely discussed and it has been uncov-
ered that oil and other non-tax revenues increase a government's survival
expectancy (Ross 2001; Smith 2004; Morrison 2009; Bueno de Mesquita and
Smith 2010). I therefore additionally include different measures for non-tax
revenues: the natural logarithm of a government's per capita oil revenues (Ross
2008) and official development aid (ODA) from the OECD countries as a
percentage of a countries GDP (Organisation for Economic Cooperation and

Table 9.9 Robustness. Exports to China and leadership duration

	(1)	(2)	(3)	(4)	(5)	(6)
Exports to China$_{t-1}$	−0.039***	−0.049***	−0.029**	−0.042***	−0.043***	−0.038***
	(0.013)	(0.013)	(0.014)	(0.014)	(0.013)	(0.014)
W	1.274**	1.062*	0.629	1.317**	1.256**	1.210*
	(0.614)	(0.629)	(0.704)	(0.635)	(0.628)	(0.619)
S	−1.305***	−1.227***	−1.016***	−1.297***	−1.143***	−1.257***
	(0.337)	(0.347)	(0.354)	(0.344)	(0.327)	(0.345)
W*ln(t)	0.897**	0.932***	1.346***	0.841**	0.804**	0.904**
	(0.360)	(0.359)	(0.425)	(0.362)	(0.358)	(0.362)
Oil rents/c$_{t-1}$ (ln)	−0.005					
	(0.009)					
ODA$_{t-1}$ (% GDP)		−0.062*				
		(0.035)				
Agricultural Exports$_{t-1}$			−0.009			
			(0.007)			
Exports to US$_{t-1}$ (% total trade, ln)				0.060*		
				(0.035)		
Subsahara					−0.455***	
					(0.155)	
East Asia					0.089	
					(0.250)	
South Asia					0.689***	
					(0.265)	
Observations	1717	1717	1408	1703	1717	1651
Countries	132	132	125	131	132	127
Log Likelihood	−1339	−1338	−1171	−1325	−1332	−1320
Chi-squared	93	92	91	97	137	87

Note: Robust standard errors clustered by country. Additional control variables included, but not shown. * p<0.1, ** p<0.05, *** p<0.01

Development 2010).[3] Because of the wider coverage, I also control for the natural logarithm of a country's oil reserves in billion barrels, instead of its oil revenues (US Energy Information Administration 2010). These variables are all lagged by one year and then included one by one (Models 1 and 2 in Tables 9.9 and 9.10). A government's oil revenues do not seem to have any effect on leadership duration (Model 1), and this is essentially the same when a country's oil reserves are used instead of its oil revenues (not shown). While development aid has a significant stabilizing effect on leadership duration (Models 2 in Tables 9.9 and 9.10), this does not affect the impact that *Exports to China* exerts on leadership durability.

Next, I investigate whether the stabilizing effect of export dependence on China is connected to the type of goods that a country exports by including the volume of agricultural raw materials as a share of a country's total merchandise exports, lagged by one year (World Bank 2010). As can be seen in Model 3 in

Table 9.10 Robustness. Exports to China and leadership duration

	(1)	(2)	(3)	(4)	(5)	(6)
Exports to China$_{t-1}$	−0.077***	−0.078***	−0.052**	−0.075***	−0.082***	−0.066***
	(0.018)	(0.020)	(0.023)	(0.020)	(0.022)	(0.020)
Exports$_{t-1}$ *Democracy	0.057***	0.051**	0.043	0.057**	0.059**	0.049**
	(0.022)	(0.023)	(0.026)	(0.024)	(0.025)	(0.024)
Democracy	0.396	0.278	0.141	0.306	0.395	0.308
	(0.321)	(0.320)	(0.303)	(0.319)	(0.281)	(0.317)
Democracy*ln(t)	0.643***	0.642***	0.751***	0.639***	0.603***	0.632***
	(0.169)	(0.168)	(0.160)	(0.166)	(0.151)	(0.168)
Oil rents/c$_{t-1}$ (ln)	−0.002					
	(0.009)					
ODA$_{t-1}$ (% GDP)		−0.048*				
		(0.027)				
Agricultural Exports$_{t-1}$			−0.014**			
			(0.006)			
Exports to US$_{t-1}$ (% total trade, ln)				0.059*		
				(0.034)		
Subsahara					−0.425***	
					(0.162)	
East Asia					0.275	
					(0.233)	
South Asia					0.839***	
					(0.308)	
Observations	1907	2038	1646	2022	2038	1958
Countries	133	133	126	132	133	128
Log Likelihood	−1496	−1619	−1380	−1606	−1609	−1599
Chi-squared	108	102	76	108	104	96

Note: Robust standard errors clustered by country. Additional control variables included, but not shown. * p<0.1, ** p<0.05, *** p<0.01

Table 9.10, this variable indeed significantly prolongs a leader's duration in power in the regression with *Democracy*, without, however, affecting China's impact on *Leadership Duration*. Moreover, I test whether China's impact depends on the exporter's importance for China by controlling for the volume of bilateral trade expressed as a share of China's total trade (lagged by one year; results are not shown). And, I test whether the effect is driven by exporters that are internationally isolated by including their exports to the US, expressed as a share of total trade and lagged by one year. While neither control impacts on the stabilizing effect of export dependence on China, a country's export dependence on the US is found to increase the hazard of leadership failure in Models 4, see Tables 9.9 and 9.10.

In addition to checking for omitted variables, I also re-estimate the regressions with different estimation procedures. I replicate the model with a Weibull regression and by running a logit estimation with time splines (Beck *et al.* 1998; Carter and Signorino 2010). The results are very similar to the results in Table 9.6 (results are not shown, but are available upon request).

Finally, I test whether the effect is, in fact, driven by China's tightening trade relations with Africa and included a number of regional dummies. The results of Model 5 in Tables 9.9 and 9.10 suggest that leadership duration in sub-Saharan African countries is generally longer, while it is generally shorter for South Asian leaders (as indicated by the significant negative and positive coefficients). However, the stabilizing effect of *Exports to China* remains unaffected. Model 6 in Tables 9.9 and 9.10 shows that the results are robust when the most extreme observations are excluded from the sample. As mentioned earlier, most of the countries in the sample export less than 5 per cent of their overall trade to China, on average. However, a few countries, notably Sudan, Zimbabwe, Congo, Angola and Mongolia, export up to 35 per cent of their total trade to China. In order to make sure that the stabilizing effect of trade with China is not created because of these few unrepresentative, but potentially influential, cases, I exclude these five cases from the sample.

In sum, the finding that export dependence on China increases leadership survival in autocracies is very robust. Neither the inclusion of additional explanatory variables, nor the exclusion of extreme observations, nor using different estimation procedures challenged this finding.

As has been shown, the effect of export dependence on China is robust to all these alternative model specifications. However, one potential problem, the possibility of reverse causality and endogeneity, has yet to be addressed extensively. A first attempt to address this problem consisted in lagging the independent variables. By ensuring that the model correctly reflects the chronology of events, the lagged variables generally help to reduce the risk of reverse causality. A more rigorous attempt would be to include instrumental variables and so to tackle possible endogeneity. However, this approach requires identifying plausible instruments first, and this can be a very complicated issue. Thus far, I have not succeeded in coming up with adequate instruments that would fulfil all the requirements.

In addition to a statistical solution, one can also address the endogeneity problem with plausible reasoning. As China is renowned as a proponent of sovereignty and non-interference, endogeneity should occur primarily as a result of leadership vulnerability, whereby leaders strive for Chinese protection when they feel vulnerable. Accordingly, leaders who are uncertain about whether they will survive in power, strengthen their ties with China in order to prevent their own failure. A good example is Burma's provision of oil concessions to Chinese oil corporations after China deflected international pressure on the Burmese government, as discussed in Chapter 4. According to Chinese analysts, the Iranian government seemed to have adopted a similar strategy, to deliberately 'bind' Chinese companies to Iran – partly with the aim of safeguarding Chinese protection against UN sanctions against Iran (International Crisis Group 2010c).

As a result of such protection-seeking behaviour, the relationship between leadership failure and exports to China could be affected by endogeneity as it is partly driven by a leader's anticipation of being removed from office. If this were the case, endogeneity would lead to a positive relationship between leadership failure and exports to China, i.e. endogeneity would bias the findings upwards. However, my results suggest a negative relationship. Thus, if endogeneity plays out, it partly cancels out the negative relationship revealed here. With no endogeneity at play, in contrast, the true negative correlation between leadership failure and exports should be even stronger.

Conclusion and discussion of findings

This chapter attempted to investigate China's impact on autocratic longevity and to assess whether external interaction, linkages with, or support from China is more beneficial to the survival of autocratic small-coalition than democratic large-coalition leaders (hypothesis 3). This quantitative investigation was based on an actor-centred understanding of autocratic longevity. Accordingly, it assessed this question on the basis of the survival of individual leaders in power. It presented and investigated four different types of linkages to China: high-level diplomacy, arms transfers, economic cooperation and export dependence on China. The comprehensive investigation provided a complex picture of the nexus between leader survival and linkages with China as an autocratic major power.

My results suggest that the impact of China's rise on leadership survival is mixed. Rather than providing a conclusive answer to the controversial debate about the nature of China's rise, these findings confirm that the impact of China's rise is highly ambiguous. It is particularly interesting to note that the economic aspects of China's rise seem to have stronger political consequences than other, often hotly debated, forms of diplomatic or political aspects.

It is shown that trade dependence does have an impact. Most strikingly, export dependence on China has a stabilizing effect on leader survival in other autocracies. Export dependence on China, that is, exports to China in relation to a country's overall trade, improve the prospects for leaders to remain in power, and this effect is much stronger for autocrats than for democrats. Interestingly, earlier research has found that trade dependence inhibits democratization, but this effect was found to be independent of the trade partner's regime type (Teorell 2010). However, when including exports to the US, my results clearly indicate different effects for China and the US. Various other tests showed that my finding is very robust and holds for various modifications of the initial model and alternative estimation procedures.

This finding is particularly interesting against the background of other investigations of China's strategic use of economic interdependence. Particularly in the regional context, China has been pushing for economic integration, as much with an eye on political as on economic objectives (Ravenhill and Jiang 2009; Kastner and Saunders 2012). Such instrumentalization of economic interdependence seems to increasingly take on global dimensions. Recent studies have found, for example, that the Chinese government systematically punishes governments for officially receiving the Dalai Lama by reducing Chinese imports from these countries (Fuchs and Klann 2013). At the same time, for African and Latin American countries, trade with China was found to relate to converging voting behaviour with Chinese positions in the UN (Flores-Macías and Kreps 2013). Given the speed with which bilateral trade between China and some countries in the developing world has been increasing in recent years, these findings are highly relevant – even though one should keep in mind that, in the vast majority of countries, bilateral trade with China does not yet reach extraordinary volumes in relation to their overall trade.

As to the underlying mechanisms of why export dependence leads to leader survival in autocracies, my own findings are somewhat puzzling. It can be said with some confidence that the stabilizing effect of export dependence on China is not reflecting a spurious relation between trade openness and political stability. However, the expectation that rentier effects, whereby export dependence partly reflects the reliance on extractive resources, could explain the impact of export dependence on leader survival was not directly supported by the analysis. Previous research has found that this kind of income generated by resource extraction prolongs authoritarian longevity (Ross 2001; Smith 2004). Yet, when different alternative rents were included in the analysis, this did not weaken the effect of export dependence on China. At this point, further investigations into the mechanism of this relationship are required. In any event, the insights from the above-cited research would suggest that there is a systematic relationship between bilateral trade, compliance with Chinese interests and survival in office – even if this could not be directly tested here.

However, the analysis did not find evidence that other forms of linkages influenced leadership survival. Neither for high-level diplomacy, nor for arms transfers from China, nor for Chinese economic cooperation could any effect on leader survival be shown. Given the heated debate about China's rise, this finding is as important and relevant as the previous one as it suggests that the effect of China on autocratic longevity appears to be exaggerated. While media reports often link China's engagement, especially in the developing world, to all kinds of issues of bad governance and authoritarianism, the analysis suggests that these outcomes are, in fact, not attributable to China. Here, the analysis reminds us that high profile cases, such as the Chinese attempt to ship weapons to Zimbabwe in the aftermath of Zimbabwe's 2008 disputed elections, tend to shape perceptions of China's foreign behaviour (Beresford 2008). These cases cause much publicity – in fact, the Chinese container ship was unable to unload, because of international protests, and had to return to China – but they may not adequately reflect the reality of China's impact (BBC News 2008). In reality, China is still a rather minor weapon exporter when compared to other arms sellers such as the US or Russia.

In view of the theoretical argument, the claim that autocratic small-coalition leaders benefit more from external interaction than democratic large-coalition leaders is only partly supported. It appears that the form of support and linkage matters for whether or not external interaction helps leaders to survive in power. This is also where the investigation has its limitations. I admit that the linkages and aspects of bilateral interaction investigated here remain rather rough. As I am a pioneer in attempting to assess this aspect of the impact of China's rise, the approach should certainly be understood as a first approximation to the topic.

Notes

1   Due to rounding errors, the database of the Stockholm International Peace Research Institute base does not add up to 100 per cent. Therefore, this measure can exceed 100 per cent.
2   For example, the timing of leadership turnover in China is now scheduled by internal rules, such as term limits and age restrictions. These have led to shorter tenures for the party leaders and more frequent leadership turnovers to party-bred successors. With the last leadership turnover in 2012, the tenures of Hu Jintao and Jiang Zemin, the fourth and third leadership generations in China, have been limited to two five-years terms, in contrast to 16 years of rule under Deng Xiaoping and 27 years of dictatorship under Mao Zedong. Another classical example of internally regulated leadership turnover is Mexico during the Cold War, where an autocratic regime endured from the 1940s until the 1990s. Here, a core element of the highly institutionalized authoritarian regime consisted of a succession mechanism that restricted the president's time in power to one electoral cycle of six years. At the end of each cycle, the president had the privilege to nominate his successor, an arrangement that gave continuity to the regime (Faust 2007a: 322).
3   Because this database contains only those countries that receive development assistance, missing values for all other countries were replaced by zero.

Part IV
So what?
Findings, reflections and conclusions

10 Conclusion

This book has examined the role of China in autocratic longevity throughout the world. Does China profit from the persistence of other autocratic regimes? Do China's leaders strategically target other autocrats with cooperation? And to what extent is linkage to China a cause of autocratic longevity for other autocrats?

In order to answer these questions, the book presented a theoretical framework that helps explain what we should expect from China with regard to its relationship to other autocracies. Based on a political economy perspective and relying, to a large extent, on selectorate theory, the framework is explicitly actor-centred. It gives great weight to the actor constellation in a country and the distribution of material resources by political leaders to secure their position in power. These material incentives to survive in power deliver an explanation for why one should expect China's leaders to be interested in autocratic survival elsewhere and how such interests may translate into the prolongation of autocratic rule.

According to this theoretical argument, autocratic leaders are easier to influence from the outside and, therefore, autocratic rule elsewhere is beneficial to external players as it allows them to exploit autocratic countries for their own interest. However, the fact that China is ruled by autocratic elites adds another layer to such purely materialist argumentation. As autocrats are vulnerable to spillover effects and diffusion from protest, revolution or transition to democracy in nearby autocratic countries, autocratic stability elsewhere is in the self-interest of autocratic elites. These considerations should make the Chinese government prefer others to be autocratic too, and to lend their support to autocratic regimes under pressure. Given China's powerful position as a member of the UN Security Council, this might also lead other autocrats to actively seek protection from China against liberalist international intervention.

These very same domestic structures and incentives also impact on whether and how external interaction with authoritatian states affects the survival in power of a given autocrat. Outside linkages and interaction at the international level should, in principle, be beneficial to any government that can capitalize on the benefits of cooperation and redistribute the created resources among its supporters. To what degree such external interaction advances the power of specific political actors over others should largely depend on the competitiveness and the domestic institutional constraints that define how freely actors can use these benefits to bolster their specific support groups. By choosing specific interaction partners and by interacting only selectively, external actors have some influence on the distribution of power in a given country.

From this theoretical thinking, three main arguments were derived to be investigated empirically. First, in line with the exploitation argument, one should expect that China is more successful in realizing its interests in small-coalition (autocratic) systems than in large-coalition (democratic) systems (hypothesis 1). Second, if the possibility for exploitation creates an interest in collaborating with other autocrats, then one should observe that China specifically targets autocratic systems in its international interactions (hypothesis 2). Finally, since the effect of external interaction on the domestic distribution of power is expected to be dependent on the pre-existing power distribution and institutional constraints, it is hypothesized that external interaction should be more beneficial to less constrained small-coalition-winning (autocratic) leaders than to more constrained large-coalition (democratic) leaders (hypothesis 3).

Subsequently, the book investigated the validity of these claims. In an in-depth study of China's approach towards countries with large- and small-coalition systems, the book compared the patterns of Chinese interactions with and targeting of specific groups of actors in autocracies versus non-autocracies. In order to do so, the case studies identified the members of the winning coalition in each of the cases. Then, they illustrated how – in contradiction to China's rhetoric – the Chinese policy of non-interference, which concentrates all interaction on a country's government, de facto takes sides and translates into support for the incumbent leadership in autocratic countries. Chinese engagement is responsive to the specific needs of a given leader in power and his respective winning coalition. Thus, the case studies qualitatively illustrated that China's cooperation de facto shores up the power position of incumbent autocratic regimes. This is likely to contribute to autocratic survival, even though the case studies did not assess to what extent this support is vital for a leader's survival in power.

Comparing China's success in realizing a set of three distinct Chinese foreign policy goals in Burma, Cambodia and Mongolia, the case studies provided evidence widely in support of hypothesis 1. With regard to all three issue areas, the 'one China' policy, access to natural resources and China's geopolitical interests, the Chinese leaderhip seemed to find it easier to realize its interests in the small-coalition systems of Burma and Cambodia, while it faced much resistance in Mongolia. The case study comparison also found some indications for Chinese adaptation to the distribution patterns in the counterpart as a means to increase the responsiveness to Chinese interests. While the Chinese government was more inclined to target the political and economic elites in Burma and Cambodia, it seemed more concerned with addressing the broader population in Mongolia. The finding that small-coalition countries are prone to external exploitation offers a powerful motivation for a preference for small-coalition systems – even though this does not prove that any preference for a specific regime type exists in China's leaders' minds.

Though it was not my aim to examine the intentions of China's leaders, the question of whether regime type translates into specific cooperation with autocracies received further attention. This question was addressed by quantita-tively examining the drivers of China's external engagement and interaction with other countries. This examination focused on the question of whether small-coali-tion systems are specifically targeted by China. As a measurement for such targeting, the study relied on China's economic cooperation with other countries, a blend of private and state assistance and FDI from China. My investigation found that the Chinese government, indeed, tends to specifically target autocratic countries in the sense that they are more likely to be the recipients of such coop-eration. Moreover, Chinese economic cooperation is strongly determined by the recipient's compliance with the 'one China' policy, and it is oriented towards large markets, i.e. targeted towards populous (and poor) countries. Resource wealth also makes the Chinese government more inclined to provide economic cooperation, at least when a global sample of countries is compared.

Finally, the book investigated whether China is a cause of autocratic longevity. My quantitative analysis delivered mixed findings as to this question. On the one hand, China indeed has an impact on the survival of autocratic leaders if they are dependent on exports to China. As the statistical analysis shows, exports to China in relation to a country's overall trade prolongs political survival for autocratic leaders, while this effect is much weaker for democratic leaders. On the other hand, it could not be observed that other forms of cooperation such as Chinese arms transfers, economic cooperation or high-level diplomacy prolong a leader's survival in power – be they democratic or autocratic.

Implications and need for further research

The book's empirical findings have some important implications. The first, highly relevant implication concerns our understanding of how Chinese leaders deal with political regime type and political stability elsewhere. It is important to acknowledge that, much in line with its foreign policy rhetoric, Chinese govern-ments in the post-Mao era have thus far refrained from direct external interference into the domestic politics elsewhere. However, the finding that coali-tion size varies with the degree of compliance suggests that there are, indeed, incentives for external actors to cultivate or prop up small-coalition systems else-where in the world. With China's economic rise, and its growing economic engagement elsewhere, it is becoming increasingly difficult to maintain this non-interference policy. Increasing flows of Chinese investments to autocratic countries, such as Angola, Iran and Sudan, over the last decade have created vested interests in the stability of these countries. This changing context of China's foreign engagement is underlined by the finding that non-democratic countries were more likely to be the recipients of Chinese projects of economic cooperation. Thus, in combination, both parts of the investigation suggest that the incentives for Chinese policymakers to protect existing autocratic ruling elites under the disguise of political stability are changing and now extend far beyond its regional neighbourhood. It is not to be expected that the Chinese leadership will give up the principle of non-interference anytime soon. However, under the slogan 'influence without interference' this principle has already become more flexible while the Chinese leaders have become more inclined to negotiate and mediate between competing elites (Large 2009).

Even so, the study cautions against an interpretation that unqualifiedly equates the Chinese desire for political stability with a preference for the status quo or political stagnation. As a lesson learnt from its own domestic experience, the Chinese government considers economic development and welfare to be a corner-stone of political legitimacy and a crucial contribution to autocratic stability. The case study of Burma vividly illustrates that the Chinese leaders advocated grad-ual political reforms and the transition to a civilian leadership in order to increase the domestic and international legitimacy of the regime. This is in line with obser-vations on China's position on other authoritarian or politically unstable regimes, for example on North Korea (Shambaugh 2008).

Finally, the positive and negative findings with regard to the effect of linkages with China on leader survival are highly relevant for the current discussion on external autocracy promotion and on the debate about the broader implications of China's rise in the field of IR. Rather than solving the controversy over the nature of China's rise, my contribution consists of the insight that the impact of China's rise on leader survival is highly ambiguous. Strikingly, it is China's economic power that has political consequences, rather than other, highly debated forms of political linkages.

On the one hand, the study shows that China's economic rise is increasingly felt and does have political repercussions elsewhere in the world. As discussed in Chapter 9, the finding that export dependence on China increases leadership survival in autocracies is particularly interesting against the background of other investigations of China's strategic use of economic interdependence, which seems increasingly to be employed at a global level. In combination with the insights from other research, my finding suggests that bilateral trade, compliance with Chinese interests and survival in office are indeed systematically related. As a broader implication of this, the world should be prepared to see that an increas-ingly wealthy China can (and will) strategically throw its economic weight around.

On the other hand, equally relevant is the lack of evidence that would show that other, highly debated forms of linkages with China – such as prestige diplo-macy, arms transfers, or economic assistance – do prolong autocratic survival. This is widely in line with earlier research that views China's external relations to be, in many respects, not much different from that of other international actors, and in any event no worse than Western powers (Meyersson *et al.* 2008; Brautigam 2009; Melnykovska *et al.* 2012; De Soysa and Midford 2012; Fuchs and Klann 2013; Hackenesch 2014). This lack of evidence supports the perspec-tive that the impact and influence China has on others tends to be overestimated, and is sometimes even misreported. Such findings call for more prudent and cool-headed discussions of and dealings with China's new role in international relations. They also imply that more self-reflection and less hypocrisy are in order when judging China.

In any event, the ambiguity of the book's findings call for more research to further our understanding of the impact of China's rise on other autocracies, and on IR more generally. There are several issues that follow-up research could or should investigate. Firstly, such a research agenda should seek to provide a more fine-grained picture of the patterns of China's foreign behaviour, particularly with regard to the cooperation with other autocracies. As China's proactive engagement with the outside world in its current form is a rather recent phenomenon, there is still much to be learnt about the specific behaviour of China. Thereby, questions about the content and quality of cooperation with regard to various aspects are relevant. For example, thus far, we do not know much about the content of party-to-party exchanges between authoritarian countries, or of Chinese training programmes for foreign government officials. What are the purpose and the impli-cations of such interactions? Do they constitute a transmission belt to exchange on how to manage the challenges of autocratic governance and to share the CCP's experience in enhancing its organizational capacity? Moreover, in the field of security cooperation, we require a better understanding of whether and to what extent China proliferates its domestic surveillance system to other countries, or how closely it cooperates with regard to aspects of internal security and what this means for domestic opposition groups. Finally, while the 'Beijing Consensus' has become a buzzword in the development aid community, the ideational implica-tions of China's rise are rather ill-understood. Some scholars argue that China unintentionally exports its own developmental model to other developing coun-tries (Jiang 2009). And, even if China's centralized developmental model is not widely emulated elsewhere, from a more constructivist perspective it would be worthwhile to investigate the implications of China's developmental success as it offers a rhetoric to justify authoritarian standpoints or frame political debates.

Secondly, with regard to the broader debate on the external factors of regime type and of external regime type promotion – including democracy and autocracy promotion alike – scholars need to rethink the role of intentionality and identity of the external actor and the focus on interactions that are deliberately designed to bolster authoritarianism or promote democracy elsewhere. When investigating China's foreign relations, existing studies on the behaviour of other authoritarian major powers such as Russia, Iran or Venezuela (Tolstrup 2009; Ambrosio 2009; Burnell 2010; Vanderhill 2013) can offer a valuable starting point. However, as becomes apparent in the case of China, and given the Chinese self-perception, many of those activities, which can potentially impact on the political structures elsewhere, can and are perfectly justified without reference, or even in opposi-tion, to any deliberate agenda of intereference or autocracy promotion. For example, China's increasing cooperation in the field of media may have little to do with the explicit intention to influence the political landscape elsewhere. Yet, even if primarily aimed at portraying China positively abroad, it may potentially have negative implications for media freedom and the plurality of media else-where. By the same token, attempts to promote democracy abroad are often badly countered by alternative, competing foreign interests of the very same external player or may have some very different effects from those intended.

Therefore, assessing the effect of external factors is as crucial as the mapping of activities that have the potential to impact on regime type elsewhere. This holds, in particular, for the autocracy promotion debate, which, compared to the study of democratization, has made fewer attempts to rigorously assess the effectiveness of external factors. Here, the challenges are manifold. Not only is it difficult to find ways to capture the more qualitative aspects of such interaction and to find suitable ways to systematically assess their impact in a comparative qualitative or quantitative manner, but, as can be learnt from the long history of democratization studies, it is also extremely difficult to trace and isolate the causal mechanisms that are eventually responsible for the outcome.

Appendix
Sample

Country	Leader	From	To	Democracy	W	S
Albania	Berisha	1992	1997	0	0.75	1
Albania	Nano	1997	1998	0	0.75	1
Albania	Majko	1998	1999	0	0.75	1
Albania	Meta	1999	2002	1	0.75	1
Albania	Nano	2002	2005	1	0.75	1
Albania	Berisha	2005	2010	1	.	.
Algeria	Kafi	1992	1994	0	0.25	0
Algeria	Zeroual	1994	1999	0	0.5	1
Algeria	Bouteflika	1999	2010	0	.	.
Angola	Dos Santos	1979	2010	0	.	.
Argentina	Menem	1988	1999	1	0.75	1
Argentina	De la Rúa	1999	2001	1	0.75	1
Argentina	Rodríguez Saá	2001	2002	1	0.75	1
Argentina	Duhalde	2002	2003	1	0.75	1
Argentina	Kirchner	2003	2007	1	.	.
Argentina	Fernández de Kirchner	2007	2010	1	.	.
Armenia	Ter-Petrosyan	1991	1998	0	0.75	1
Armenia	Kocharian	1998	2008	0	.	.
Australia	Keating	1991	1996	1	1	1
Australia	Howard	1996	2007	1	.	.
Australia	Rudd	2007	2010	1	.	.
Austria	Vranitzky	1986	1997	1	1	1
Austria	Klima	1997	2000	1	1	1
Austria	Schüssel	2000	2007	1	.	.
Austria	Gusenbauer	2007	2008	1	.	.
Azerbaijan	Aliyev	1993	2003	0	0.5	1
Azerbaijan	Aliyev	2003	2010	0	.	.
Bangladesh	Zia	1991	1996	1	0.75	1
Bangladesh	Wazed	1996	2001	1	0.75	1
Bangladesh	Zia	2001	2006	1	0.75	1

Country	Leader	From	To	Democracy	W	S
Bangladesh	I. Ahmed	2006	2007	0	.	.
Bangladesh	F. Ahmed	2007	2009	0	.	.
Belarus	Lukashenko	1994	2010	0	.	.
Belgium	Dehaene	1992	1999	1	1	1
Belgium	Verhofstadt	1999	2008	1	.	.
Benin	Soglo	1991	1996	1	0.75	1
Benin	Kerekou	1996	2006	1	0.75	1
Benin	Boni	2006	2010	1	.	.
Bolivia	Paz Zamora	1989	1993	1	0.75	1
Bolivia	Sánchez de Lozada	1993	1997	1	0.75	1
Bolivia	Banzer Suárez	1997	2001	1	0.75	1
Bolivia	Quiroga Ramírez	2001	2002	1	0.75	1
Bolivia	Sánchez de Lozada	2002	2003	1	0.75	1
Bolivia	Mesa	2003	2005	1	0.75	1
Bolivia	Rodríguez Veltzé	2005	2006	1	0.75	1
Bolivia	Morales	2006	2010	1	.	.
Brazil	Franco	1992	1994	1	0.75	1
Brazil	Cardoso	1995	2003	1	0.5	1
Brazil	Da Silva	2003	2010	1	.	.
Bulgaria	Berov	1992	1994	1	0.75	1
Bulgaria	Indzhova	1994	1995	1	0.75	1
Bulgaria	Videnov	1995	1997	1	0.75	1
Bulgaria	Kostov	1997	2001	1	0.75	1
Bulgaria	Saksgoburggotski	2001	2005	1	0.75	1
Bulgaria	Stanishev	2005	2009	1	.	.
Burkina Faso	Campaore	1987	2010	0	.	.
Burundi	Buyoya	1987	1993	0	.	1
Burundi	Kinigi	1993	1994	0	.	1
Burundi	Ntibantunganya	1994	1996	0	0.25	1
Burundi	Buyoya	1996	2003	0	.	.5
Burundi	Nkurunziza	2005	2010	1	.	.
Cambodia	Hun Sen	1985	1993	0	0.75	1
Cambodia	Ranariddh	1993	1997	0	0.25	1
Cambodia	Hun Sen	1997	2010	0	.	.
Cameroon	Biya	1982	2010	0	.	.
Canada	Mulroney	1984	1993	1	1	1
Canada	Chretien	1993	2003	1	1	1
Canada	Martin	2003	2006	1	1	1
Canada	Harper	2006	2010	1	.	.
Central African Republic	Kolingba	1981	1993	0	0.75	1
Central African Republic	Patasse	1993	2003	0	0	0

Country	Leader	From	To	Democracy	W	S
Central African Republic	Bozize	2003	2010	0	.	.
Chad	Deby	1990	2010	0	.	.
Chile	Aylwin	1990	1994	1	0.75	1
Chile	Frei Ruiz-Tagle	1994	2000	1	0.75	1
Chile	Lagos Escobar	2000	2006	1	1	1
Chile	Bachelet Jeria	2006	2010	1	.	.
Colombia	Trujillo	1990	1994	1	0.75	1
Colombia	Pizano	1994	1998	1	0.75	1
Colombia	Arango	1998	2002	1	0.75	1
Colombia	Uribe Velez	2002	2010	1	.	.
Congo	Lissouba	1992	1997	0	0	0
Congo	Nguesso	1997	2010	0	.	.
Costa Rica	Calderón Fournier	1990	1994	1	1	1
Costa Rica	Figueres	1994	1998	1	1	1
Costa Rica	Rodríguez	1998	2002	1	1	1
Costa Rica	De la Espriella	2002	2006	1	1	1
Costa Rica	Arias	2006	2010	1	.	.
Croatia	Tudjman	1990	1999	0	.	1
Croatia	Pavletic	1999	2000	1	0.75	1
Croatia	Mesic	2000	2010	1	.	.
Cuba	Castro	1959	2010	0	.	.
Czech Republic	Klaus	1993	1997	1	1	1
Czech Republic	Tosovsky	1997	1998	1	1	1
Czech Republic	Zeman	1998	2002	1	1	1
Czech Republic	Spidla	2002	2004	1	1	1
Czech Republic	Gross	2004	2005	1	1	1
Czech Republic	Paroubek	2005	2006	1	0.75	1
Czech Republic	Topolánek	2006	2009	1	.	.
Côte d'Ivoire	Houphouet-Boigny	1960	1993	0	0.5	1
Côte d'Ivoire	Bédié	1993	1999	0	.	1
Côte d'Ivoire	Guei	1999	2000	0	0.75	1
Côte d'Ivoire	Gbagbo	2000	2010	0	.	.
DR Congo	Mobutu	1965	1997	0	.	0
DR Congo	L. Kabila	1997	2001	0	.	.5
DR Congo	J. Kabila	2001	2010	0	.	.
Denmark	Schluter	1982	1993	1	1	1
Denmark	N. Rasmussen	1993	2001	1	1	1
Denmark	F. Rasmussen	2001	2009	1	.	.
Dominican Republic	Balaguer	1986	1996	1	0.75	1
Dominican Republic	Fernandez Reyna	1996	2000	1	0.75	1

Country	Leader	From	To	Democracy	W	S
Dominican Republic	Mejia	2000	2004	1	0.75	1
Dominican Republic	Fernandez Reyna	2004	2010	1	.	.
Ecuador	Durán-Ballén	1992	1996	1	0.75	1
Ecuador	Bucaram Ortiz	1996	1997	1	0.75	1
Ecuador	Alarcón	1997	1998	1	0.75	1
Ecuador	Mahuad	1998	2000	1	0.75	1
Ecuador	Noboa	2000	2003	1	0.75	1
Ecuador	Gutiérrez	2003	2005	1	0.75	1
Ecuador	Palacio González	2005	2007	0	.	.
Ecuador	Correa Delgado	2007	2010	0	.	.
Egypt	Mubarak	1981	2010	0	.	.
El Salvador	Cristiani	1989	1994	1	0.75	1
El Salvador	Calderón Sol	1994	1999	1	0.75	1
El Salvador	Flores	1999	2004	1	0.75	1
El Salvador	Saca González	2004	2009	1	.	.
Estonia	Laar	1992	1994	1	0.75	1
Estonia	Tarand	1994	1995	1	0.75	1
Estonia	Vahi	1995	1997	1	0.75	1
Estonia	Siimann	1997	1999	1	0.75	1
Estonia	Laar	1999	2002	1	0.75	1
Estonia	Kallas	2002	2003	1	0.75	1
Estonia	Parts	2003	2005	1	0.75	1
Estonia	Ansip	2005	2010	1	.	.
Ethiopia	Meles	1991	2010	0	.	.
Finland	Koivisto	1981	1994	1	1	1
Finland	Ahtisaari	1994	2000	1	1	1
Finland	Halonen	2000	2010	1	.	.
France	Mitterand	1981	1995	1	1	1
France	Chirac	1995	2007	1	.	.
France	Sarkozy	2007	2012	1	.	.
Gabon	Bongo	1967	2009	0	.	.
Gambia	Jawara	1965	1994	0	0	1
Gambia	Jammeh	1994	2010	0	.	.
Georgia	Shevardnadze	1992	2003	0	0.75	0
Georgia	Saakashvili	2004	2007	1	.	.
Georgia	Burdzhanadze	2007	2008	1	.	.
Ghana	Rawlings	1981	2001	1	0.75	1
Ghana	Kufuor	2001	2009	1	.	.
Greece	Mitsotakis	1990	1993	1	1	1
Greece	Papandreou	1993	1995	1	1	1
Greece	Tsokhatzopulos	1995	1996	1	1	1

Country	Leader	From	To	Democracy	W	S
Greece	Simitis	1996	2004	1	1	1
Greece	Karamanlis	2004	2009	1	.	.
Guatemala	Serrano Elías	1991	1993	0	0.75	1
Guatemala	De León Carpio	1993	1996	1	0.75	1
Guatemala	Arzú Yrigoyen	1996	2000	1	0.75	1
Guatemala	Portillo	2000	2004	1	0.75	1
Guatemala	Berger	2004	2008	1	.	.
Guinea	Conte	1984	2008	0	.	.
Guinea-Bissau	Vieira	1980	1999	0	.	1
Guinea-Bissau	Ialá	2000	2003	0	0.25	0
Guinea-Bissau	Vieira	2005	2009	1	.	.
Haiti	Cedras	1991	1994	1	0.75	1
Haiti	Aristide	1994	1996	1	0.75	1
Haiti	Preval	1996	2001	0	0.5	1
Haiti	Aristide	2001	2004	0	.	1
Haiti	Préval	2006	2010	0	.	.
Honduras	Callejas	1990	1994	1	0.75	1
Honduras	Reina	1994	1998	1	0.75	1
Honduras	Flores	1998	2002	1	0.75	1
Honduras	Maduro	2002	2006	1	0.75	1
Honduras	Zelay	2006	2009	1	.	.
Hungary	Antall	1990	1993	1	1	1
Hungary	Boross	1993	1994	1	1	1
Hungary	Horn	1994	1998	1	1	1
Hungary	Orban	1998	2002	1	1	1
Hungary	Medgyessy	2002	2004	1	1	1
Hungary	Gyurcsány	2004	2009	1	.	.
India	Rao	1991	1996	1	0.75	1
India	Gowda	1996	1997	1	0.75	1
India	Gujral	1997	1998	1	0.75	1
India	Vajpayee	1998	2004	1	0.75	1
India	Singh	2004	2010	1	.	.
Indonesia	Suharto	1966	1998	0	0.5	1
Indonesia	Habibie	1998	1999	1	0.75	1
Indonesia	Wahid	1999	2001	1	0.75	1
Indonesia	Megawati	2001	2004	1	0.75	1
Indonesia	Yudhoyono	2004	2010	1	.	.
Iran	Rafsanjani	1989	1997	0	0.75	1
Iran	Khatami	1997	2005	0	0.5	1
Iran	Ahmadinejad	2005	2010	0	.	.
Ireland	Reynolds	1992	1994	1	1	1
Ireland	Bruton	1994	1997	1	1	1
Ireland	Ahern	1997	2008	1	.	.

Country	Leader	From	To	Democracy	W	S
Israel	Rabin	1992	1995	1	0.75	1
Israel	Peres	1995	1996	1	0.75	1
Israel	Netanyahu	1996	1999	1	1	1
Israel	Barak	1999	2001	1	1	1
Israel	Sharon	2001	2006	1	1	1
Israel	Olmert	2006	2009	1	.	.
Italy	Amato	1992	1993	1	1	1
Italy	Ciampi	1993	1994	1	1	1
Italy	Berlusconi	1994	1995	1	1	1
Italy	Dini	1995	1996	1	1	1
Italy	Prodi	1996	1998	1	1	1
Italy	D'Alema	1998	2000	1	1	1
Italy	Amato	2000	2001	1	1	1
Italy	Berlusconi	2001	2006	1	1	1
Italy	Prodi	2006	2008	1	.	.
Japan	Miyazawa	1991	1993	1	1	1
Japan	Hosokawa	1993	1994	1	1	1
Japan	Murayama	1994	1996	1	1	1
Japan	Hashimoto	1996	1998	1	1	1
Japan	Obuchi	1998	2000	1	1	1
Japan	Mori	2000	2001	1	1	1
Japan	Koizumi	2001	2006	1	1	1
Japan	Abe	2006	2007	1	.	.
Japan	Fukuda	2007	2008	1	.	.
Jordan	Hussein	1952	1999	0	0.25	1
Jordan	Abdullah II	1999	2010	0	.	.
Kazakhstan	Nazarbaev	1990	2010	0	.	.
Kenya	Moi	1978	2002	1	0.75	1
Kenya	Kibaki	2002	2010	1	.	.
Kuwait	Dschabir al-Ahmad al-Dschabir as-Sabah	1991	2006	0	0.25	1
Kuwait	Sabah al-Ahmad al-Dschabir as-Sabah	2006	2010	0	.	.
Kyrgyzstan	Akayev	1990	2005	0	0.75	1
Kyrgyzstan	Bakiyev	2005	2010	0	.	.
Lao	Phounsavanh	1992	1998	0	0.5	1
Lao	Siphandon	1998	2006	0	0.5	1
Lao	Choummaly Sayasone	2006	2010	0	.	.
Latvia	Gailis	1994	1995	1	0.75	1
Latvia	Skele	1995	1997	1	0.75	1
Latvia	Krasts	1997	1998	1	0.75	1
Latvia	Kristopans	1998	1999	1	0.75	1

Country	Leader	From	To	Democracy	W	S
Latvia	Skele	1999	2000	1	0.75	1
Latvia	Berzins	2000	2002	1	0.75	1
Latvia	Repse	2002	2004	1	0.75	1
Latvia	Kalvitis	2004	2007	1	.	.
Latvia	Godmanis	2007	2009	1	.	.
Lebanon	Lahoud	1998	2007	1	.	.
Lebanon	Siniora	2007	2008	1	.	.
Liberia	Taylor	1997	2003	0	.	.5
Liberia	Bryant	2003	2006	1	0.5	1
Liberia	Johnson-Sirleaf	2006	2010	1	.	.
Libyan Arab Jamahiriya	Qaddafi	1969	2010	0	.	.
Lithuania	Brazauskas	1992	1998	1	1	1
Lithuania	Adamkus	1998	2003	1	1	1
Lithuania	Paksas	2003	2004	1	1	1
Lithuania	Adamkus	2004	2009	1	.	.
Madagascar	Ratsiraka	1975	1993	1	0.75	1
Madagascar	Zafy	1993	1996	1	0.75	1
Madagascar	Ratsirahonana	1996	1997	1	0.75	1
Madagascar	Ratsiraka	1997	2002	1	0.75	1
Madagascar	Ravalomanana	2002	2009	1	.	.
Malawi	Banda	1964	1994	1	0.75	1
Malawi	Muluzi	1994	2004	1	0.75	1
Malawi	Mutharika	2004	2010	1	.	.
Malaysia	Mahatir	1981	2003	0	0.75	1
Malaysia	Badawi	2003	2009	1	.	.
Mali	Konare	1992	2002	1	0.75	1
Mali	Touré	2002	2010	1	.	.
Mauritania	Taya	1984	2005	0	0.5	1
Mauritania	Vall	2005	2007	0	.	.
Mauritania	Abdellahi	2007	2008	0	.	.
Mauritius	Jugnauth	1982	1995	1	1	1
Mauritius	Ramgoolam	1995	2000	1	1	1
Mauritius	Jugnauth	2000	2003	1	1	1
Mauritius	Bérenger	2003	2005	1	1	1
Mauritius	Ramgoolam	2005	2010	1	.	.
Mexico	Salinas	1988	1994	0	0.75	1
Mexico	Zedillo	1994	2000	1	0.75	1
Mexico	Fox	2000	2006	1	0.75	1
Mexico	Calderón	2006	2010	1	.	.
Moldova	Snegur	1990	1997	1	0.75	1
Moldova	Lucinschi	1997	2001	1	0.75	1
Moldova	Tarlev	2001	2008	1	.	.

Country	Leader	From	To	Democracy	W	S
Mongolia	Ochirbat	1990	1997	1	1	1
Mongolia	Bagabandi	1997	2005	1	1	1
Mongolia	Enkhbayar	2005	2009	1	.	.
Morocco	Hassan II	1961	1999	0	0.25	1
Morocco	Muhammad VI	1999	2010	0	.	.
Mozambique	Chissano	1986	2005	0	0.75	1
Mozambique	Guebuza	2005	2010	0	.	.
Myanmar	Than Shwe	1992	2010	0	.	.
Nepal	Koirala	1991	1994	0	0.75	1
Nepal	Man Mohan	1994	1995	0	0.75	1
Nepal	Deuba	1995	1997	0	0.75	1
Nepal	Thapa	1997	1998	0	0.75	1
Nepal	Koirala	1998	1999	1	0.75	1
Nepal	Bhatterai	1999	2000	1	0.75	1
Nepal	Koirala	2000	2001	1	0.75	1
Nepal	Deuba	2001	2002	0	0.25	0
Nepal	Chand	2002	2003	0	0.25	0
Nepal	Thapa	2003	2004	0	0.25	0
Nepal	Deuba	2004	2005	0	0.25	0
Nepal	Gyanendra	2005	2006	1	0.75	0
Nepal	Koirala	2006	2008	1	.	.
Netherlands	Lubbers	1982	1994	1	1	1
Netherlands	Kok	1994	2002	1	1	1
Netherlands	Balkenende	2002	2010	1	.	.
New Zealand	Bolger	1990	1997	1	1	1
New Zealand	Shipley	1997	1999	1	1	1
New Zealand	Clark	1999	2008	1	.	.
Nicaragua	Chamorro	1990	1997	1	0.75	1
Nicaragua	Aleman	1997	2002	1	0.75	1
Nicaragua	Bolanos	2002	2007	1	.	.
Nicaragua	Ortega	2007	2010	1	.	.
Niger	Ousmane	1993	1996	0	0.25	1
Niger	Mainassara	1996	1999	0	0.75	0
Niger	Mamadou	1999	2010	1	.	.
Nigeria	Babangida	1985	1993	0	0	0
Nigeria	Abacha	1993	1998	0	.	0
Nigeria	Abubakar	1998	1999	0	0.75	1
Nigeria	Obasanjo	1999	2007	0	.	.
Nigeria	Yar'Adua	2007	2010	0	.	.
Norway	Brundtland	1990	1996	1	1	1
Norway	Jagland	1996	1997	1	1	1
Norway	Bondevik	1997	1998	1	1	1
Norway	Bondevik	1998	2000	1	1	1

Country	Leader	From	To	Democracy	W	S
Norway	Stoltenberg	2000	2001	1	1	1
Norway	Bondevik	2001	2005	1	1	1
Norway	Stoltenberg	2005	2010	1	.	.
Oman	Qabus	1970	2010	0	.	.
Pakistan	Sharif	1990	1993	1	0.75	1
Pakistan	Bhutto	1993	1996	1	0.75	1
Pakistan	Khalid	1996	1997	1	0.75	1
Pakistan	Sharif	1997	1999	0	0	0
Pakistan	Musharraf	1999	2008	0	.	.
Panama	Endara	1990	1994	1	1	1
Panama	Balladares	1994	1999	1	1	1
Panama	Moscoso	1999	2004	1	1	1
Panama	Torrijos	2004	2009	1	.	.
Paraguay	Pedotti	1989	1993	1	0.75	1
Paraguay	Wasmosy	1993	1998	1	0.75	1
Paraguay	Cubas	1998	1999	1	0.75	1
Paraguay	González Macchi	1999	2003	1	0.75	1
Paraguay	Duarte	2003	2008	1	.	.
Peru	Fujimori	1990	2000	0	.	1
Peru	Toledo	2001	2006	1	0.75	1
Peru	García	2006	2010	1	.	.
Philippines	Ramos	1992	1998	1	0.75	1
Philippines	Estrada	1998	2001	1	0.75	1
Philippines	Macapagal-Arroyo	2001	2010	1	.	.
Poland	Walesa	1990	1995	1	0.75	1
Poland	Kwasniewski	1995	2005	1	1	1
Poland	Kaczynski	2005	2010	1	.	.
Portugal	Soares	1986	1996	1	1	1
Portugal	Sampaio	1996	2006	1	1	1
Portugal	Cavaco Silva	2006	2010	1	.	.
Republic of Korea	Roh T.	1988	1993	1	0.75	1
Republic of Korea	Kim Y.	1993	1998	1	0.75	1
Republic of Korea	Kim D.	1998	2003	1	0.75	1
Republic of Korea	Roh M.	2003	2008	1	.	.
Romania	Vacariou	1992	1996	1	0.75	1
Romania	Ciorbea	1996	1998	1	0.75	1
Romania	Vasile	1998	1999	1	0.75	1
Romania	Isarescu	1999	2000	1	0.75	1
Romania	Nastase	2000	2004	1	0.75	1

Country	Leader	From	To	Democracy	W	S
Romania	Basescu	2004	2008	1	.	.
Russian Federation	Yeltsin	1991	1999	0	0.75	1
Russian Federation	Putin	2000	2008	0	.	.
Rwanda	Habyarimana	1973	1994	0	0	.5
Rwanda	Kagame	1994	2010	0	.	.
Saudi Arabia	Fahd	1982	1996	0	0.25	.5
Saudi Arabia	Abdullah	1996	2010	0	.	.
Senegal	Diouf	1981	2000	1	0.75	1
Senegal	Wade	2000	2010	1	.	.
Sierra Leone	Strasser	1992	1996	0	0.75	1
Sierra Leone	Kabbah	1996	1997	0	.	0
Sierra Leone	Koroma	1997	1998	0	.	0
Sierra Leone	Kabbah	1998	2007	1	.	.
Sierra Leone	Koroma	2007	2010	1	.	.
Singapore	Goh	1990	2004	0	0.75	1
Singapore	Lee	2004	2010	0	.	.
Slovakia	Meciar	1994	1998	1	0.75	1
Slovakia	Dzurinda	1998	2006	1	1	1
Slovakia	Fico	2006	2010	1	.	.
Slovenia	Drnovsek	1992	2000	1	1	1
Slovenia	Drnovsek	2000	2002	1	1	1
Slovenia	Rop	2002	2004	1	1	1
Slovenia	Jansa	2004	2008	1	.	.
South Africa	Mandela	1994	1999	1	0.75	1
South Africa	Mbeki	1999	2008	1	.	.
Spain	González	1982	1996	1	1	1
Spain	Aznar	1996	2004	1	1	1
Spain	Zapatero	2004	2010	1	.	.
Sri Lanka	Premadasa	1989	1993	0	0.75	1
Sri Lanka	Wijetunge	1993	1994	0	0.75	1
Sri Lanka	Kumaratunga	1994	2005	0	0.75	1
Sri Lanka	Rajapakse	2005	2010	1	.	.
Sudan	Al-Bashir	1989	2010	0	.	.
Sweden	Bildt	1991	1994	1	1	1
Sweden	Carlsson	1994	1996	1	1	1
Sweden	Persson	1996	2006	1	1	1
Sweden	Reinfeldt	2006	2010	1	.	.
Syrian Arab Republic	H. Al-Assad	1971	2000	0	.5	1
Syrian Arab Republic	B. Al-Assad	2000	2010	0	.	.

Country	Leader	From	To	Democracy	W	S
Tajikistan	Rakhmonov	1992	2010	0	.	.
Thailand	Leekpai	1992	1995	1	0.75	1
Thailand	Silpa-Archa	1995	1996	1	0.75	1
Thailand	Chavalit	1996	1997	1	0.75	1
Thailand	Leekpai	1997	2001	1	0.75	1
Thailand	Thaksin	2001	2006	0	0.5	0
Thailand	Surayud	2006	2008	0	.	.
The former Yugoslav Republic of Macedonia	Crvenkovski	1992	1998	1	0.75	1
The former Yugoslav Republic of Macedonia	Georgievski	1998	2002	1	0.75	1
The former Yugoslav Republic of Macedonia	Crvenkovski	2002	2004	1	0.75	1
The former Yugoslav Republic of Macedonia	Buckovski	2004	2006	1	0.75	1
The former Yugoslav Republic of Macedonia	Gruevski	2006	2010	1	.	.
Togo	Eyadema	1967	2005	0	0.5	1
Togo	Gnassingbé	2005	2010	0	.	.
Tunisia	Ben Ali	1987	2010	0	.	.
Turkey	Demirel	1991	1993	1	0.75	1
Turkey	Ciller	1993	1996	1	0.75	1
Turkey	Erbakan	1996	1997	1	0.75	1
Turkey	Yilmaz	1997	1999	1	0.75	1
Turkey	Ecevit	1999	2002	1	0.75	1
Turkey	Gul	2002	2003	1	0.75	1
Turkey	Erdogan	2003	2010	1	.	.
Turkmenistan	Niyazov	1990	2006	0	0.5	1
Turkmenistan	Berdimuhamedow	2006	2010	0	.	.
Uganda	Museveni	1986	2010	0	.	.
Ukraine	Kuchma	1994	2005	1	0.75	1
Ukraine	Yushchenko	2005	2010	1	.	.
United Arab Emirates	An-Nahayan I	1971	2004	0	0.25	. 5
United Arab Emirates	An-Nahayan II	2004	2010	0	.	.
United Kingdom	Major	1990	1997	1	1	1
United Kingdom	Blair	1997	2007	1	.	.

Country	Leader	From	To	Democracy	W	S
United Kingdom	Brown	2007	2010	1	.	.
Tanzania	Mwinyi	1985	1995	0	0.75	1
Tanzania	Mkapa	1995	2005	0	0.75	1
Tanzania	Kikwete	2005	2010	0	.	.
United States	Bush	1989	1993	1	1	1
United States	Clinton	1993	2001	1	1	1
United States	Bush, Jr	2001	2009	1	.	.
Uruguay	Lacalle	1990	1995	1	1	1
Uruguay	Sanguinetti	1995	2000	1	1	1
Uruguay	Batlle	2000	2005	1	1	1
Uruguay	Vázquez	2005	2010	1	.	.
Uzbekistan	Karimov	1990	2010	0	.	.
Venezuela	Pérez	1989	1993	1	0.75	1
Venezuela	Velasquez	1993	1994	1	0.75	1
Venezuela	Caldera	1994	1999	1	0.75	1
Venezuela	Chavez	1999	2010	0	.	.
Viet Nam	Do Muoi	1991	1997	0	.	.
Viet Nam	Phieu	1997	2001	0	.	.
Viet Nam	Manh	2001	2010	0	.	.
Zambia	Chiluba	1991	2002	0	0.75	1
Zambia	Mwanawasa	2002	2008	1	.	.
Zimbabwe	Mugabe	1980	2010	0	.	.

References

Agwaandorjiin, S. (1999) *Demokratisierungschancen in der Mongolei*. Marburg: Tectum Verlag.

Alden, C. (2007) *China in Africa*. London, New York, Cape Town: Zed Books.

Alesina, A. and Dollar, D. (2000) Who Gives Foreign Aid to Whom and Why? *Journal of Economic Growth*, 5(1), 33–63.

Almond, G. and Verba, S. (1963) *The Civic Culture: Political Attitudes and Democracy in Five Nations*. Princeton: Princeton University Press.

Alvarez, M., Cheibub, J. A., Limongi, F. and Przeworski, A. (1996) Classifying Political Regimes. *Studies in Comparative International Development*, 31(1), 3–36.

Ambrosio, T. (2009) *Authoritarian Backlash: Russian Resistance to Democratization in the Former Soviet Union*. Farnham: Ashgate.

Amnesty International (2009) Impunity and Injustice are Legacy of Deadly July Riots in Mongolia. Retrieved 24 July 2013, from www.amnesty.org/en/news-and-updates/report/impunity-and-injustice-are-legacy-deadly-july-riots-mongolia-20091218

An, M., Bush, S., Lake, B., Lopez, S., McCants, A., Sawyer, J., Skidmore, P. and Velasco, C. (2008) *Idealism without Illusions*. New Jersey: Woodrow Wilson School of Public and International Affairs.

AsiaNews.it (2004) World Buddhist Summit: Appeals to Boycott Myanmar's Military Regime. Retrieved 26 January 2012, from www.asianews.it/view4print.php?l=en&art=1923

Aung, H. (2009, 7 September) Burma's New Constitution Privileges Soldiers above Civilians. *The Irrawaddy*.

Baabar, B. (2009) A Country without Much Hope [translated from Mongolian]. Retrieved 14 March 2011, from http://economics.gogo.mn/news/55237

Bader, J. (2013) The Political Economy of External Exploitation. A Comparative Investigation of China's Foreign Relations. *Democratization*, DOI: 10.1080/13510347.2013.795550, pp. 1–21.

Bader, J. and Kästner, A. (2013) Externe Autokratieförderung? Das autokratiefördernde Potential russischer und chinesischer Außenpolitik. In S. Kailitz and P. Köllner (eds), *Autokratien im Vergleich* (Politische Vierteljahresschrift Sonderheft 47 ed.). Baden-Baden: Nomos, pp. 564–86.

Bader, J., Grävingholt, J. and Kästner, A. (2010) Would Autocracies Promote Autocracy? A Political Economy Perspective on Regime-type Export in Regional Neighbourhoods. *Contemporary Politics*, 16(1), 81–100.

Baily, G. (2007) Burma: From Colonisation to Brutalisation. *CIPS Electronic Briefing Paper*, 5, 30 December 2010.

Banks, A. (2007) *Cross-National Times-Series Data Archive User's Manual*. Jerusalem, Israel: Databanks International; see www.databanksinternational.com

Barkmann, U. B. (2006) Zur Entwicklung der politischen Eliten – am Beispiel der Mandatsträger der MRVP in der Großen Staatsversammlung (1992–2005). In U. B. Barkmann (ed.), *Die Rolle der politischen Parteien im Transformationsprozess der Mongolei*. Ulaanbaatar: Konrad-Adenauer-Stiftung, pp. 293–6.

Batbajar, B. (2006) Politische Parteien oder Bürgerbewegung? – Widersprüche in der heutigen Politik – Die politische Krise in der Mongolei. In U.B. Barkmann (ed.), *Die Rolle der politischen Parteien im Transformationsprozess der Mongolei*. Ulaanbaatar: Konrad-Adenauer-Stiftung, pp. 281–6.

Batbayar, T. (2003) Foreign Policy and Domestic Reform in Mongolia. *Central Asian Survey*, 22(1), 45–59.

Batchimeg, M. (2005a) Future Challenges for the PRC and Mongolia. *China Brief*, 5(10).

Batchimeg, M. (2005b) Mongolia-China Relations and its Implications on Mongolia–U.S. Relations. In R. A. Scalapino (ed.), *A Comprehensive U.S.–Mongolia Partnership: Challenges and Opportunities*. Ulaanbaatar: The Institute for Strategic Studies, pp. 46–59.

Batmonkh, S. (2007, 26 July) Closure Order on Chinese-owned Plants. *The UB Post*.

BBC News (2007, 29 September) Burma Junta's Bunker Mentality. *BBC News*.

BBC News (2008, 19 April) Zimbabwe Arms Ship Quits S-Africa. *BBC News*.

BBC News (2010, 15 July) Burma Junta Support Group USDA Disbands. *BBC News*.

Beck, N., Katz, J. N. and Tucker, R. (1998) Taking Time Seriously: Time-Series-Cross-Section Analysis with a Binary Dependent Variable. *American Journal of Political Science*, 42(4), 1260–88.

Bellin, E. (2004) The Robustness of Authoritarianism in the Middle East. *Comparative Politics*, 36(2), 139–57.

Beresford, D. (2008, 18 April) Chinese Ship Carries Arms Cargo to Mugabe Regime. *The Guardian*.

Berthélemy, J. (2011) *China's Engagement and Aid Effectiveness in Africa* (Working Paper Series No. 129). Tunis: African Development Bank Group.

Blagov, S. (2005) Mongolia Drifts Away from Russia Towards China. *China Brief*, 5(10).

Blaydes, L. and Kayser, M. (2011) Counting Calories: Democracy and Distribution in the Developing World. *International Studies Quarterly*, 55(4), 887–908.

Bond, S. R. and Malik, A. (2009) Natural Resources, Export Structure, and Investment. *Oxford Economic Papers*, 61(4), 675–702.

Box-Steffensmeier, J. M. and Jones, B. S. (1997) Time is of the Essence: Event History Models in Political Science. *American Journal of Political Science*, 41(4), 1414–61.

Brambor, T., Clark, W. R. and Golder, M. (2006) Understanding Interaction Models: Improving Empirical Analyses. *Political Analysis*, 14(1), 63–82.

Braumoeller, B. F. (2004) Hypothesis Testing and Multiplicative Interaction Terms. *International Organization*, 58(4), 807–20.

Brautigam, D. (2008) *China's African Aid: Transatlantic Challenges*. Washington, DC: The German Marshall Fund of the United States.

Brautigam, D. (2009) *The Dragon's Gift*. Oxford: Oxford University Press.

Brinks, D. and Coppedge, M. (2006) Diffusion is no Illusion. *Comparative Political Studies*, 39(4), 463–89.

Brooker, P. (2009) *Non-Democratic Regimes* (2nd edn). New York: Palgrave Macmillan.

Brown, F. (1992) Cambodia in 1991. *Asian Survey*, 32(1), 83–90.

Bueno de Mesquita, B. and Root, H. (2002) The Political Roots of Poverty. *The National Interest*, 68(Summer), 27–38.

Bueno de Mesquita, B. and Smith, A. (2007) Foreign Aid and Policy Concessions. *Journal of Conflict Resolution*, 51(2), 251–84.

Bueno de Mesquita, B. and Smith, A. (2009) A Political Economy of Aid. *International Organization*, 63(2), 309–40.

Bueno de Mesquita, B. and Smith, A. (2010) Leader Survival, Revolutions, and the Nature of Government Finance. *American Journal of Political Science*, 54(4), 936–50.

Bueno de Mesquita, B. and Smith, A. (2011) *The Dictator's Handbook: Why Bad Behavior is Almost Always Good Politics*. New York: Public Affairs.

Bueno de Mesquita, B., Smith, A., Siverson, R. M. and Morrow, J. D. (2003) *The Logic of Political Survival*. Cambridge and London: The MIT Press.

Bulag, U. E. (2009) Mongolia in 2008: From Mongolia to Mine-golia. *Asian Survey*, 49(1), 129–34.

Bulag, U. E. (2010) Mongolia in 2009: From Landlocked to Land-linked Cosmopolitan. *Asian Survey*, 50(1), 97–103.

Bünte, M. (2008) Myanmar: Autoritarismus im Wandel. *Südostasien Aktuell*, 2, 75–88.

Burgos, S. and Ear, S. (2010) China's Strategic Interests in Cambodia. Influence and Resources. *Asian Survey*, 50(3), 615–39.

Burma News International (2010, 6 September) Sino-Burmese Talks 'On Key Issues'. *Burma News International*.

Burnell, P. (2006) *Promoting Democracy Backwards*. Madrid: FRIDE.

Burnell, P. (2010) *Is There a New Autocracy Promotion?* Madrid: FRIDE.

Byambasuren, B. (2006) *Peace Operations Engagement of the Mongolian Armed Forces*. Ulaanbaatar: The Institute for Strategic Studies.

Callahan, M. (2012) The Generals Loosen Their Grip. *Journal of Democracy*, 23(4), 120–31.

Cambodian Human Rights Action Committee (2009) *Losing Ground. Forced Evictions and Intimidation in Cambodia*. Phnom Penh: The Cambodian Human Rights Action Committee.

Campi, A. (2004) *Modern Mongolian-Chinese Strategic Relations: Challenges for the New Century*. Ulaanbaatar: The Institute for Strategic Studies.

Campi, A. (2005) Sino-Mongolian Relations from Beijing's Viewpoint. *China Brief*, 5(10).

Cardoso, F. H. and Faletto, E. (1979) *Dependency and Development in Latin America*. Berkeley, CA: University of California Press.

Carothers, T. (1999) *Aiding Democracy Abroad*. Washington, DC: Carnegie Endowment for International Peace.

Carothers, T. (2006) The Backlash against Democracy Promotion. *Foreign Affairs*, 85(2), 55–68.

Carter, D. B. and Signorino, C. S. (2010) Back to the Future: Modeling Time Dependence in Binary Data. *Political Analysis*, 18(3), 271–92.

Chan, S. (2008) *China, the U.S., and the Power Transition Theory: A Critique*. New York: Routledge.

Chanda, N. (2002) China and Cambodia: In the Mirror of History. *Asia-Pacific Review*, 9(2), 1–11.

Cheibub, J. A., Gandhi, J. and Vreeland, J. R. (2010) Democracy and Dictatorship Revisited. *Public Choice*, 143(1), 67–101.

Chenyang, L. and Fook, L. L. (2009) China's Policies towards Myanmar: A Successful Model for Dealing with the Myanmar Issue? *China: An International Journal*, 7(2), 255–87.

Cheung, Y., de Haan, J., Qian, X. and Yu, S. (2012) China's Outward Investment in Africa. *Review of International Economics*, 20(2), 202–20.

China Daily (2009) Wrong Stance on Tibet Hinders Ties with China. Retrieved 24 July 2013, from www.chinadaily.com.cn/china/2009-03/05/content_7538147.htm

Chinese Government (2009) Top Lawmakers of China, U.S. Meet on Wide-Ranging Issues. Retrieved 24 July 2013, from www.gov.cn/misc/2009-05/27/content_1326253.htm

Chiozza, G. and Goemans, H. E. (2003) Peace through Insecurity: Tenure and International Conflict. *The Journal of Conflict Resolution*, 47(4), 443–67.

Chung, J. H. (2009) East Asia Responds to the Rise of China: Patterns and Variations. *Pacific Affairs*, 82(4), 657–75.

Clapp, P. (2007a) *Burma's Long Road to Democracy*. Washington, DC: United States Institute of Peace.

Clapp, P. (2007b) *Building Democracy in Burma*. Washington, DC: United States Institute of Peace.

Cock, A. R. (2010a) Anticipating an Oil Boom: The Resource Curse Thesis in the Play of Cambodian Politics. *Pacific Affairs*, 83(3), 525–46.

Cock, A. R. (2010b) External Actors and the Relative Autonomy of the Ruling Elite in Post-UNTAC Cambodia. *Journal of Southeast Asian Studies*, 41(2), 241–65.

Conrad, C. R. (2011) Constrained Concessions: Beneficent Dictatorial Responses to the Domestic Political Opposition. *International Studies Quarterly*, 55(4), 1167–87.

Correlates of War Project (2007) *Direct Contiguity Data, 1816–2006. Version 3.1*. Online: http://correlatesofwar.org

Council for the Development of Cambodia. (2010) The Cambodia ODA Database. Retrieved 30 December 2010, from http://cdc.khmer.biz/

Crispin, S. W. (2007, 26 January) Cambodia's Coming Energy Bonanza. *Asia Times Online*.

Croissant, A. (2008) The Perils and Promises of Democratization through United Nations Transitional Authority. *Democratization*, 15(3), 649–68.

Croissant, A. and Kamerling, J. (2013) Why Do Military Regimes Institutionalize? Constitution-making and Elections as Political Survival Strategy in Myanmar. *Asian Journal of Political Science*, 21(2), 105–25.

Dahl, R. (1971) *Polyarchy*. New Haven, CT: Yale University Press.

Dalailama.com (2013) His Holiness the Dalai Lama sends congratulations to the Australian Prime Minister and the President of Mongolia. Retrieved 24 July 2013, from www.dalailama.com/news/post/971-his-holiness-the-dalai-lama-sends-congratulations-to-the-australian-prime-minister-and-the-president-of-mongolia

Davenport, C. (2007) State Repression and Political Order. *Annual Review of Political Science*, 10(June), 1–23.

Davies, M., Edinger, H., Tay, N. and Naidu, S. (2008) *How China Delivers Development Assistance to Africa*. Stellenbosch: Centre for Chinese Studies.

De Soysa, I. and Midford, P. (2012) Enter the Dragon! An Empirical Analysis of Chinese versus US Arms Transfers to Autocrats and Violators of Human Rights, 1989–2006. *International Studies Quarterly*, 56(4), 843–56.

Demirbag, M., Tatoglu, E. and Oyungerel, A. (2005) Patterns of Foreign Direct Investments in Mongolia, 1990–2003. *Eurasian Geography and Economics*, 46(4), 306–18.

Diamond, L. (2008) The Democratic Rollback. *Foreign Affairs*, 87(2), 36–48.

Diamond, L. (2012) The Need for a Political Pact. *Journal of Democracy*, 23(4), 138–49.

Dierkes, J. (2011) Asia Pacific Memo #52 Current Convulsions in Mongolia's Political Party Landscape. Retrieved 24 July 2013, from www.asiapacificmemo.ca/ mongolian-politics

Downs, A. (1957) *An Economic Theory of Democracy*. New York: Harpers and Collins.

Dreher, A. and Fuchs, A. (forthcoming) Rogue Aid? An Empirical Analysis of China's Aid Allocation. *Canadian Journal of Economics*.

Dukalskis, A. (2009) Stateness Problems or Regime Unification? Explaining Obstacles to Democratization in Burma/Myanmar. *Democratization*, 16(5), 945–68.

Ear, S. and Hall, J. (2008, 28 July 2008) Managing Democracy: Cambodia's Free Press Under Fire. *International Herald Tribune*, p. 8.

Easterly, W. (2002) The Cartel of Good Intentions: the Problem of Bureaucracy in Foreign Aid. *Journal of Economic Policy Reform*, 5(4), 223–50.

Easterly, W., Satyanath, S. and Berger, D. (2008) Superpower Interventions and their Consequences for Democracy: An Empirical Inquiry. *NBER Working Paper Series, 13992*.

Embassy of the PRC (2012) Review on Bilateral Relations. Retrieved 1 December 2013, from http://mm.china-embassy.org/eng/zmgx/zzgx/t174785.htm

Embassypages.com (2013) Taiwan – Embassies and Consulate. Retrieved 24 July 2013, from www.embassypages.com/taiwan

Emmanuel, N. (2010) Undermining Cooperation: Donor-Patrons and the Failure of Political Conditionality. *Democratization*, 17(5), 856–77.

Englehart, N. A. (2012) Two Cheers for Burma's Rigged Election. *Asian Survey*, 52(4), 666–86.

Escribà-Folch, A. (2012) Authoritarian Responses to Foreign Pressure: Spending, Repression, and Sanctions. *Comparative Political Studies*, 45(6), 683–713.

Ezrow, N. and Frantz, E. (2011) *Dictators and Dictatorships. Understanding Authoritarian Regimes and their Leaders*. New York: Continuum.

Farah, D. and Mosher, A. (2010) *Winds From the East*. Washington, DC: Center for International Media Assistance.

Faust, J. (2007a) Autocracies and Economic Development: Theory and Evidence from 20th Century Mexico. *Historical Social Research*, 32(4), 305–29.

Faust, J. (2007b) Democracy's Dividend: Political Order and Economic Productivity. *World Political Science Review*, 3(2), pp.1–26.

Flores-Macías, G. A. and Kreps, S. E. (2013) The Foreign Policy Consequences of Trade: China's Commercial Relations with Africa and Latin America, 1992–2006. *The Journal of Politics*, 75(2), 357–71.

Food and Agriculture Organization of the United Nations (2005) *Global Forest Resources Assessment 2005. FAO Forestry Paper 147*. Rome: Food and Agriculture Organization of the United Nations.

Foster, V., Butterfield, W., Chen, C. and Pushak, N. (2009) *Building Bridges: China's Growing Role as Infrastructure Financier for Sub-Saharan Africa*. Washington, DC: The World Bank.

Freedom House (2006) Freedom in the World – Mongolia. Retrieved 30 December 2012, from www.freedomhouse.org/report/freedom-world/2006/mongolia#.U1rWEVd7Z3E

Freedom House (2011) Freedom in the World – Mongolia. Retrieved 30 December 2012, from www.freedomhouse.org/report/freedom-world/2011/mongolia#.U2E5YFd7Z3E

Frost, S. (2004) Chinese Outward Direct Investment in Southeast Asia: How Big are the Flows and What Does it Mean for the Region? *The Pacific Review*, 17(3), 323–40.

Fuchs, A. and Klann, N. H. (2013) Paying a Visit: The Dalai Lama Effect on International Trade. *Journal of International Economics*, 91(1), pp.164–77.

Fukuyama, F. (1995) The Primacy of Culture. *Journal of Democracy*, 6(1), 7–14.

Fullbrook, D. (2006, 6 September) China's Growing Influence in Cambodia. *Asia Times Online*.

Gallagher, M. and Hanson, J. (2013) Authoritarian Survival, Resilience and the Selectorate Theory. In M. Dimitrov (eds), *Why Communism did not Collapse: Understanding Authoritarian Regime Resilience in Asia and Europe*. New York: Cambridge University Press, pp. 185–204.

Gandhi, J. and Przeworski, A. (2006) Cooperation, Cooptation, and Rebellion under Dictatorship. *Economics and Politics*, 18(1), 1–26.

Gandhi, J. and Przeworski, A. (2007) Authoritarian Institutions and the Survival of Autocrats. *Comparative Political Studies*, 40(11), 1279–1301.

Ganesan, N. (2011) Myanmar-China Relations: Interlocking Interests but Independent Output. *Japanese Journal of Political Science*, 12(1), 95–111.

Gartner, S. and Regan, P. (1996) Threat and Repression: The Non-Linear Relationship between Government and Opposition. *Journal of Peace Research*, 33(3), 273–87.

Gat, A. (2007) The Return of Authoritarian Great Powers. *Foreign Affairs*, 86(4), 59–69.

Geddes, B. (1999) Authoritarian Breakdown: Empirical Test of a Game Theoretic Argument. *The Annual Meeting of the American Political Science Association*, Atlanta.

Geddes, B., Wright, J. and Frantz, E. (forthcoming) Autocratic Breakdown and Regime Transitions: A New Data Set. *Perspective on Politics*.

Gerring, J. (2006) *Case Study Research: Principles and Practices*. Cambridge: Cambridge University Press.

Gershman, C. and Allen, M. (2006) New Threats to Freedom: The Assault on Democracy Assistance. *Journal of Democracy*, 17(2), 36–51.

Gilpin, R. (1996) The Nature of Political Economy. In C. R. Goddard, J. T. Passe-Smith and J. G. Conklin (eds), *International Political Economy*. Boulder, CO: Lynne Rienner Publishers, pp. 9–24.

Gleditsch, K. S. and Ward, M. (2006) Diffusion and the International Context of Democratization. *International Organization*, 60(3), 911–33.

Global Witness (2005) *A Choice for China. Ending the Destruction of Burma's Northern Frontier Forests*. Washington, DC: Global Witness.

Global Witness (2007) *Cambodia's Family Tree: Illegal Logging and the Stripping of Public Assets by Cambodia's Elite*. Washington, DC: Global Witness.

Global Witness (2009a) Dramatic Decrease in Illegal Timber Trade between Burma and China but Smuggling Continues. Retrieved 30 July 2013, from www.globalwitness.org/library/dramatic-decrease-illegal-timber-trade-between-burma-and-china-smuggling-continues

Global Witness (2009b) *Country for Sale. How Cambodia's Elite has Captured the Country's Extractive Industries*. Washington, DC: Global Witness.

Goemans, H. E., Gleditsch, K. S. and Chiozza, G. (2009) Introducing Archigos: A Dataset of Political Leaders. *Journal of Peace Research*, 46(2), 269–83.

Gottesmann, E. R. (2004) *Cambodia after the Khmer Rouge: Inside the Politics of Nation Building*. New Haven, CT and London: Yale University Press.

Green, E. (1986) China and Mongolia: Recurring Trends and Prospects for Change. *Asian Survey*, 26(12), 1337–63.

Grimm, S. and Leininger, J. (2012) Not all Good Things go Together: Conflicting Objectives in Democracy Promotion. *Democratization* 19(3), Special Issue, pp. 391–414.

Grimm, S., Rank, R., McDonald, M. and Schickerling, E. (2011) *Transparency of Chinese Aid. An Analysis of the Published Information on Chinese External Financial Flows.* Stellenbosch: Publish What You Fund and Centre for Chinese Studies.

Guo, X. (2007, March) Towards Resolution: China in the Myanmar Issue. *Silkroad Paper.*

Hackenesch, C. (2014) *The EU Meets China in African Authoritarian Regimes. The Politics of Cooperating on Governance Reforms in the 21st Century.* Dissertation. Berlin: Free University Berlin.

Hadenius, A. (2007) Pathways from Authoritarianism. *Journal of Democracy*, 18(1), 143–57.

Hadenius, A. and Teorell, J. (2006) *Authoritarian Regimes: Stability, Change, and Pathways to Democracy, 1972–2003. Working paper 331.*

Halper, S. (2010) *The Beijing Consensus.* New York: Basic Books.

Harris, S. (2005) China's Regional Policies: How Much Hegemony? *Australian Journal of International Affairs*, 59(4), 481–92.

Hawkins, D., Nielson, D., Bergevin, A., Hearn, A. and Becky, P. (2010) Codebook for Assembling Data on China's Development Finance. Retrieved 1 May 2011, from www.aiddata.org/research/china

Heaton, W. R. (1992) Mongolia in 1991. *Asian Survey*, 32(1), 50–5.

Heder, S. (2011) Cambodia in 2010: Hun Sen's Further Consolidation. *Asian Survey*, 51(1), 208–14.

Heinrich Böll Stiftung (2013) Cambodia before the Parliamentary Elections: Leave Nothing to Chance or the Voters. Retrieved 30 July 2013, from www.boell.de/worldwide/asia/asia-cambodia-parliamentary-elections-leave-nothing-to-chance-or-the-voters-18017.html

Herbst, J. (2000) *States and Power in Africa: Comparative Lessons in Authority and Control.* Princeton, NJ: Princeton University Press.

Hermann, C. F. (1990) Changing Course: When Governments Choose to Redirect Foreign Policy. *International Studies Quarterly*, 34(1), 3–21.

Heston, A., Summers, R. and Aten, B. (2011) *Penn World Table Version 7.0* Center for International Comparisons of Production, Income and Prices at the University of Pennsylvania.

Hlaing, K. Y. (2005) Myanmar in 2004: Why Military Rule Continues. In C. K. Wah and D. Singh (eds), *Southeast Asian Affairs 2005.* Singapore: Institute of Southeast Asian Studies, pp. 231–56.

Holliday, I. (2009) Beijing and the Myanmar Problem. *The Pacific Review*, 22(4), 479–500.

Holliday, I. (2013) Myanmar in 2012: Toward a Normal State. *Asian Survey*, 53(1), 93–100.

Hongwei, F. (2012) The 1967 Anti-Chinese riots in Burma and Sino–Burmese Relations. *Journal of Southeast Asian Studies*, 43(2), 234–56.

Hood, S. (1990) Beijing's Cambodia Gamble and the Prospects for Peace in Indochina: The Khmer Rouge or Sihanouk? *Asian Survey*, 30(10), 977–91.

Hook, S. W. and Zhang, G. (1998) Japan's Aid Policy Since the Cold War: Rhetoric and Reality. *Asian Survey*, 38(11), 1051–66.

Hubbard, P. (2007) *Aiding Transparency: What we can Learn about China EXIM Bank's Concessional Loans.* Washington, DC: Center for Global Development.

Hughes, C. (2003) *The Political Economy of Cambodia's Transition, 1991–2001.* London and New York: Routledge Curzon Taylor & Francis Group.

Hughes, C. (2009) Cambodia in 2008: Consolidation in the Midst of Crisis. *Asian Survey*, 49(1), 206–12.

Huntington, S. P. (1968) *Political Order in Changing Societies.* New Haven, CT: Yale University Press.

Huntington, S. P. (1996) *The Clash of Civilizations and the Remaking of World Order.* New York: Simon and Schuster.

Inglehart, R. and Welzel, C. (2009) How Development Leads to Democracy – What we Know about Modernization. *Foreign Affairs*, 88(March/April), 33–48.

International Crisis Group (2009) *China's Myanmar Dilemma.* (Asia Report No. 177). Brussels: International Crisis Group.

International Crisis Group (2010a) *The Myanmar Elections.* Jakarta/Brussels: International Crisis Group.

International Crisis Group (2010b) *China's Myanmar Strategy: Elections, Ethnic Politics and Economics.* Beijing/Jakarta/Brussels: International Crisis Group.

International Crisis Group (2010c) *The Iran Nuclear Issue: The View from Beijing.* (Asia Briefing No. 100). Beijing/Brussels: International Crisis Group.

International Crisis Group (2012) *Myanmar: The Politics of Economic Reform* (Asia Report No 231). Jakarta/Brussels: International Crisis Group.

International Department CCP (2013a) Liu Yunshan Meets Mongolian People's Party Delegation. Retrieved 31 July 2013, from www.idcpc.org.cn/english/news/ 130327.htm

International Department CCP (2013b) Mongolia Takes Ties with China as Top Priority: PM. Retrieved 31 July 2013, from www.idcpc.org.cn/english/news/130710.htm

International Department CCP (2013c) P2P News. Retrieved 21 December 2013, from www.idcpc.org.cn/index.htm

International Monetary Fund (2010) *Direction of Trade.* Washington, DC: International Monetary Fund.

Isham, J., Woolcock, M., Pritchett, L. and Busby, G. (2005) The Varieties of Resource Experience: Natural Resource Export Structures and the Political Economy of Economic Growth. *The World Bank Economic Review*, 19(2), 141–74.

Jackson, N. J. (2010) The Role of External Factors in Advancing Non-Liberal Democratic Forms of Political Rule. *Contemporary Politics*, 16(1), 101–18.

Jagan, L. (2009, 1 September) Border War Rattles China-Myanmar Ties. *Asia Times Online.*

Jeldres, J. A. (2003) China-Cambodia: More than Just Friends? Retrieved 21 December 2013, from www.atimes.com/atimes/Southeast_Asia/EI16Ae03.html

Jiang, W. (2009) Fuelling the Dragon: China's Rise and Its Energy and Resources Extraction in Africa. *The China Quarterly*, 199, pp. 585–609.

Job, B. L. and Williams, E. (eds) (2009) *CSCAP Regional Security Outlook 2009–2010.* Singapore: Council for Security Cooperation in the Asia Pacific.

Johnston, A. I. (2003) Is China a Status-Quo Power? *International Security*, 27(4), 5–56.

Kagan, R. (2006) League of Dictators? Retrieved 2 May 2013, from http://carnegieendowment.org/2006/04/30/league-of-dictators/8a

Kagan, R. (2008) *The Return of History and the End of Dreams.* New York: Alfred A. Knopf.

Kang, D. (2007) *China Rising: Peace, Power, and Order in East Asia.* New York: Columbia University Press.

Kastner, S. L. and Saunders, P. C. (2012) Is China a Status Quo or Revisionist State? Leadership Travel as an Empirical Indicator of Foreign Policy Priorities. *International Studies Quarterly*, 56(1), 163–77.

Keefer, P. and Knack, S. (2007) Boondoggles, Rent-Seeking, and Political Checks and Balances: Public Investment under Unaccountable Governments. *The Review of Economics and Statistics*, 89(3), 566–72.

Khirghis, M. (2005) U.S.–Mongolian Comprehensive Partnership: Opportunities and Challenges. In R. A. Scalapino (ed.), *A Comprehensive U.S.–Mongolia Partnership: Challenges and Opportunities*. Ulaanbaatar: The Institute for Strategic Studies, pp. 31–45.

Kingdom of Cambodia. (1993) The Constitution of the Kingdom of Cambodia. Retrieved 31 July 2013, from http://cambodia.ohchr.org/klc_pages/KLC_files/section_001/section_01_01_ENG.pdf

Kleine-Ahlbrandt, S. and Small, A. (2008) China's New Dictatorship Diplomacy. *Foreign Affairs*, 87(1), 38–56.

Knack, S. (2001) Aid Dependence and the Quality of Governance: Cross-Country Empirical Tests. *Southern Economic Journal*, 68(2), 310–29.

Kobayashi, T. (2008) *Evolution of China's Aid Policy*. Tokyo: Japan Bank for International Cooperation.

Koesel, K. J. and Bunce, V. (2013) Diffusion-proofing: Russian and Chinese Responses to Waves of Popular Mobilizations against Authoritarian Rulers. *Perspectives on Politics*, 11(3), 753–68.

Kopinski, D., Polus, A. and Taylor, I. (2011) Contextualising Chinese Engagement in Africa. *Journal of Contemporary African Studies*, 29(2), 129–36.

Kramer, T. (2009) *From Golden Triangle to Rubber Belt? The Future of Opium Bans in the Kokang and Wa Regions*. Drug Policy Briefing No. 29. Amsterdam: Transnational Institute.

Kurlantzick, J. (2007) *Charm Offensive – How China's Soft Power is Transforming the World*. New Haven, CT and London: Yale University Press.

Kurlantzick, J. (2008) Asia's Democracy Backlash. *Current History*, 107(712), 375–80.

Kurtenbach, E. (2007, 25 May) China Steelmakers Plan Cambodia Investment. *The Associated Press*

Lake, D. (2006) International Political Economy. A Maturing Interdiscipline. In B. Weingast and D. Wittman (eds), *The Oxford Handbook of Political Economy*. Oxford: Oxford University Press, pp. 757–77.

Lake, D. and Baum, M. (2001) The Invisible Hand of Democracy: Political Control and the Provision of Public Services. *Comparative Political Studies*, 34(6), 587–621.

Lall, M. (2006) Indo-Myanmar Relations in the Era of Pipeline Diplomacy. *Contemporary Southeast Asia*, 28(3), 424–46.

Landman, T., Larizza, M. and Mc Evoy, C. (2005) *State of Democracy in Mongolia*. Ulaanbaatar: 'Democracy Development in Mongolia: Challenges and Opportunities' Conference 30 June–1 July 2005.

Large, D. (2009) China's Sudan Engagement: Changing Northern and Southern Political Trajectories in Peace and War. *China Quarterly*, 199, pp. 610–26.

Lee, P. K., Chan, G. and Chan, L. (2009) China's 'Realpolitik' Engagement with Myanmar. *China Security*, 5(1), 105–26.

Leeds, B. A. (1999) Domestic Political Institutions, Credible Commitments, and International Cooperation. *American Journal of Political Science*, 43(4), 979–1002.

Leeson, P. T. and Dean, A. M. (2009) The Democratic Domino Theory: An Empirical Investigation. *American Journal of Political Science*, 53(3), 533–51.

Leeson, P. T. and Sobel, R. S. (2008) Weathering Corruption. *Journal of Law and Economics*, 51(4), 667–81.

Lemke, D. (2003) Power Transition Theory and the Rise of China. *International Interactions*, 29, 269–71.

Lerner, D. (1958) *The Passing of Traditional Society*. New York: Free Press.

Levitsky, S. and Way, L. (2005) International Linkage and Democratization. *Journal of Democracy*, 16(3), 20–33.

Levitsky, S. and Way, L. (2010) *Competitive Authoritarianism. Hybrid Regimes After the Cold War*. Cambridge: Cambridge University Press.

Li, J. (2011) Chinese Investment in Mongolia: An Uneasy Courtship between Goliath and David. Retrieved 24 July 2013, from www.eastasiaforum.org/2011/02/02/ chinese-investment-in-mongolia-an-uneasy-courtship-between-goliath-and-david/

Li, M. (2007) *China's Proactive Engagement in Asia: Economics, Politics and Interactions.* Singapore: The S. Rajaratnam School of International Studies.

Lijphart, A. (1984) *Patterns of Majoritarian and Consensus Government in Twenty-One Countries*. New Haven, CT: Yale University Press.

Lintner, B. (2002) *Blood Brothers. The Criminal Underworld of Asia*. New York: Palgrave Macmillan.

Linz, J. J. (2000) *Authoritarian and Totalitarian Regimes*. Boulder, CO: Lynne Rienner.

Lipset, S. M. (1960) Economic Development and Democracy. In S. M. Lipset (ed.), *Political Man: The Social Basis for Politics*. New York: Anchor Books, pp. 45–76.

Lipton, M. (1977) *Why Poor People Stay Poor: Urban Bias in World Development*. Cambridge, MA: Harvard University Press.

Liu, J. (1993) PRC Agreements with Foreign Countries. Monthly Data Supplement January–December. *China Aktuell.*

Liu, J. (1994) PRC Agreements with Foreign Countries. Monthly Data Supplement January–December. *China Aktuell.*

Liu, J. (1995) PRC Agreements with Foreign Countries. Monthly Data Supplement January–December. *China Aktuell.*

Liu, J. (1996) PRC Agreements with Foreign Countries. Monthly Data Supplement January–December. *China Aktuell.*

Liu, J. (1997) PRC Agreements with Foreign Countries. Monthly Data Supplement January–December. *China Aktuell.*

Liu, J. (1998) PRC Agreements with Foreign Countries. Monthly Data Supplement January–December. *China Aktuell.*

Liu, J. (1999) PRC Agreements with Foreign Countries. Monthly Data Supplement January–December. *China Aktuell.*

Liu, J. (2000) PRC Agreements with Foreign Countries. Monthly Data Supplement January–December. *China Aktuell.*

Liu, J. (2001) PRC Agreements with Foreign Countries. Monthly Data Supplement January–December. *China Aktuell.*

Liu, J. (2002) PRC Agreements with Foreign Countries. Monthly Data Supplement January–December. *China Aktuell.*

Liu, J. (2003) PRC Agreements with Foreign Countries. Monthly Data Supplement January–December. *China Aktuell.*

Liu, J. (2004) PRC Agreements with Foreign Countries. Monthly Data Supplement January–December. *China Aktuell.*

Liu, J. (2005) PRC Agreements with Foreign Countries. Monthly Data Supplement January–December. *China Aktuell.*

Liu, J. (2006) PRC Agreements with Foreign Countries. Monthly Data Supplement January–December. *China Aktuell.*

Liu, J. (2007) PRC Agreements with Foreign Countries. Monthly Data Supplement January–December. *China Aktuell.*

Liu, J. (2008) PRC Agreements with Foreign Countries. Monthly Data Supplement January–December. *China Aktuell.*

Lum, T. (2007) *Cambodia: Background and U.S. Relations.* Washington, DC: Congressional Research Service.

Lum, T., Morrison, W. and Vaughn, B. (2008) *China's 'Soft Power' in Southeast Asia.* Washington, DC: Congressional Research Service.

Magaloni, B. (2008) Credible Power-Sharing and the Longevity of Authoritarian Rule. *Comparative Political Studies*, 41(4/5), 715–41.

Magaloni, B. and Kricheli, R. (2010) Political Order and One-Party Rule. *Annual Review of Political Science*, 13(May), 123–43.

Mansfield, E. D., Milner, H. V. and Rosendorff, B. P. (2000) Free to Trade: Democracies, Autocracies, and International Trade. *American Political Science Review*, 94(2), 305–21.

Marks, P. (2000) China's Cambodia Strategy. *Parameters*, 30(3), 92–108.

Marshall, M. G. and Jaggers, K. (2013) *Polity IV Project: Political Regime Characteristics and Transitions, 1800–2012.* Vienna, VA: Center for Systemic Peace.

Mashbat, O. S. (2007) *International Politics of the Reincarnation of the Dalai Lama.* Monterey, CA: Naval Postgraduate School.

Matthews, B. (2006) Myanmar's Human and Economic Crisis and its Regional Implications. In D. Singh, and L. C. Salazar (eds), *Southeast Asian Affairs 2006.* Singapore: Institute of Southeast Asian Studies, pp. 208–23.

Maung, A. M. (2007) *Sino-Myanmar Economic Relations since 1988.* Working Paper Series No. 86. Singapore: National University of Singapore, Asia Research Institute.

McCargo, D. (2005) Cambodia: Getting away with Authoritarianism? *Journal of Democracy*, 16(4), 98–112.

McGillivray, F. and Smith, A. (2000) Trust and Cooperation through Agent-Specific Punishments. *International Organization*, 54(4), 809–24.

McGillivray, F. and Smith, A. (2004) The Impact of Leadership Turnover on Trading Relations between States. *International Organization*, 58(3), 567–600.

McGillivray, F. and Smith, A. (2006) Credibility in Compliance and Punishment: Leader Specific Punishment and Credibility. *Journal of Politics*, 68(2), 248-258.

Medeiros, E. S. and Fravel, M. T. (2003) China's New Diplomacy. *Foreign Affairs*, 82(6), 22–35.

Melnykovska, I., Plamper, H. and Schweickert, R. (2012) Do Russia and China Promote Autocracy in Central Asia? *Asia Europe Journal*, 10(1), 75–89.

Mendee, J. (2010) Broad Gauge versus Narrow Gauge: The Politics of Dimension in Mongolia's Railroad System. Retrieved 24 July 2013, from www.asiapacificmemo.ca/mongolia-gauging-inner-asian-tensions-over-railways

Mendee, J. (2012) Why Mongolia's Mining Strategy is not a Mistake. Retrieved 24 July 2013, from http://blogs.ubc.ca/mongolia/2012/why-mongolias-china-mining-strategy-is-not-a-mistake/

Mengin, F. (2007) *La présence chinoise au Cambodge. Contribution à une économie politique violente rentière et inégalitaire.* Les études du CERI 133. Paris: Science Po.

Merkel, W. (2010) Are Dictatorships Returning? Revisiting the 'Democratic Rollback' Hypothesis. *Contemporary Politics*, 16(1), 17–32.

Meyersson, E., i Miquel, G. P. and Qian, N. (2008) *The Rise of China and the Natural Resource Curse in Africa.* Unpublished manuscript.

Middleton, C. (2008) *Cambodia's Hydropower Development and China's Involvement.* Berkeley/Phnom Penh: River Coalition in Cambodia, International Rivers.

Milner, H. V. (1997) *Interests, Institutions, and Information: Domestic Politics and International Relations*. Princeton, NJ: Princeton University Press.

Milner, H. V. (1999) The Political Economy of International Trade. *Annual Review of Political Science*, 2(June), 91–114.

Milner, H. V. (2006) The Digital Divide. The Role of Political Institutions in Technology Diffusion. *Comparative Political Studies*, 39(2), 176–99.

Milner, H. V. and Kubota, K. (2005) Why the Move to Free Trade? Democracy and Trade Policy in the Developing Countries. *International Organization*, 59(1), 107–43.

Ministry of Economic Development (2013) International. Retrieved 24 July 2013, from www.investmongolia.com/fiftanew/contents.php?id=1&sId=2&lang=Eng

Ministry of Foreign Affairs of the PRC (2010) Bilateral Relations. Retrieved 16 November 2010, from www.fmprc.gov.cn/eng/wjb/zzjg/yzs/gjlb/2742/

Moe, W. (2010a, 17 August) Shan State Railway to Suppress Armed Ethnic Groups: Rights Groups. *The Irrawaddy*.

Moe, W. (2010b, 11 September) Taiwanese Spies on Burmese Soil? *The Irrawaddy*.

Möller, K. (1998) Cambodia and Burma. *Asian Survey*, 38(12), 1087–104.

Mongolian Mining Journal (2009, 13 July) Exporting the Tavan Tolgoi Coal: Choosing the Best Way Out. Retrieved 13 December 2010, from http://en.mongolianminingjournal.com/content/15640.shtml

Moore, B. (1960) *Social Origins of Dictatorship and Democracy*. Boston, MA: Beacon Press.

Moore, W. (2000) The Repression of Dissent: A Substitution Model of Government. *The Journal of Conflict Resolution*, 44(1), 107–27.

Moravcsik, A. (1997) Taking Preferences Seriously: A Liberal Theory of International Politics. *International Organization*, 51(4), 513–53.

Morrison, K. M. (2009) Oil, Nontax Revenue, and the Redistributional Foundations of Regime Stability. *International Organization*, 63(1), 107–38.

Mydans, S. (2008a, 25 July) Cambodian Leader is Expected to Win Election. *International Herald Tribune*.

Mydans, S. (2008b, 28 July) Cambodia's Premier is Poised for Election Victory. *International Herald Tribune*

Naim, M. (2007) Rogue Aid. *Foreign Policy*, March-April(159), 95–6.

Naing, S. Y. (2008, 17 March) Burmese Monks Condemn Crackdown on Tibetan Monks. *The Irrawaddy*.

Naing, S. Y. (2010, 18 August) Election Doubtful in Areas Controlled by Ceasefire Groups. *The Irrawaddy*.

Narangoa, L. (2012a) Mongolia in 2011: Resources Bring Friends and Wealth. *Asian Survey*, 52(1), 81–7.

Narangoa, L. (2012b) Mongolia's 2012 Parliamentary Election. Retrieved 21 December 2013, from www.eastasiaforum.org/2012/07/10/mongolias-2012-parliamentary-election/

Nathan, A. J. and Scobell, A. (2012) *China's Search for Security*. New York: Columbia Universtiy Press. Kindle edition.

National Bureau of Statistics of China. (2010) *China Statistical Yearbook*. Beijing: China Statistics Press.

Nielsen, R. and Nielson, D. (2010) *Triage for Democracy: Selection Effects in Governance Aid*. Annual Meeting of the Political Science Association, Washington, DC.

Niksch, L. A. (2007) *Burma-U.S. Relations*. Washington, DC: Congressional Research Service.

Norman, C. S. (2009) Rule of Law and the Resource Curse: Abundance versus Intensity. *Environmental and Resource Economics*, 43(2), 183–207.

Nye, J. S., Jr (2008) Public Diplomacy and Soft Power. *The Annals of the American Academy of Political and Social Science*, 616(16), 94–109.

Olson, M. (1965) *The Logic of Collective Action: Public Goods and the Theory of Groups.* Cambridge, MA: Harvard University.

Olson, M. (1982) *The Rise and Decline of Nations: Economic Growth, Stagflation and Social Rigidities.* New Haven, CT: Yale University Press.

Olson, M. (1993) Dictatorship, Democracy, and Development. *American Political Science Review*, 87(3), 567–76.

Ooluun, B. (2009a, 13 May) Is V. Putin's Visit a Big Geopolitical Move? *The Mongol Messenger.*

Ooluun, B. (2009b, 20 May) Russian Railway Establishes Joint Venture in Mongolia. *The Mongol Messenger.*

Organisation for Economic Cooperation and Development. (2010) International Development Statistics. Creditor Reporting System. Retrieved 30 December 2010, from http://stats.oecd.org/BrandedView.aspx?oecd_bv_id=dev-data-en&doi=dev-cred-data-en

Organski, A. F. K. (1968) *World Politics* (2nd edn). New York: Knopf.

Osborne, M. (2006) *The Paramount Power.* Double Bay, NSW: Lowy Institute for International Policy.

Paal, D. (2013) The United States and Asia in 2012: Domestic Politics Takes Charge. *Asian Survey*, 53(1), 12–21.

People's Daily Online (2007) Chinese Ship-Building Company Delivers Marine Equipments to Cambodia. Retrieved 14 July 2010, from http://english.people.com.cn/90001/90776/90883/6298603.html

People's Daily Online (2013) Myanmar Youth Delegation Heads to China for Cultural Exchange. Retrieved 1 December 2013, from http://english.peopledaily.com.cn/90782/8348189.html

Peou, S. (2000) *Intervention & Change in Cambodia Towards Democracy?* New York: St Martin's Press.

Perry, P. (2005) Corruption in Burma and the Corruption of Burma. In N. Tarling (ed.), *Corruption and Good Governance in Asia.* London and New York: Routledge, pp. 186–97.

Plaut, E. and Chan Thul, P. (2006, 8 April) The New Emperors. Chinese Business and Politics: A Growing Influence in Cambodia. *Cambodia Daily Weekend.*

Pomfret, R. (2000) Transition and Democracy in Mongolia. *Europe-Asia Studies*, 52(1), 149–60.

Prohl, W. and Sumati, L. (2008) *Voter's Voices: People's Perception of Mongolia's Political and Economic Transition as Reflected in Opinion Polls from 1995 to 2007.* Ulaanbaatar: Munkhin Useg.

Przeworski, A. and Limongi, F. (1997) Modernization: Theories and Facts. *World Politics*, 49(2), 155–83.

Przeworski, A., Alvarez, M. E., Cheibub, J. A. and Limongi, F. (2000) *Democracy and Development. Political Institutions and Well-Being in the World, 1950–1990.* Cambridge: University Press.

Puddington, A. (2007) The 2006 Freedom House Survey: The Pushback against Democracy. *Journal of Democracy*, 18(2), 125–37.

Puddington, A. (2010) The Freedom House Survey for 2009. *Journal of Democracy*, 21(2), 136–50.

Putnam, R. D. (1988) Diplomacy and Domestic Politics. *International Organization*, 42(3), 427–60.

Putnam, R. D., Leonardi, R. and Nanetti, R. (1993) *Making Democracy Work: Civic Traditions in Modern Italy*. Princeton, NJ: Princeton University Press.

Pye, L. (1985) *Asian Power and Politics*. Cambridge, MA: Belknap.

Ravenhill, J. and Jiang, Y. (2009) China's Move to Preferential Trading: A New Direction in China's Diplomacy. *Journal of Contemporary China*, 18(58), 27–46.

Reeves, J. (2011) Mongolia's Environmental Security. *Asian Survey*, 51(3), 453–71.

Reeves, J. (2012) Mongolia's Evolving Security Strategy: Omni-Enmeshment and Balance of Influence. *The Pacific Review*, 25(5), 589–612.

Reeves, J. (2013) Sino-Mongolian Relations and Mongolia's Non-Traditional Security. *Central Asian Survey*, 32(2), 175–88.

Reilly, B. (2013) Southeast Asia: In the Shadow of China. *Journal of Democracy*, 24(1), 156–64.

Reilly, J. and Na, W. (2007) China's Corporate Engagement in Africa. In M. Kitissou (ed.), *Africa in China's Global Strategy*. London: Adonis and Abbey Publishers, pp. 132–55.

Reuters (2011) China Agrees $500 Million Loan to Mongolia. Retrieved 25 July 2013, from http://in.reuters.com/article/2011/06/16/china-mongolia-loan-idINL3E7HG1Y020110616

Richardson, S. (2010) *China, Cambodia, and the Five Principles of Peaceful Coexistence*. New York: Columbia University Press.

Rith, S. and Cochrane, L. (2005, 21 October) Cambodia's Army: Best Friends with China, Vietnam. *Phnom Penh Post*.

Roberts, D. (2002) Democratization, Elite Transition, and Violence in Cambodia, 1991–1999. *Critical Asian Studies*, 34(4), 520–38.

Ros, C. (2000) *Cambodge, La répétition de l'histoire*. Paris: Éditions You-Feng.

Rosendorff, B. P. and Vreeland, J. R. (2006) Democracy and Data Dissemination: The Effect of Political Regime on Transparency. *First Annual International Political Economy Society Conference*, Princeton University.

Ross, M. L. (2001) Does Oil Hinder Democracy? *World Politics*, 53(3), 325–61.

Ross, M. L. (2008) Replication Data for: Oil, Islam, and Women. Retrieved 31 December 2012, from http://thedata.harvard.edu/dvn/dv/mlross/faces/study/StudyPage.xhtml?globalId=hdl:1902.1/14307

Ross, R. (1992) China and Post-Cambodia Southeast Asia. *The Annals of the American Academy of Political and Social Science*, 519(1), 52–66.

Rossabi, M. (2005a) Beijing's Growing Politico-Economic Leverage over Ulaanbaatar. *China Brief*, 5(10).

Rossabi, M. (2005b) *Modern Mongolia – From Khans to Commissars to Capitalists*. Berkeley and Los Angeles, CA, and London: University of California Press.

Ruisheng, C. (2010) Handling Relations with Myanmar in a Chinese Way. *The Hague Journal of Diplomacy*, 5(4), 405–13.

Russett, B. M. and Oneal, J. R. (2001) *Triangulating Peace: Democracy, Interdependence, and International Organizations*. New York: Norton.

Rustow, D. (1970) Transitions to Democracy: Towards a Dynamic Model. *Comparative Politics*, 35(1), 51–66.

Sachs, J. D. and Warner, A. M. (1999) The Big Push, Natural Resource Booms and Growth. *Journal of Development Economics*, 59(1), 43–76.

Sachs, J. D. and Warner, A. M. (2001) Natural Resources and Economic Development: The Curse of Natural Resources. *European Economic Review*, 45(4–6), 827–38.

Sartori, G. (1976) *Parties and Party Systems: A Framework for Analysis*. Cambridge: Cambridge University Press.

Schedler, A. (2006) *Electoral Authoritarianism. The Dynamics of Unfree Competition*. Boulder, CO and London: Lynne Rienner Publishers.

Schraeder, P. J., Hook, S. W. and Taylor, B. (1998) Clarifying the Foreign Aid Puzzle: A Comparison of American, Japanese, French, and Swedish Aid Flows. *World Politics*, 50(2), 294–323.

Seekins, D. M. (2010) Myanmar in 2009: A New Political Era? *Asian Survey*, 50(1), 195–202.

Selth, A. (1996) Burma and the Strategic Competition between China and India. *Journal of Strategic Studies*, 19(2), 213–30.

Selth, A. (2003) *Burma's China Connection and the Indian Ocean Region*. Canberra: The Australian National University, Strategic and Defence Studies Centre.

Shambaugh, D. (2008) *China's Communist Party*. Berkeley and Los Angeles, CA, and London: University of California Press.

Shinebayar, P. (2010, 24 August) Mongolia is Least Attractive for Mining. *The UB Post*.

Sieren, F. (2008) *Der China Schock. Wie sich Peking die Welt gefügig macht*. Berlin: Econ.

Simmons, B. and Elkins, Z. (2004) The Globalization of Liberalization: Policy Diffusion in the International Political Economy. *American Political Science Review*, 98(1), 171–89.

Smith, A. (2009) Political Groups, Leader Change, and the Pattern of International Cooperation. *Journal of Conflict Resolution*, 53(6), 853–77.

Smith, B. (2004) Oil Wealth and Regime Survival in the Developing World, 1960–1999. *American Journal of Political Science*, 48(2), 232–46.

Smith, M. (2007, 15 November) The Politics of Doing Business with a Brutal Regime. *Bangkok Post*.

Sneath, D. (2010) Political Mobilization and the Construction of Collective Identity in Mongolia, *Central Asian Survey*, 29(3), 251–67.

Sok, H. (2005) *The Political Economy of Development in Cambodia – How to Untie the Knot of Poverty?* Phnom Penh: Economic Institute of Cambodia.

South China Morning Post. (2010, 7 July) South China Sea Becomes Beijing's Latest 'Core Interest'. *South China Morning Post*

State Council (2003) White Paper on China's Policy on Mineral Resources. Retrieved 16 November 2013, from www.china.org.cn/e-white/20031223/index.htm

State Council (2004) White Paper on China's National Defense in 2004. Retrieved 16 November 2013, from www.china.org.cn/e-white/20041227/index.htm

State Council (2008) White Paper on China's Defense in 2008. Retrieved 16 November 2013, from www.china.org.cn/government/whitepaper/node_7060059.htm

State Council (2011a) White Paper on China's Foreign Aid. Retrieved 1 October 2012, from www.gov.cn/english/official/2011-04/21/content_1849913.htm

State Council (2011b) White Paper on China's Peaceful Development. Retrieved 3 March 2014, from http://english.gov.cn/official/2011-09/06/content_1941354.htm

Steinberg, D. I. (2010) The United States and Myanmar: A 'Boutique Issue'? *International Affairs*, 86(1), 175–94.

Stockholm International Peace Research Institute. (2008) *Arms Transfer Database*. Stockholm: Stockholm International Peace Research Institute.

Storey, I. (2006) China's Tightening Relationship with Cambodia. *China Brief*, 6(9).

Storey, I. (2007) Burma's Relation with China: Neither Puppet nor Pawn. *China Brief*, 7(3).

Storey, I. (2009) Emerging Fault Lines in Sino-Burmese Relations: The Kokang Incident. *China Brief*, 9(18), 5–8.

Sumiyabazar, C. (2006, 6 September) A Religious Visit is on. *The UB Post*.

Sumiyabazar, C. (2009, 11 September) MCC Begins Reallocation of Rail Project Funds. *The UB Post*.

Sumiyabazar, C. (2010, 4 June) Wen Woes Stronger Links. *The UB Post*.

Sun, Y. (2012) China's Strategic Misjudgement on Myanmar. *Journal of Current Southeast Asian Affairs*, 31(1), 73–96.

Svensson, J. (2003) Foreign Aid and Rent-Seeking. *Journal of International Economics*, 51(2), 435–61.

Svolik, M. (2012) *The Politics of Authoritarian Rule*. Cambridge: Cambridge University Press.

Taipei Economic and Cultural Representative Office. (2012) Taiwan Targets Myanmar for Trade. Retrieved 24 July 2013, from www.taiwanembassy.org/US/ct.asp?xItem=330641&ctNode=2300&mp=12

Taylor, I. (2006) China's Oil Diplomacy in Africa. *International Affairs*, 82(5), 937–59.

Teorell, J. (2010) *Determinants of Democratization. Explaining Regime Change in the World, 1972–2006*. Cambridge: Cambridge University Press.

The Associated Press (2010a, 17 July) China Gives 257 Military Trucks to Cambodia. *The Associated Press*.

The Associated Press (2010b, 13 September) Burma Wins Key Support from China. *The Irrawaddy*.

The China Post (2002, 27 February) Major Taipei Decision Alters Mongolia's Status. *The China Post*.

The China Post (2009, 16 January) Mongolia asks China for US$3 billion Crisis Loan. *The China Post*.

The Conference Board (2011) Total Economy Database. Retrieved 30 December 2011, from www.conference-board.org/data/economydatabase/

The Economist (2012, 6 October) Less Thunder out of China. Relations with Myanmar. *The Economist*, p. 60.

The Economist Intelligence Unit (1996) *China. Mongolia. 1st quarter*. London: EIU.

The Economist Intelligence Unit (1997a) *China. Mongolia. 4th quarter*. London: EIU.

The Economist Intelligence Unit (1997b) *China. Mongolia. 1st quarter*. London: EIU.

The Economist Intelligence Unit (1998a) *China. Mongolia. 1997/1998*. London: EIU.

The Economist Intelligence Unit (1998b) *China. Mongolia. 2nd quarter*. London: EIU.

The Economist Intelligence Unit (1999) *China. Mongolia. 2nd quarter*. London: EIU.

The Economist Intelligence Unit (2000) *China. Mongolia. May 2000*. London: EIU.

The Economist Intelligence Unit (2003) *Country Report Mongolia. November 2003*. London: EIU.

The Economist Intelligence Unit (2005a) *Country Profile Mongolia*. London: EIU.

The Economist Intelligence Unit (2005b) *Country Report Mongolia. December 2005*. London: EIU.

The Economist Intelligence Unit (2010) *Country Report Mongolia. May 2010*. London: EIU.

The Shwe Gas Movement (2010) Chronology of Events Related to the Shwe Project 1988 to 2009. Retrieved 30 December 2010, from www.shwe.org/chronology/

The UB Post (2003a, 7 February) Chinese Donate to Elderly. *The UB Post*.

The UB Post (2003b, 13 March) China Funds Free Trade Zone. *The UB Post*.

The UB Post (2003c, 21 November) Democratic Party Meets with Chinese Communists to Discuss Relations. *The UB Post*.

The UB Post (2009a, 21 January) Exporting the Tavan Tolgoi Coal: Choosing the Best Way Out. *The UB Post.*

The UB Post (2009b, 7 August) Chinese Military Exercises. *The UB Post.*

Tin, M. M. T. (2003) Myanmar and China: A Special Relationship? In D. Singh and C. K. Wah (eds), *Southeast Asian Affairs 2003*. Singapore: Institute of Southeast Asian Studies, pp. 189–210.

Tin, M. M. T. (2005a) Dreams and Nightmares: State Building and Ethnic Conflict in Myanmar (Burma). In K. Snitwongse and W. S. Thompson (eds), *Ethnic Conflicts in Southeast Asia*. Singapore: Institute of Southeast Asian Studies, pp. 65–108.

Tolstrup, J. (2009) Studying a Negative External Actor: Russia's Management of Stability and Instability in the 'Near Abroad'. *Democratization*, 16(2), 922–44.

Transparency International (2009) Corruption Perception Index. Retrieved 30 December 2010, from www.transparency.org/research/cpi/cpi_2009

Tsenddoo, B. (2010, 13 May) From Russian Mongolia to the Russian-Chinese Mongolia. *Daily News.*

Tucker, S. (2008, 8 March) Confucius Institute Aims to Change Famously Frosty Attitudes. *The UB Post.*

Tullock, G. (1987) *Autocracy*. Boston, MA: Kluwer Academic.

Tully, J. (2005) *A Short History of Cambodia: From Empire to Survival*. Crows Nest, NSW: Allen & Unwin.

Turnell, S. (2011) Fundamentals of Myanmar's Macroeconomy: A Political Economy Perspective. *Asian Economic Policy Review*, 6(1), 136–53.

Turnell, S. (2012) Myanmar in 2011: Confounding Expectations. *Asian Survey*, 52(1), 157–64.

Um, K. (1994) Cambodia in 1993. *Asian Survey*, 34(1), 72–81.

Um, K. (1995) Cambodia in 1994. *Asian Survey*, 35(1), 76–83.

Un, K. (2012) Cambodia in 2011: A Thin Veneer of Change. *Asian Survey*, 52(1), 202–9.

Un, K. (2013) Cambodia in 2012: Beyond the Crossroads? *Asian Survey*, 53(1), 142–9.

US Energy Information Administration (2010) International Energy Statistics. Retrieved 31 December 2012, from www.eia.gov/cfapps/ipdbproject/iedindex3.cfm?tid=5&pid=57&aid=6&cid=regions&syid=1990&eyid=2013&unit=BB

US Geology Survey (2008) International Minerals Statistics and Information. Minerals Yearbook (Volume III – Area Reports: International). Retrieved 8 November 2010, from http://minerals.usgs.gov/minerals/pubs/country/.

Vanderhill, R. (2013) *Promoting Authoritarianism Abroad*. Boulder, CO and London: Lynne Rienner Publishers.

Vreeland, J. R. (2008) Political Institutions and Human Rights: Why Dictatorships Enter into the United Nations Convention Against Torture. *International Organization*, 62(1), 65–101.

Wachman, A. M. (2009) *Mongolia's Geopolitical Gambit: Preserving a Precarious Independence While Resisting 'Soft Colonialism'* (EAI Fellows Program Working Paper 18). Seoul: The East Asia Institute.

Wallerstein, I. (1974) *The Modern World System: Capitalist Agriculture and the Origins of the European World-Economy in the 16th Century*. New York: Academic Press.

Waltz, K. N. (1979) *Theory of International Politics*. Reading, MA: Addison-Wesley.

Wang, F. (2005) Beijing's Incentive Structure: The Pursuit of Preservation, Prosperity, and Power. In Y. Deng and F. Wang (eds), *China Rising – Power and Motivation in Chinese Foreign Policy*. Lanham, MD: Rowman and Littelfield Publishers, pp. 19–49.

Wang, P. (2009) Mongolia's Delicate Balancing Act. *China Security*, 5(2), 20–33.

Wang, W. (2006) Mongolia's Role between the US and China. 529th MTAC Commissioner Meeting and the 1082nd Administrative Meeting. Retrieved 30 December 2010, from www.mtac.gov.tw/mtacbooke/upload/09501/0202/e2.pdf

Weder, B. and Alesina, A. (2002) Do Corrupt Governments Receive Less Foreign Aid? *American Economic Review*, 92(4), 1126–37.

Wen, J. (2004) 'Carrying Forward the Five Principles of Peaceful Coexistence in the Promotion of Peace and Development'. Speech by Wen Jiabao Premier of the State Council of the People's Republic of China at Commemorating the 50th Anniversary of The Five Principles of Peaceful Coexistence. Retrieved 25 October 2012, from www.fmprc.gov.cn/eng/topics/seminaronfiveprinciples/t140777.htm

Weng, L. (2010, 18 October) Border Closure Costing Millions. *The Irrawaddy*.

Whitehead, L. (1996) *The International Dimensions of Democratization*. Oxford: Oxford University Press.

Wintrobe, R. (1990) The Tinpot and the Totalitarian: An Economic Theory of Dictatorship. *The American Political Science Review*, 84(3), 849–72.

Wintrobe, R. (1998) *The Political Economy of Dictatorship*. Cambridge: Cambridge University Press.

Wintrobe, R. (2001) How to Understand and Deal with Dictatorship: An Economist's View. *Economics of Governance*, 2(1), 35–58.

Wolf Jr., C., Wang, X. and Warner, E. (2013) *China's Foreign Aid and Government-Sponsored Investment Activities Scale, Content, Destinations, and Implications*. Washington, DC: RAND National Defense Research Institute.

Wood, R. M. and Gibney, M. (2010) The Political Terror Scale (PTS): A Re-introduction and a Comparison to CIRI. *Human Rights Quarterly*, 32(2), 367–400.

World Bank (2010) *World Development Indicators*. World Bank.

World Wide Religious News (2007) Cambodian Official Says Dalai Lama Still Not Welcome. Retrieved July 12 2010, from http://wwrn.org/articles/24087/

Wright, J. (2008) Do Authoritarian Institutions Constrain? How Legislatures Affect Economic Growth and Investment. *American Journal of Political Science*, 52(2), 322–43.

Wright, J. (2009) How Foreign Aid can Foster Democratization in Authoritarian Regimes. *American Journal of Political Science*, 53(3), 552–71.

Xinhua (2008a) China Offers Further Aid to Cyclone-Hit Myanmar. Retrieved 30 December 2009, from http://news.xinhuanet.com/english/2008-05/08/content_8131097.htm

Xinhua (2008b) PM Blasts Taiwan for Attempt to Reopen Representative Office in Cambodia. Retrieved 30 December 2009, from http://news.xinhuanet.com/english/2008-03/13/content_7784912.htm

Xinhua (2008c) Cambodia Rejects Taiwan's Bid to Open Business Representative Office. Retrieved 30 December 2009, from http://news.xinhuanet.com/english/2008-01/09/content_7390738.htm

Xinhua Economic News (2007) CNOOC Signs PSC Contract with Cambodia [-for offshore Block F]. Retrieved 12 July 2010, from http://ki-media.blogspot.com/2007/06/cnooc-signs-psc-contract-with-cambodia.html

Yahuda, M. (1996) The International Standing of the Republic of China on Taiwan. *The China Quarterly, Special Issue: Contemporary Taiwan*, 148, 1319–39.

Yunling, Z. and Shiping, T. (2005) China's Regional Strategy. In D. Shambaugh (ed.), *Power Shift*. Berkeley, CA: University of California Press, pp. 48–68.

Zarni, D. (2010, 4 October) Why Soldiers Don't Rebel in Than Shwe's Burma. *The Irrawaddy*.

Zeeuw, J. De. (2005) Projects Do Not Create Institutions: The Record of Democracy Assistance in Post-Conflict Societies. *Democratization*, 12(4), 481–504.

Zhao, H. (2007) *China and India Courting Myanmar for Good Relations*. Singapore: East Asian Institute.

Zin, M. (2012) Burmese Attitude toward Chinese: Portrayal of the Chinese in Contemporary Cultural and Media Works. *Journal of Current Southeast Asian Affairs*, 31(1), 115–31.

Index

Kampuchean People's Revolutionary
    Party 68–9, 73
Khin Nyunt 45, 50, 56
Khmer Rouge: fighters 71; regime 66, 68,
    74, 127; tribunal 80
Kokang: incident 57, 60–1; region 56, 61;
    see also ceasefire group

leadership: duration 154–5, 161–75 (*see
    also* survival); failure 155–6, 171,
    174–6; military *see* military; survival
    see survival; turnover 21, 50, 93,
    154–5, 161, 171, 178
legitimacy 23–4, 57, 70, 72, 100, 130,
    132–3, 135–6, 184
leverage: economic 103–4; Western 84;
    Chinese 111; Russian 114
liberalization *see* reforms, democratization
linkage 9, 11, 22; to China 3–8, 154–7,
    159, 161, 163–4, 170, 176–7, 181, 184

Malacca: strait 118; dilemma 117, 120
Mao Zedong 26, 42, 52, 154, 178, 183
Maung Aye 45, 50–1
military: support 52, 60, 67, 77–8, 157;
    assistance 54, 77–8, 83, 94, 118, 121,
    133–4, 142, 156; government in Burma
    55, 58–9, 64, 118–19; leadership 41,
    44–6, 50; regime *see* regime
mining 63, 74, 79, 91, 94, 96–7, 106–7,
    109, 111–16; *see also* Oyu Tolgoi,
    Tavan Tolgoi, natural resources
minorities: ethnic 41, 48, 51–2, 56, 59–60,
    74, 90, 101; Chinese ethnic 36
modernization theory 4
Mongolian's People's Revolutionary Party
    (MPRP) 87–9

National Assembly *see* parliament in
    Cambodia
National League for Democracy (NLD)
    44, 47–8, 50–1, 58–9, 132
natural gas 39, 55, 105; *see also* natural
    resources, resource endowment, oil
natural resources 14, 23, 35–9, 42, 116,
    118, 124–5, 131, 142, 146–7, 150–2,
    173; extraction in Burma 54–5, 62, 65,
    105–7; extraction in Cambodia 84,
    107–10; extraction in Mongolia 95,
    110–14; *see also* oil, natural gas,
    timber, hydropower, mining
Ne Win 43–4
negative externalities 23–5
non-interference 12, 52, 133, 156, 175,

182–3; *see also* Five principles of
    peaceful co-existence
non-tax revenue 10, 72; *see also* rent-
    seeking
North Korea 118, 157, 184

oil 3, 39, 47, 54–5, 63, 67, 73, 77, 96,
    105–11, 116–18, 129, 143, 145–6, 148,
    152, 160, 162, 172–5; reserves 39,
    145–6, 152, 162, 173; *see also* natural
    resources
oligarch 86–7, 91–4, 96, 115;
    oligarchization 86, 91–2
One China policy 14, 35, 37, 99–104, 124,
    145, 147, 152, 183; *see also* Taiwan
Opposition: political 8, 15, 18; against
    Chinese interests 112, 116, 126;
    China's approach towards 132–5;
    Chinese international 13, 185; domestic
    political opposition in Burma 40–2,
    44–8, 50–9, 63–5, 119; domestic
    political opposition in Cambodia 67–9,
    80, 84; domestic political opposition in
    Mongolia 88–9, 91, 94, 96
Organisation for Economic Cooperation
    and Development (OECD) 142–3, 151,
    172
Oyu Tolgoi 111–12, 115; *see also* mining

parliament: in Cambodia 69, 77, 81; in
    Mongolia 88–90, 111–14; *see also*
    elections
patronage: in Burma 45, 63; in Cambodia
    71–3, 77; *see also* corruption, rent-
    seeking
People's Liberation Army (PLA) 52–3,
    56–7, 60, 120
Phnom Penh 40, 67–8, 79–81, 85, 101–2,
    104, 132, 138
pipelines: gas 106, 118, 124; oil 63, 118;
    see also construction of pipelines
political economy 6, 13, 15–17, 26, 33,
    130, 181
power: major 3–6, 11–15, 40, 114, 121,
    127, 136, 176, 185; monopoly of 18, 25,
    41, 66, 70; soft 12, 84, 127–9; *see also*
    autocratic power, distribution of power
preferences: policy 20, 25, 90, 126, 130,
    154
preferential treatment: China towards
    Burma 54, 64; of Chinese companies
    abroad 105, 108, 110, 125; China
    towards Cambodia 78; of winning-
    coalition members 17, 20